ALLEN J. LIEBEROFF is director
of *Profit Research,*
a Beverly-Hills-based
career and business research organization.

ALLEN J. LIEBEROFF

good jobs

HIGH PAYING OPPORTUNITIES
working for yourself or for others

A SPECTRUM BOOK

PRENTICE-HALL, INC., *Englewood Cliffs, New Jersey 07632*

Library of Congress Cataloging in Publication Data

LIEBEROFF, ALLEN J
    Good jobs.

    A Spectrum Book
    Includes index.
        1. Vocational guidance. 2. Occupations.
    3. Vocational guidance—United States. I. Title.
    HF5381.L44   331.7′02   78-1775
    ISBN 0-13-360297-4
    ISBN 0-13-360289-3 pbk.

A SPECTRUM BOOK

Printed in the United States of America

10   9   8   7   6   5   4   3   2   1

PRENTICE-HALL INTERNATIONAL, INC., *London*
PRENTICE-HALL OF AUSTRALIA PTY. LIMITED, *Sydney*
PRENTICE-HALL OF CANADA, LTD., *Toronto*
PRENTICE-HALL OF INDIA PRIVATE LIMITED, *New Delhi*
PRENTICE-HALL OF JAPAN, INC., *Tokyo*
PRENTICE-HALL OF SOUTHEAST ASIA PTE. LTD., *Singapore*
WHITEHALL BOOKS LIMITED, *Wellington, New Zealand*

Contents

3

Construction Trades 31

4

Technical Services and Trades 69

5

Paramedicine 135

6

Creative Fields 200

7

Special Fields 258

8

Administrative and Clerical Fields 273

9

Food Service Industry 297

Preface

This book is written for people who want autonomy in their life's work. There are numerous well-paying and satisfying careers that many people are unaware of. Many of these opportunities can be trained for in a relatively short period of time at little or no expense to the trainee. After one completes an educational program to acquire a particular skill described in this volume, one will find not only is there a demand for the acquired skill in today's and tomorrow's work force, but, in addition, many of these skills can be adapted to a business of one's own. This can provide not only the potential for large financial gains, but also the opportunity for an individual to develop his or her own potential for success, free from the entanglements of the corporate structure.

Each business opportunity mentioned is followed by methods by which the practitioner can inexpensively and successfully start and promote that business. The presentation satisfies a twofold purpose in writing this book. First, the unemployment rate can be reduced by showing people how they can create their own jobs and businesses. Second, because all of the business opportunities discussed can be initiated with very little financial investment and continued with little overhead, they, therefore, can work to reduce the inflationary spiral in this country by offering formidible competition to the giant industries that tend to control our economy. This is possible because many of the business opportunities discussed serve both the private individual and small businesses usually on a free-lance, fee-for-service basis, thus allowing an overall lower business overhead. By reducing the operating costs of the businesses served, such service enables many organizations that normally would not have survived to grow and prosper. These businesses can then provide new jobs to other people, decreasing the need for massive government employment programs. Again, they can also offer strong competition to other firms, thus tending to hold down inflation. In effect, we will still have a spiral, but the spiral will be reversed to have a positive effect on our economy rather than a negative effect. Today, we have gigantic unions controlling gigantic industries resulting in a gradual control of everybody—with nobody winning.

It should be pointed out that in no way is this book against big business or unions. These institutions have been responsible, and will continue to be responsible, for the survival of this country. However, this author feels that more competition from the small independent businessperson is necessary to maintain an economic balance of power that is also necessary for the survival of our nation. Keep in mind that years ago when small business operations were more prevalent, there was less inflation. An individual involved in his or her own business enterprise can enjoy many of the tax benefits of the larger corporations. In this way the private sector of our society can effect to varying degrees its own tax reforms.

It should be further pointed out that when individuals do something that they like and they can see a possible way of controlling their own destiny, this generally gives them an increased sense of identity and purpose enhancing their ability to succeed in other areas of their lives.

Many of the opportunities presented in this book can be learned with as little as three months of training and can be practiced on a part-time basis with excellent income results. Although some of them may appear far remote from your eventual career goals, do not overlook them. Very often they can provide an excellent source of revenue while undergoing a more sophisticated training program or while starting a business as a result of that training program.

Some people may be more prepared than they realize for new jobs and careers. There are many ways for an individual to adapt his or her present occupation into a newer, more exciting, and more financially rewarding career. For the college student or graduate who seems to be going nowhere, this book describes many ways to harness one's college training to a financially rewarding and satisfying career.

Whether a training program requires a two-year junior college curriculum, a trade school curriculum, a four-year liberal arts program, or just some on-the-job experience with no formal training needed, remember one thing—college, no matter what the level, is never a waste of time. Even if you undertake an opportunity far remote from your educational background, any exposure you have had to the academic world can give you the polish and poise to succeed in that endeavor, whether it be in a mechanical, business, or administrative capacity. It should be noted that the wages, business profits, and expenses quoted are for the year 1977. As inflation continues these figures will most likely rise in proportion to the overall inflationary rate.

With all of its problems, the United States is still the land of opportunity and resources, with a depressed economy presenting as many opportunities as a buoyant one. There are many people who have the potential for success—they just need the opportunities exposed to them so that they can tap the resources. *That is the purpose of this book.* If the reading of this book can provide a person with just one opportunity for success, this author will be deeply gratified.

This book is dedicated to the loving memory of my dear friend, Mr. Herb Newman. Although called from this earth suddenly and unexpectedly, Herb had the satisfaction and enjoyment of discovering and succeeding in his own special talent. He was one of the nation's finest songwriters and record producers: "The Wayward Wind," "The Birds and the Bees," "So This Is Love," "Doll House," "Mr. Custer," "Tall Oak Tree," and many others either written or produced by Herb earned him 34 gold records.

I was fortunate to have had Herb recognize and encourage a talent in me. This book is written to allow people to recognize their own aptitudes and cultivate the opportunities resulting from them.

1

Introduction

HOW TO USE THIS BOOK

First, you have to find a career endeavor that suits your personality. To help you do this, a job description is given for every field investigated. You must decide whether or not you would like the type of work described. If not, continue on to another area until you find one more suitable to your temperament. Once you find a field you like, the "battle" has been half won. The mere fact that you enjoy what you are doing makes you a more industrious and ambitious worker.

After the job description the "training requirements" are described. These differ from job to job. Sometimes a career field can be learned merely by working in it and then utilizing everything you learn to promote yourself into a higher financial position.

Some jobs require an apprenticeship in order to qualify for

senior positions. If an apprenticeship is required, keep one thing in mind: in contrast to a four-year university program, you do not pay any money for apprenticeship training. In fact, all apprenticeship programs pay you while you are learning your trade. In fields where it is difficult to get into an apprenticeship program, we describe other alternatives available to you in order to qualify for certification and top money in that particular field.

Many good career fields require approximately two years of academic training to qualify for a desirable job. Much or even all of this training can be acquired in a junior college program at very little cost. The tuition charges at many junior colleges are very low; at some schools all that is required for a resident of the community served by the college is to pay for books.

Qualified vocational and technical schools provide an excellent source of training for many high-paying trades.

Many high schools and universities offer night school programs for people who want to learn a new career or supplement their existing one with increased training. If it is difficult for you to attend classes because of family or present job commitments, accredited home study programs may be the answer. Many provide excellent occupational programs for the industrious student. In this manner a student can proceed to achieve educational goals at a pace that is convenient for that individual. By not being rushed through a course, one may even get more out of it than if actual classes were attended. After each assignment is studied and completed, it is evaluated by the home study school, and corrections and suggestions for improvement are sent back to the student. In some ways a home study course is almost like receiving private tutor lessons.

In addition to private or commercial home study programs, many colleges and universities, through their extension divisions, offer home study courses that award credits toward college degrees. The National University Extension Association offers a "Guide to Correspondence Study" (50¢) which lists courses available through its member schools. To receive this booklet, write:

National University Extension Association
One Dupont Circle, N.W.
Washington, D.C. 20036

HOW TO
CHOOSE A GOOD SCHOOL

No matter what type of school you decide to attend, there are many ways to find out whether a particular institution is qualified to give you the quality of training you require.

The first thing to do is to check with a high school guidance department in your area. The staff usually keeps abreast of the better educational programs available. However, do not stop there. Ask the people employed in the career field you pick for their recommendation of a good school.

For most careers or jobs discussed in this book the official organizations that represent these fields are listed. Write to them for the names of qualified schools in that particular field. When considering a school, see if it is approved for veterans by the Veterans Administration.

There are official organizations whose job it is to investigate the quality of teaching in various types of schools and then to give official accreditation to those qualifying. Writing to these agencies can provide you with valuable information as to the educational quality of the member schools. The following is a list of accrediting organizations for various types of schools:

Junior Colleges:
American Association of Community
and Junior Colleges
One Dupont Circle, N.W.
Suite 410
Washington, D.C. 20036

Trade and Technical Schools:
*National Association of Trade
and Technical Schools*
2021 L Street, N.W.
Washington, D.C. 20036

Business and other Private Schools:
*Association of Independent
Colleges and Schools*
1730 M Street, N.W.
Washington, D.C. 20036

Home Study Programs:
National Home Study Council
1601 Eighteenth Street, N.W.
Washington, D.C. 20009

University Home Study Extension Programs:
National University Extension Association
One Dupont Circle, N.W.
Washington, D.C. 20036

The state department of education at each state's capitol can furnish information about approved technical institutes, junior colleges, and other institutions offering post-high school training in various career specialties. Some of these institutions offer a vast array of career training courses. For example, the Los Angeles Community Colleges provide 350 career choices at nine of the system's member schools. The tuition is free to residents.

The nearest local office of your state employment service can provide details on training programs operated under the Manpower Development and Training Act.

Contact your local Better Business Bureau or chamber of commerce for information about schools, particularly privately operated ones. While these agencies will not recommend any schools, they can tell you approximately how long a school has been in operation and its record of complaints.

Take at least one comprehensive aptitude test covering your field of interest.

Investigate the courses and their costs of instruction for several schools in the field in which you are interested. Compare them with each other. If the schools you are considering are specialty trade schools, compare them to the available junior and community colleges in your area offering these courses. You may find that in many cases the institutions offering the highest quality education require the smallest financial outlay.

Arrange to visit several schools. Examine their facilities to determine what up-to-date equipment they have for student use. Request permission to speak to several students. Check into the educational backgrounds of the teachers. See if they assist the students rather than simply lecture. Find out what the teacher-to-student ratio is. In addition, request the names and addresses of recent graduates from the school and their areas of training. Determine how long the school has been in existence.

For private schools, read all contracts or other binding agreements before signing. Make sure that the school's refund policy, in cases of cancellation, is clearly spelled out. Make certain that you understand everything in the contract and that it contains all agreements that may have been presented orally. If you are uncertain on any points, request written clarification, and, if necessary, obtain outside assistance in reviewing the final contract prior to signing.

Be cautious with schools employing extravagant or misleading advertising or high-pressure salesmen. Avoid any school that tries to pressure you to sign a contract immediately. Be wary of schools that do not require an entrance aptitude test or that offer a test so simple or short as to make its worth seem questionable.

There are many fine trade, technical, business, and vocational schools offering excellent training that can lead to satisfying and financially rewarding careers. However, there are unscrupulous operators in every field, and it is necessary to take steps to avoid them.

2

Mechanical Trades

AUTOMOTIVE MECHANIC

There are millions of cars on the nation's highways. Someone has to fix them. It might as well be you.

The automotive field represents one of the greatest sources for financial success. For a young person who has mechanical ability and is willing to work hard, the opportunities as an *automobile mechanic* are unlimited. This is especially true if you desire to go into business for yourself. A well-trained technician can earn an excellent salary, or go beyond that as a self-employed practitioner in one of the many automotive repair specialties. For the employed mechanic, wages are well above the national average. They are paid on an hourly, weekly, or flat-rate basis.

Today a car is a necessity for almost every adult in this country. The automobile is such a complex machine that it requires a variety of highly trained mechanics to keep it in good running condition.

Due to inflation and the high cost of new cars, many people are not trading in their old ones as often as they used to. It is cheaper to repair a malfunction in an old car than to go out and buy a new one. A car that is kept under proper repair will often run as well as a new one, if not better. Many consumers are now following this principle. The result is a very bright future for the skilled mechanic.

Many years ago one mechanic would do most of the work on a car. Today, as in medicine, many mechanics specialize in just one field or in several closely related areas of automobile maintenance. This practice benefits both the repairperson and the consumer.

The consumers can be assured of top-notch workmanship, for they are getting a mechanic thoroughly trained in a car's particular malfunction. The repairperson is benefitted in two ways: first, all mental and physical energies can be concentrated in one special field and can be learned in a relatively short period of time; second, if one goes into business for oneself, the financial investment in a specialty repair shop will be considerably less than in an all-around shop.

The automotive repair field can be broken down into nine major categories:

1. Engine tune-up
2. Electrical repair
3. Front end and brake work
4. Automatic transmission repair
5. Radiator and air conditioning repair
6. Muffler installation
7. Auto-body painting
8. Automotive body repair
9. Auto upholstery installation and repair (automobile trimming)

The first six specialties can be learned together in a two-year auto mechanic program at an accredited automotive trade school. This program will touch on each of these specialities. After graduation and about two years' practical experience, the new mechanic can work in all or specialize in just one or several of them.

The last three categories are special trades in themselves and require special training for each one.

We will now give a brief description of the work involved in each of the categories. Then we will discuss the potential wages paid plus the capital needed to enter one of these specialities as an independent businessperson. We will conclude the discussion by considering the earning potential that is waiting.

Engine Tune-up

The proper functioning of the engine and all its parts are the prime concerns of an automotive tune-up. The repairperson adjusts the ignition, timing, and valves and adjusts or replaces spark plugs, distributor points, and other parts to ensure efficient engine performance. Often, scientific test equipment is used to locate and repair malfunctions in the fuel and ignition systems.

Electrical Repair

Many of a car's components run on electricity. The car's electrical system consists of a maze of wires, gauges, and mechanical devices. There are many possible areas where a malfunction might occur. The electrical specialist, assisted by a variety of diagnostic and repair equipment, will locate and repair these malfunctions. Numerous electrical shops engage in a lucrative sideline of rebuilding and reselling worn-out generators.

Front End and Brake Repair

There are technicians who specialize in aligning and balancing wheels and repairing steering and suspension systems. They frequently use special alignment equipment and wheel-balancing machines. Most garages and general repair shops do not like to get involved with this highly specialized work and will send this type of work out to a specialty shop. These technicians will also adjust brakes, replace brake linings, repair hydraulic cylinders, and make other repairs on the brake systems.

Automatic Transmission Repair

Automatic transmission specialists work on gear trains, couplings, hydraulic pumps, and other parts of automatic transmissions. These are complex mechanisms; their repair requires considerable experience and training, including a knowledge of hydraulics.

Radiator and Air Conditioning Repair

Radiator mechanics clean radiators, locate and solder leaks, and install new radiator cores. They may also repair heaters and air conditioners and solder leaks in gasoline tanks.

Muffler Installation

The muffler is an important part of the exhaust system. It is not only vital to the proper operation of an automobile, but it is also a safety factor that concerns the passengers. The muffler installer replaces defective mufflers and pipes on motor vehicles.

As mentioned previously, the preceding skills can be learned in a good comprehensive two-year automotive mechanic's program at a good trade school or junior college. In some states junior colleges in the state system offer this program free of charge. The only costs are student fees and books.

The following three skills require specialized training in each category.

Auto-body Painting

Automobile painters make old and damaged vehicles "look like new." These skilled workers repair vehicles that have lost the luster of their original paint jobs as well as the repaired portions of vehicles damaged in traffic accidents. To repair an automobile for painting, a painter must first rough sand it to remove the original paint and the rust that has developed on the body. A spray gun is used to apply primer coats to the automobile surface. After the primer is dried, the surface is sanded until it is smooth. A good painter must be an expert in mixing paints to match the color of the car and an expert in handling the spray gun. Automobile painting is usually learned on the job until top proficiency is achieved.

Automotive Body Repair

Every time an automobile is involved in an accident, whether large or small, repair work is provided for the skilled auto-body repairperson.

This technician is a skilled craftsperson who repairs damaged vehicles by straightening bent frames, removing dents, welding torn metal, and replacing ruined parts. Special machines are used to align damaged frames and body sections. Usually, the repairperson will chain or clamp the machine to the damaged metal and apply hydraulic pressure to straighten it. Some repair people specialize in only straightening frames.

Pneumatic metal-cutting guns and acetylene torches are used to remove badly damaged sections of body panels, and welding equipment is used to install new sections. The repairperson has an array of other tools to push out and repair dents.

After being restored to its original shape, the repaired surface is sanded for painting. Some shops have their own painting facilities on the premises, while others will send the work out to shops that specialize in auto painting.

As you can see, there is a great deal of cooperation among repair shops in readying a vehicle for use again.

An auto-body mechanic can often learn this craft on the job; however, it is highly recommended that he or she go to a good trade school for the basic education. The school-trained mechanic can usually count on a better job after graduation.

With some overtime, an auto-body repair person can usually make about $20,000 per year and the demand for these technicians is great.

Automobile Trimming

The *automobile trimmer* is basically an upholsterer for the seats and related items found in a car. Automobile trimmers, often assisted by installation men, replace, repair, and custom make automobile seats, seat covers, door panels, convertible tops, and other items found in the car. The installer assists the trimmer in the installation of the finished product.

To make these items, the trimmer first determines the dimensions of each piece of vinyl, leatherette, broadcloth, or other material to be used and marks the material for cutting. Although trimmers follow standard designs for most items, they may use their own creations, or the original designs specified by customers. After the material is cut and fitted, heavy-duty sewing machines are used to stitch the pieces together. Finished pieces are stretched and pulled to fit snugly and then are trimmed of excess material.

Because of today's high prices, many people who do a lot of auto travel find it necessary to buy economy cars with just the bare essentials, including seats that are uncomfortable on long trips. An automobile trimmer can do an excellent business in offering to upholster the basic seat to provide the motorist with a more comfortable and enjoyable ride.

In addition to automobile work, trimmers may make truck seat cushions, tarpaulins, boat covers, and seats for buses, motorcycles, and small airplanes.

Because much of the work involves measuring, cutting, and fitting geometric designs, many auto trimmers find it convenient to apply their talents to the cutting and installation of automobile glass. This talent and service can add immeasurably to the income of the auto trimmer who owns and operates his or her own shop.

Most trimmers, and also installers, learn their skills on the job. However, someone who has gone through training as a furniture upholsterer should find it easy to transfer the skills to the automotive field.

Beginners usually learn the trade on the job—first learning to do installation work. To qualify as an installer generally takes from three to six months of work experience. However, it will then require from two-and-a-half to three years to become a skilled trimmer. Even though the training may be somewhat lengthy, keep in mind that you are usually earning at least a subsistence salary until fully qualified.

SALARY AND EMPLOYMENT OPPORTUNITIES

We have tried to give you a general description of the many specialties and opportunities in the automotive field. There is plenty of room for the ambitious and well-trained person to grow in this lucrative field. Very often success will be achieved through advancement into supervisory positions, for those preferring to work for a large organization, or success may come from the ownership of one's own shop.

Employed mechanics are paid on a variety of bases. Some are paid by the hour, some by the week, and some by each individual repair job they complete. At any rate, a good mechanic in any of the specialties discussed, can earn anywhere from $8 to $11 per hour, depending on the locality in which one works.

For the craftsperson desiring to work his or her own shop and be his or her own boss, the financial possibilities are almost limitless. Good technicians with some expertise in business can make salaries anywhere from $20,000 to $30,000 per year and even more, if they are willing to promote themselves. Of course, you will have to save up or borrow some capital to get started.

The following is a list of the specialties discussed, plus the average investment necessary to go into business for yourself:

Tune-up shop	$13,000
Electrical shop	9,000
Wheel-alignment and brake repair shop	12,000
Transmission repair shop	13,000
Radiator and auto-airconditioning shop	4,400
Muffler shop	11,000
Auto paint shop	9,000
Auto-body shop	11,000
Upholstery shop	4,800

These figures are for the year 1977. They will undoubtedly go up at a rate paralleling that of the general economy. Do not be discouraged, as your profit margin can also be increased if necessary. The figures include equipment and beginning inventories. Most shops do not have to carry large inventories as most automobile repair parts can be obtained in less than twenty-four hours from auto distributors who specialize in supplying independent shops. Rent is not included in these figures. However, our investigators have shown that a good structure can be rented for about $300 to $400 per month. Vacated gasoline stations make excellent structures to house practically any kind of shop.

If you desire to go into business for yourself but your cash situation is insufficient, you might consider leasing work space in one of the work areas of a busy gasoline station. Many gas stations are limited to the types of mechanical work performed, and if your specialty does not conflict with the services that the gas station already performs, it is possible to rent space at a reasonable cost, as the service you will render can greatly enhance the image of the station.

Once the technician has set up shop, there are many things that can be done to promote and ensure success.

First, remember, most gas stations are limited in the types of repair work performed. Much of the repair work is usually farmed out to the specialty repair shops. The specialty repair shop bills the gasoline station at a fee that represents a small trade discount. The customer gets the total bill from the gas station. The gas station owner is entitled to make a small profit on the work done by thus saving the car owner a lot of time in having to go from one shop to another to get the necessary repairs.

The beginning shop owner should contact all of the many service stations in the area to advise them of the excellent work done and of the reasonable profit being allowed. Once the service stations are on your side, you are on your way.

Another good source of business is to contact the automobile insurance companies. This is especially true for automobile-body repairers. Most auto-body damage is due to accidents, and it is usually the insurance companies that pay the bill. It is wise to contact the many auto insurance agencies to advise them of the expert work that you do and the fair prices that you charge. This can lead to recommendations for cars damaged in your area.

You do not have to wait for business to come into your shop to make money. It is quite possible for auto repairers to buy broken-down cars at auctions at very low prices, fix them up at their own cost, and resell them for a handsome profit. Very often at various times of the year used-car dealers, government agencies, and auto-rental companies auction off cars that are no longer useful to them.

Due to the need for better gas mileage, cars of the future will be equipped with more sophisticated carburetion and ignition systems. It is expected that by 1985 an additional 200,000 highly skilled mechanics will be needed just to service these systems.

As you can see, the opportunities for financial success in the automotive repair field are infinite. You can learn these crafts inexpensively, and even get paid while you learn in preparation for the bigger money. All it takes is a reasonable amount of training and YOU.

DIESEL MECHANIC

Because of the emphasis on energy conservation, many vehicles and other types of machines are being made to run by diesel power. *Diesel mechanics* maintain and repair diesel engines used to power large construction machinery, electric generators, trucks, buses, railroad locomotives, ships, tractors, and a variety of other diesel-powered equipment, such as compressors and pumps used in oil well drilling rigs and irrigation systems.

The principal differences between the diesel engine and the common gasoline engine are in the fuel and ignition systems. Diesel engines have no carburetors or electrical ignition systems; they have a fuel-injection system. No spark ignites the vaporized fuel at the end of the compression stroke as it does in gasoline engines. The diesel engine is constructed so that the heat of compression is sufficient to cause the fuel to burn at the proper time. When an engine needs repairs or an overhaul, it is brought into the shop or the mechanic goes to its location.

Using various testing devices, such as injector testing apparatus, the mechanic inspects and tests the engine to determine the causes of faulty operation. After diagnosing the trouble, deciding what must be done, and how best to do it, the engine is sometimes disassembled to reach the trouble spot.

If a part is worn or defective, the mechanic must properly disassemble the engine to remove the part. He or she must then repair or replace it. In repairing a part, the mechanic may use welding equipment or hand and power metalworking tools. It may be necessary to drill, scrape, or otherwise work the metal part.

In replacing a worn or defective part of an engine, the mechanic may alter a new part to make it fit or completely fabricate (make) a new part. A good mechanic can often make emergency repairs to put an essential engine back in service while waiting for part replacements. After the engine is reassembled, it is started for a performance test run. This may include connecting the engine to a dynamometer to determine the power output of the engine throughout its various speed ranges.

Many mechanics make all types of diesel engine repairs, while others specialize, for example, in rebuilding engines or in repairing fuel-injection systems, turbochargers, cylinder heads, or starting systems. Some also repair large natural gas engines used to power generators and other industrial equipment.

TRAINING REQUIREMENTS

Most diesel mechanics first learn to repair gasoline engines. A description of this type of work has been discussed under the Engine Tune-up section of Automotive Repair. After becoming proficient in gasoline engine repair, an additional six to eight months of training in diesel equipment maintenance and repair is usually required in order for one to qualify as a diesel mechanic.

Many diesel mechanics are trained on the job through an apprenticeship program or by taking company-sponsored training programs. Correspondence courses taken while undergoing on-the-job training can also be helpful in learning diesel mechanic skills. The armed forces also train a large number of diesel mechanics.

Many junior colleges and universities offer full-time day and evening courses in diesel technology. Full-time attendance at a good trade or technical school offers comprehensive training in diesel engine maintenance and repair. Such a program generally lasts from several months to two years and provides practical experience and related classroom instruction.

During classroom study trainees will receive instruction in blueprint reading, hydraulics, welding, and other related subjects. In their practical training they learn about valves, bearings, injection systems, starting systems, cooling systems, and other parts of diesel engines.

A serious student who aspires to becoming a good diesel mechanic can map out a program of academic and on-the-job training until both the student and the employer feel enough training has been met to master most job orders.

SALARY AND EMPLOYMENT OPPORTUNITIES

A diesel mechanic generally makes from $9 to $11 an hour, plus vacation, medical, and retirement benefits, as an employee. Most users of diesel equipment lack sufficient extra equipment to get along without an engine or a piece of equipment for very long. Therefore, when an employer or customer needs essential equipment repaired, a diesel mechanic may work overtime receiving time and a half or even double time in wages.

Good diesel mechanics can also go into business for themselves, traveling to the location of large diesel engines and making the necessary repairs on the customer's premises. A mechanic who is aggressive in business can solicit the maintenance and repair business of trucking companies. This work can be done in the mechanic's own shop, or, very often, at the trucking firm's headquarters.

It is profitable even to go into a full-time business of one's own just overhauling and rebuilding diesel engines. When you consider that most diesel engines cost in the neighborhood of $15,000 at the least, many firms would prefer to overhaul their present engines, or purchase rebuilt engines, rather than buy new ones. Independent mechanics operating their own diesel maintenance and servicing businesses usually charge their customers at the rate of $20 to $25 an hour plus parts. This can add up to a sizable income for an aggressive mechanic.

Increased employment of mechanics is expected mainly because most industries that use diesel engines are expected to expand their activities in the years ahead. In addition, diesel engines will continue to replace gasoline engines. For example, small delivery trucks powered by diesel engines are expected to be used increasingly in the future. At present most large trailer trucks have diesel engines. The transportation industry is the largest in the country and alone can provide full-time employment just in the maintenance of truck engines.

Farm mechanization is expected to continue, and diesel-powered farm equipment also will become more common.

The economic advantage of the diesel engine as a source of power is one of the main reasons for the increased applications of diesel engines over gasoline engines.

BOAT MOTOR MECHANIC

Boating has become a major recreational pastime for large numbers of people from many walks of life. These include the owners of small runabouts with outboard motors to the owners and skippers of large ocean-going cabin cruisers up to 50 feet and more in length. There are over 6 million power boats in operation today—and only about 10,000 fully trained *boat motor mechanics* to keep them in repair. A problem common to most boat owners is finding competent mechanics to keep their engines in repair. A reliable motor is particularly essential in boating. Breakdowns far from shore can leave a boat stranded for hours. This can be a very frustrating and potentially dangerous predicament if the weather turns bad. Therefore, most boat owners are even more concerned with the proper repair and maintenance of their boat motors than they are with their automobile engines.

Boat motors can be divided into three main categories:

1. Outboard gasoline-powered engines consisting of two cycles with lubricating oil mixed directly with the gasoline.

2. Inboard gasoline-powered engines consisting of four, six, and sometimes even eight cylinders.

3. Inboard diesel-powered engines. These engines are usually more expensive than gasoline engines; however, the fuel they burn is less expensive than gasoline.

Some mechanics will specialize in just one of the three types of engines, while many will repair all of them.

To minimize the possibility of breakdowns, motor manufacturers recommend periodic inspections by qualified mechanics to have motors examined and repaired and to have worn or defective parts replaced. For example, the mechanics may replace ignition points, check the electrical system, adjust valves, and clean and adjust the carburetor.

When breakdowns do occur, mechanics must diagnose the cause and make the necessary repairs. This requires analytical ability as well as a thorough knowledge of the motor's operation. Some jobs require only the replacement of a single item, such as a fuel pump, while other jobs require tearing down and reassembling a motor to replace worn valves, bearings, or piston rings. Instruments such as motor analyzers, compression gauges, and other testing devices help mechanics locate faulty parts.

Mechanics are often asked to repair and/or realign propellers and propeller shafts. They may have to change the propeller to increase overall power-plant efficiency. Some mechanics install ship machinery, such as propelling mechanisms, auxiliary motors, pumps, ventilating equipment, and steering gears. A growing number of boats are now equipped with automatic tilts, power-trim controls, and other convenience features—all of which are maintained and repaired by boat mechanics.

Testing is also a part of a mechanic's job, and quite often the mechanic may take a boat out on the water to judge its performance.

TRAINING REQUIREMENTS

Gasoline- and diesel-powered boat engines have many things in common with gasoline and diesel engines used in automobiles and trucks. Therefore, a basic academic program in gasoline or diesel technology taught in many vocational and trade schools can provide an excellent background for a trainee. This should then be backed up with on-the-job training in a good marine repair shop or with a boat manufacturer.

Owners of repair shops sometimes send trainees and mechanics to factory-sponsored courses for one to two weeks. Trainees can learn the fundamentals of motor repair; mechanics can upgrade their skills and learn to repair new models. In addition, the reading of manufacturers' service manuals can help a mechanic keep up on the latest repair techniques of different engines. Training in gasoline and diesel mechanics received in the armed forces is valuable and often can be substituted for other schooling or on-the-job training.

There are a variety of opportunities available to good boat motor mechanics. Many work in the repair shops of boat dealers and marinas. Others work for boat manufacturers installing and making final adjustments and repairs on new motors. Furthermore, many prefer to open their own independent repair facilities.

Most mechanics in an employee category are paid an hourly rate or weekly salary. Others are paid a percentage of the labor charges for each repair job—usually 50 percent. In most cases a good mechanic can average approximately $11 an hour in earnings.

There are many opportunities open to the self-employed mechanic. A person who is self-employed may solicit the service work of small boat dealers who do not have their own repair facilities, may arrange to perform the warranty work for many engine and boat manufacturers, and, of course, may repair and service individually owned boats. The latter provides the largest and best source of income to the independent boat mechanic. The advertising of the services in the yellow pages of the telephone directory and in local yachting newspapers can quickly and economically put a mechanic in touch with the largest number of potential customers. Practically every marina publishes a local newspaper that is circulated to every boat owner docked at its facilities.

Skillful motor mechanics who like boats and water may find many opportunities to own a motor boat dealership. They can start by repairing motors for resale. An ambitious mechanic can start a repair business with an initial investment of from $1,000 to $5,000. The service charge can be $20 and up per hour. An even greater profit is to be derived from the rebuilding and resale of worn-out engines.

The employment outlook in the boating industry is bright. The recreational boating industry, as large as it is now, should expand even further in the future. The end result will be an even greater demand for the maritime mechanic skilled in both gasoline- and diesel-powered engines.

MOTORCYCLE MECHANIC

A challenging and satisfying career is open to the *motorcycle mechanic*. The popularity of the motorcycle continues at an increasing pace. They are quickly becoming a major means of everyday commuting and taking weekend pleasure jaunts. More than 2 million Americans own motorcycles and motor scooters. They vary in kind from the "easy-riding" adventurer to the attaché-case-toting junior executive.

Whether a cycle is purchased for the thrill of "heating up the iron" at the stoplight or simply to beat the high cost of transportation and parking, these cycles, like their four-wheeled counterpart—the automobile—require periodic servicing. Because of the large variety of makes and models and the rigid maintenance requirements, there is an acute need for skilled personnel to service these vehicles.

Most motorcycle or scooter owners rely on skilled motorcycle mechanics to keep their machines operating smoothly. Spark plugs, ignition points, brakes, and many other parts that frequently get "out of whack" have to be adjusted or replaced. These routine servicing jobs are what normally make up most of the mechanic's work load. However, a skilled mechanic must be able to find the cause of any major mechanical or electrical problem and make the necessary repairs.

In diagnosing malfunctions the mechanic will discuss the problem with the owner, take the motorcycle for a test ride, and frequently utilize special testing equipment. It may even be necessary to "strip down" some components for closer examination. Once the defective parts are located, the mechanic repairs or replaces them. Some jobs require only the replacement of a single item, such as a carburetor or electric starter, and may be completed in less than an hour. In contrast, it may take several hours for the mechanic to overhaul an engine. Motorcycle mechanics occasionally are asked to repair minibikes, go-carts, snowmobiles, outboard boat motors, lawn mowers, and other equipment powered by small gasoline engines.

TRAINING REQUIREMENTS

Motorcycle mechanics can learn their craft on the job picking up skills from experienced workers. Employers sometimes send mechanics and experienced trainees to special training courses conducted by cycle manufacturers and importers. These courses, which may last as long as two weeks, are designed to upgrade the worker's skills and provide information on repairing new models.

There are many fine trade schools offering specialized one- and two-year programs in motorcycle repair. Among the courses taught are engine diagnosis and repair; transmission diagnosis and repair; general service and tune-up; electrical system theory and repair; carburetion theory and repair; frame and wheel repairs; welding, soldering, and brazing; cylinder boring; and shop management and control.

SALARY AND EMPLOYMENT OPPORTUNITIES

Experienced mechanics in the employ of a large shop can earn up to $11 an hour. As owners of their own shop, they can charge customers on the basis of $20–$25 an hour plus parts, which usually allows a profit of approximately 30 percent. Moreover, since there is no need for hydraulic lifting equipment, a motorcycle repair shop can be opened for a lot less than an automobile repair shop.

The owner of a motorcycle repair shop can solicit the business of police departments in maintaining their cycles. Some shop owners can specialize in modifying or "customizing" motorcycles. An ambitious shop owner can contract various motorcycle manufacturers to perform warranty work for their cycles. It is possible to get the names and addresses of motorcycle owners from the state department of motor vehicles in your state so that you could then send direct-mail advertisements telling them of your expertise in motorcycle repair.

Once a mechanic is established in his or her own repair shop, he or she can take on a "franchise" selling new motorcycles. The financial opportunities are almost endless.

Since lawnmowers and other garden equipment machines operate on the same principles as motorcycles, it may be a good idea to list your services with lawn and garden shops. You also should advertise in the yellow pages of your local telephone directory.

Employment in this field is expected to grow rapidly. More and more people are turning to the motorcycle as a means of economical and enjoyable transportation in the midst of our fuel crisis. Because of the trend to higher powered machines and more complex engines, the amount of maintenance requirements per motorcycle will also rise.

TOOL AND DIE MAKER

Practically every manufacturing process starts with the talents of the skilled *tool and die maker* who makes tools and dies to go into machines from which machinists and machine operators will produce finished metal parts needed as components of finished and assembled products used in today's world.

There is a slight difference between toolmaking and

diemaking. However, both tasks are usually performed by the same individual since the same technical skills are required in both procedures. A *diemaker* makes molds and dies from which finished parts will be stamped out. The *toolmaker* makes special tools used in lathes, shapers, and planers from which finished metal parts or tools to make these parts will be made. Actually, both jobs overlap, as quite often the toolmaker is engaged in making cutting instruments from which dies will be made.

The toolmaker also constructs precision gauges for checking the accuracy of work pieces to exact specifications. Both the toolmaker and the diemaker use all types of machines such as lathes, drill presses, grinders, milling machines, planers, and shapers in making tools and dies. They work from specifications and blueprints presented by tool designers. Tool and die makers are also required to repair the dies and cutting tools they manufacture.

The machinist (discussed in the following chapter) uses these tools and dies in machines to manufacture finished parts for assembly into larger products ready for consumer use. In small shops one person may perform all three functions.

The tool and die maker is one of the most important people engaged in the manufacturing process. First, the engineer designs the product, whether it be a toaster or gigantic steam turbine. Next, the instruments and machines necessary to manufacture these products are made.

Tool and die makers are true craftspeople who control and see the results of their work. They are not cogs on a production line where machines master people. They master the machines and use them with the skill of an artist.

TRAINING REQUIREMENTS

Tool and die making requires rounded and varied training and experience usually acquired in a formal four-year apprenticeship program consisting of 2,000 hours of actual shop work and 144 hours of classroom study annually. During the shop training period the apprentice learns to operate the major machine tools, such as lathes, milling machines, grinders, and shapers, and is taught the use of hand tools for the fitting and assembling of tools, dies, gauges, jigs, fixtures, and machines.

The classroom training usually consists of shop mathematics, shop theory, mechanical drawing, tool designing, and blueprint reading. An apprentice generally starts training receiving 50 percent of a journeyman's wages and advances gradually as he or she progresses in training.

If there are no official apprenticeship programs available at the time one wants to start training in this trade, it is possible to take a two-year training program at a qualified vocational school. A good vocational school can train a student in all phases of tool and die making. After graduation the student can supplement schooling with some on-the-job training. Advice on a good trade school can be obtained from the local office of your state department of education. Information on training programs may be obtained by writing:

National Tool, Die
&Precision Machining Association
9300 Livingston Road
Washington, D.C. 20022

SALARY AND EMPLOYMENT OPPORTUNITIES

The average wage of an experienced tool and die maker is approximately $11 an hour plus vacation, medical, and retirement benefits. A small but successful machine shop may even offer profit-sharing programs to top craftspeople as their success usually depends on the skills and talents of these people.

The future of the tool and die maker is excellent. Every manufactured product in the world requires the talents and skills of a good tool and die maker in its initial development.

Moreover, whenever a product changes its style (as practically all products do), new tools and dies are required to turn out the modified product.

Tool and die makers are usually employed by large manufacturing firms, such as automobile manufacturers, or in the thousands of tool and die jobbing shops throughout the country.

Very often it is impractical for a manufacturing firm to employ every type of tool and die maker necessary for its production needs. Therefore, it is a common practice for firms to subcontract many of their tooling requirements to one of the many tool and die jobbing shops throughout the country. In fact, it is possible for a tool and die maker with some capital to open a jobbing shop and manufacture on individual order many of the tools, dies, jigs, fixtures, and other machine tool accessories required by other companies.

Today many products are made from plastic. Diemakers are in constant demand to make the metal molds and dies necessary to "stamp out" the plastic components of these products. This area provides innumerable opportunities for a good diemaker.

Many small manufacturing plants do not have their own tool and die maker. Thus, a very lucrative business can be built up by a competent maker who travels to such firms to repair broken and worn tools, dies, and other machine parts.

It is possible for a tool and die maker to move up to executive positions in a large firm. Recently, a large automobile manufacturer made a survey of its apprentice training graduates and discovered that 10 percent of them had moved on to the supervisory level of management. Many others advanced to specialists in such fields as machine and tool design and engineering.

Because of the many industries they service, and the exacting skill and craftsmanship they provide, tool and die makers should always be in great demand by our industrial society.

The energy crisis has created an even greater demand for machinists and tool and die makers as devices using and supplying energy will have to be remanufactured for even greater efficiency.

The all-around *machinist* who can set up and operate most types of machine tools uses these tools to make metal parts. The tools used in the machines very often are made by the tool and die makers discussed in the previous chapter. The metal parts made on these machines often are the final components of complex machines.

The machinist must be able to set up and operate a variety of machines, such as lathes, planers, shapers, milling machines, grinders, and many others in order to make the parts required for the work order.

A competent machinist must be able to assemble and erect complicated and expensive machines, apparatus, and equipment; select the tools and materials for each job; and plan the cutting and finishing operations from a blueprint or written specifications. Since all work must be done to close tolerances, precision measuring instruments are used, such as micrometers, to measure the accuracy of the work to thousandths or even millionths of an inch. After completing the machining operations, a machinist may use hand files and scrapers before assembling the finished parts with wrenches and screwdrivers.

Machinists also work in maintenance departments making and repairing metal parts in machines. For this they must have a broad knowledge of the way machines work. In plants that produce large numbers of metal products, highly skilled machinists specialize in layout work and mark specifications on metal for machine tool operators who do the machining operations.

TRAINING REQUIREMENTS

A four-year apprenticeship is the usual way to learn the machinist trade, but some companies have training programs for single-purpose machines that require less than four years.

Many machinists, however, learn on the job. To learn this trade on the job, it is best if the trainee has a high school background in machine shop training, mechanical drawing, mathematics, and physics.

There are many fine vocational schools throughout the country that provide extremely thorough training programs in machine shop operations. Many machine shop owners are not concerned whether or not a prospective employee has completed a four-year apprenticeship program. They are mainly concerned with the ability and proficiency the applicant possesses. Therefore, if an individual has natural talent for this trade, in many cases all that may be needed is just two years of a well-rounded machine school education to prepare for top-paying jobs.

Some companies require experienced machinists to take additional courses in mathematics and electronics at company expense so that they can service and operate numerically controlled machine tools.

SALARY AND EMPLOYMENT OPPORTUNITIES

All-around machinists have numerous opportunities. Many advance to foremen or supervisory positions. Some take additional training and become tool and die or instrument makers. A skilled machinist may open a shop or advance into other technical jobs in machine programming and tooling.

The demand for machinists will increase as the demand for machined goods, such as automobiles, household appliances, and industrial products, increases. After all, practically the whole production process starts with the machinist. The wage scale for an experienced machinist is from $7.50 to $10 an hour.

One thing that will partially offset the future demand for machinists is the expanding use of numerically controlled machine tools. These machines, which translate numbers into a series of motions or processes, reduce the time required to perform many machining operations. However, it should also be noted that the operation of these machines has to be supervised by a machinist. Moreover, these machines are extremely expensive and are not practical for many of the specialized smaller job requirements. Also, expert machinists will be needed in the building and maintenance of these numerically controlled machines.

As industries continue to use a greater volume of complex machinery and equipment, skilled machinists will be needed to build, maintain, and repair this equipment.

3

Construction Trades

The United States construction industry is the largest single industry of our total economy. It is a massive and complex industry comprised of many trades.

The craftspeople in these trades may practice their crafts as journeymen employees of large construction or industrial firms or as independent contractors in business for themselves. Only the more promising trades that offer both alternatives are discussed in this section.

Construction craftspeople represent the largest group of skilled workers in the nation's work force. They build, repair, and modernize homes and other kinds of buildings. They also work on a variety of other structures, including highways, airports, and missile launching pads.

The construction trades consist primarily of workers who have a high level of skill and a sound knowledge of their trade. They are often assisted by apprentices, tenders, and laborers.

In the United States there is always a great deal of new

construction taking place. Even in times of recession the government has passed bills to initiate new construction programs. Moreover, whenever there is a lull in new building activities, there are always opportunities for repairing and remodeling existing structures.

TRAINING REQUIREMENTS

The highest rank that workers in a particular construction trade can attain is that of *journeyman*. To attain journeyman status in most trades requires the participation in a three- to four-year apprenticeship program. Such programs usually consist of on-the-job training in all facets of the craft combined with classroom work in a vocational or trade school. Although a four-year apprenticeship program may seem lengthy, it should be noted that no money is paid out for this training. In fact, most apprentices start their training receiving 50 to 60 percent of a journeyman's wages and then receive gradual pay increases as they advance in training.

Since most construction trades are unionized, an ideal apprenticeship is that of a union-sponsored program whereby the various trade unions work jointly with unionized employers organizing broad training programs for the student apprentices. After completion of the apprenticeship program the trainee is then able to remain in the union receiving full recognition as a journeyman in the craft.

Frequently there are not any openings in a union apprenticeship program in a particular locality. This need not mean the end to a person's desire to obtain proper training and certification in a particular craft.

Numerous vocational and trade schools offer one- and two-year academic programs in the various construction trades. Many community junior colleges provide this training at little or no cost. This training can be supplemented with work experience in licensed nonunion shops until a total of four years of combined classroom and on-the-job training is attained. After this type of program is completed, the craftsperson may then be eligible to join a union as a journeyman if openings are available. If there are no openings, it is possible for that person to go into business for him- or herself as an independent contractor in the particular trade. This is accomplished by taking a state-sponsored examination in the craft for which the individual has trained. Upon passing the exam, the person receives a license certifying him or her as a licensed independent contractor for the particular craft.

The examinations are usually not too difficult for the person who has gone to a good trade school and has worked for competent employers during the on-the-job training years. Many large cities have schools that specialize in helping students prepare for the various licensing examinations. These schools can be found in the telephone directory's yellow pages under the heading of "schools" or "contractor's licensing schools."

Information concerning trade schools may be obtained from the supervisor of trade schools affiliated with the vocational education division of your state education department, located in your state capitol.

Information on apprenticeship programs can be obtained from the nearest office of your state apprenticeship agency or by writing to either of the following agencies:

U.S. Department of Labor—MA
Bureau of Apprenticeship and Training
Patrick Henry Building
Room 5000 - 601 D Street, N.W.
Washington, D.C. 20213

*Associated General Contractors
of America, Inc.*
1957 E Street, N.W.
Washington, D.C. 20006

Most trades provide payment for the journeyman employee at wages ranging from $10 to $12 per hour, depending on the particular trade and the locality in which it is practiced. In addition to the hourly rate, there are fringe benefits that usually include the receipt of time and one-half for hours worked over the usual forty-hour week, medical insurance for the workers and their families, paid vacations, and retirement programs.

All contractors and construction firms are in business to make a profit. Therefore, when they pay an employee from $10 to $12 an hour plus benefits, they usually calculate a fee to include twice this amount when presenting a bid to a prospective customer. This can allow the small independent contractor a chance to compete successfully with the larger firms.

If a particular craftsperson receives $10 an hour, the employer probably bills the customer at a rate of $20 per hour. Therefore, the independent contractor can bill time at $15 an hour, thereby making more money than he would have as a journeyman employee and yet be able to compete successfully with the larger firms. Often the small independent contractor does work for a large general contractor on a subcontract basis. There are also other ways the independent contractor can make money. For example, since most building supply firms give trade discounts to members of the building trades, an independent contractor can make a profit on the materials used on a particular job, providing the customer obtains the necessary materials through him.

Since the materials for a job are purchased after the work order has been obtained, very little money has to be tied up in large inventories. The tools necessary to perform the required work in most trades can usually be purchased for under $1,000. Therefore, an independent contractor can get started in business without a large capital investment. All of this can add up to a lucrative future for the skilled and aggressive craftsperson.

There are many avenues that the independent contractor can pursue in securing business. Many homeowners remodel and redecorate their homes to provide for more luxurious and comfortable living quarters and also to increase the property value on their homes. Businesspersons, such as retail store owners, restaurant proprietors, hotel and motel owners, are constantly remodeling and redecorating their establishments in order to attract new customers. Apartment house and office building owners do likewise in order to obtain top rental fees and top resale values when selling their structures. All of these people are potential customers for the independent contractor.

They can be reached through newspaper advertising, through the yellow pages of the local telephone directory, and by advertising in the trade journals of the various business organizations. It is wise to contact real estate offices and interior decorators to advise them of the services the craftsperson can offer their clients. Retail building supply stores very often know of people who have purchased materials from them and are now looking for a skilled craftsperson to install them.

It is possible for a worker of a particular trade, such as carpentry, to join forces with other tradespeople, such as electricians, plumbers, painters and paperhangers, to purchase a run-down home or building, fix it up to improve its appearance, and then resell it at a profit.

If the worker lacks the funds to purchase such a structure, it may be possible to get a real estate financier to buy a building, the craftsperson to improve it, and the building to be resold, with the profit split between the financier and the tradesperson. Whenever an agreement like this is made, the tradesperson should secure the services of a competent attorney to protect his or her efforts.

There are many ways for the skilled craftsperson in the construction industry to prosper. It just takes hard work, imagination, and some ingenuity.

Shelter! It is required by everybody. The demand for it is as old as life itself. Stop to consider all the different types of dwellings encountered each day—from the smallest home to the largest skyscraper. Practically every type of residential or commercial construction requires the talents of a skilled *carpenter* to facilitate its completion. In fact, it has been estimated that carpenters perform 30 percent of the total work in the construction of most dwellings.

Carpentry is the art and science of cutting, fitting, and assembling wood or other related materials in the construction of residential and commercial buildings and many other structures. Throughout history carpentry has occupied a basic position in the building industry.

Carpentry is a healthful occupation. It requires physical activity, and much of the work is done outdoors. It requires muscular coordination, ability to work off the ground, mechanical ability, good eyesight, as well as average intelligence. Carpentry also requires a willingness to work cooperatively with other tradespeople and other carpenters.

In addition to the useful skill with tools and equipment, the carpenter must be able to read and interpret blueprints and then carry out their specifications. Construction really begins with the study of blueprints. Quite often, a carpenter will be called upon to draw up the construction plans. This is especially true with the self-employed carpenter who may engage in the construction of room additions to homes and the remodeling of homes and small businesses.

There is a definite feeling of satisfaction in creating tangible things. Carpentry offers many varied experiences, and there is little danger of monotony.

There are two phases to carpentry: rough carpentry and finish carpentry. *Rough carpenters* build forms for concrete work, scaffolds, platforms, safety barricades, and small buildings for tool sheds or field offices. They erect the wood framework in buildings. They also work with heavy timbers when they are employed by some industries in building docks, bridges, and mining installations.

Finish carpenters usually install millwork (doors, moldings, cabinets, sashes, and casings) and apply finish hardware. They lay hardwood flooring; some may even specialize in just this one operation. Finish carpenters construct and erect stairways and affix molding and decorative trim. They apply accoustical material to walls and ceilings in order to soundproof rooms. They apply weather stripping to door frames, doors, sashes, and windows to provide airtight seams.

Frequently a carpenter becomes an independent contractor just specializing in certain functions, such as soundproofing, floor installation, or roofing.

Some carpenters may specialize in a special industry such as shipbuilding. *Ship carpenters* perform skilled carpentry operations in the construction of ships or in making repairs. They build wooden foundations, line up and true keel blocks, build the ship's cradle, and prepare vessels for launching. They lay decks and do the finish work as indicated by the type of vessel. They may even perform all of the carpentry necessary for repairs and new wood construction aboard a ship at sea. While it may be difficult to obtain employment working on large ships, as there are not that many built each year, the small leisure boat industry is booming.

The construction of small sail and power boats requires many carpentry principles. Carpenters may find excellent positions with companies who manufacture these boats, or they may go into business for themselves repairing boats. Many small-boat owners have a common complaint concerning the difficulty in finding competent people to repair their boats. This fact alone can provide lucrative business potentials to the enterprising carpenter who lives near a boating area.

Practically all types of factories require the services of at least one full-time carpenter to do repair work and perform alterations to facilitate new production methods.

TRAINING REQUIREMENTS

A union apprenticeship program is one of the best ways to become a well-trained carpenter. Such a program generally takes four years and includes 144 hours of classroom work per year in a recognized trade school. During this period students will work for union contractors learning and performing a variety of jobs, along with their classroom work, until they become proficient in the performance of all of the duties of carpenters. During the apprenticeship they receive 50 to 60 percent of a journeyman's wages and gradually advance in pay as the status of journeyman is approached.

As mentioned previously, however, it may be difficult to enroll in a union apprenticeship program in your area. If this situation is encountered, it is still possible to get excellent training by attending a good trade or vocational school. The carpentry program usually lasts two years and gives the student an excellent background in all phases of carpentry. This schooling can then be backed up by working for various nonunion contractors for another two years to supplement the classroom work.

After the completion of the trade school and the on-the-job experience program it may be possible to get accepted into a union as a journeyman carpenter. If again the doors are closed, the carpenter can then take the state exam to become a licensed independent contractor. As an independent contractor, the carpenter is permitted to go into business soliciting and performing various construction assignments. The earning potential as an independent contractor will be discussed in the next section. Information concerning trade schools may be secured from the supervisor of trade schools, vocational education division, or your state education department, located in your state capitol.

A journeyman carpenter receives about $9 to $11 per hour plus fringe benefits. As a foreman or supervisor for a large construction company, one may be paid as much as $15 to $20 per hour.

Most large contracting firms who employ journeymen carpenters, when giving a potential customer an estimate, have to bill the carpenter's labor at a rate of about $20 per hour in order to pay for overhead expenses and allow a decent profit for the construction firm. This leaves room for the small licensed independent contractor to solicit job orders from homeowners and businesspeople requiring room addition or remodeling services.

In this capacity the independent contractor can bill time at approximately $14 per hour and still compete with the larger contractors. Moreover, the larger contractors very often do not care to go after the smaller jobs.

The small independent contractor can even do subcontracting work for the larger general contractors. For instance, an independent contractor may specialize in floor or roof installation and perform this work on a subcontract basis for general contractors who are not equipped to perform these specialties.

A licensed independent contractor may build small homes for people, set up a remodeling and room addition business, and solicit repair work from small factories who do not employ a full-time carpenter on their staff. There are many avenues one can take as an independent.

It is even possible for a carpenter to enter into an agreement with a financial backer to purchase a run-down home or apartment house at a low price, fix it up, and then sell it at a substantial profit. Sometimes the financial backer will put up all of the purchase money for the dwelling, the carpenter then improves it, and when the property is sold, the profit is split evenly. When this type of an agreement is made, it is advisable for the carpenter to seek the services of an attorney for protection in business dealings with others.

As you can see, if a skilled carpenter uses ingenuity and imagination, there are many paths to travel toward financial success and independence.

ELECTRICIAN

Heat, light, power, air conditioning, and refrigeration components all operate through electrical systems that are assembled, installed, and wired by construction *electricians*. These craftspeople also install electrical machinery, electronic equipment, controls, and signal and communication systems.

Practically every new device developed and used by various industries operates on complex electrical principles. Business and industry are depending more and more on the experienced electrical craftsperson to build, install, and repair electrical equipment.

Lighting plays an important part in the interior decoration of homes, stores, and offices. Proper lighting fixtures provide not only the correct lighting for these types of structures, but the design of the fixtures as well plays an important role in providing an aesthetic atmosphere. Consequently, whenever any type of building is remodeled, the lighting system is usually upgraded. Also, whenever new electronic equipment is added to a facility (such as computers for offices, machines for factories, or X-ray equipment for hospitals), new wiring systems usually have to be installed. This all adds up to a profitable and secure future for the qualified electrical craftsperson. Construction electricians follow blueprints and specifications for most installations. They are sometimes even called upon to design an electrical system for a building.

To install wiring, electricians bend and fit conduit (tubes for electric wires) inside partitions, walls, or other concealed areas. They then pull insulated wires or cables through the conduit to complete the circuit between outlets and switches. In lighter construction, such as housing, plastic-covered wire is generally used rather than conduit. In any case, electricians connect the wiring to circuit breakers, transformers, or other components. Wires are jointed by soldering or mechanical means. When the wiring is finished, the electricians test the circuits for proper connections and grounding.

Experienced electricians can handle many types of electrical work. For example, many take jobs as maintenance electricians in factories. Others work as electricians in shipbuilding and aircraft manufacturing. The electric sign business requires the talents of electricians, especially for installation work.

TRAINING REQUIREMENTS

To become a skilled electrician requires an apprenticeship program usually lasting four years. The program combines on-the-job training with 144 hours per year of related classroom instruction. The classroom work usually includes electrical layout, blueprint reading, mathematics, and electrical theory, including electronics.

After completing their apprenticeships, many journeymen electricians enroll in courses in advanced electronics to keep abreast of the latest developments in this rapidly changing field. While these advanced courses may require the relinquishing of some spare time, they may also lead to the handling of very intricate job assignments that few people may be able to handle and thus to higher payments.

The International Brotherhood of Electrical Workers and the National Electrical Contractor's Association have jointly developed an extensive apprenticeship program. Apprentice programs are conducted under written agreement between the apprentice and the local joint union-management apprenticeship committee that supervises the training.

If one is unable to get into an apprenticeship program, it is still possible to qualify in this craft. As with the other trades mentioned in this book, the determined individual can go through a two-year electrician's program in a good trade or technical school and then supplement this with on-the-job training, after which one may then be able to get accepted into a union local. If that is not possible, one may qualify for an electrical contractor's license and go into business privately.

Information on training programs may be obtained by writing:

*International Brotherhood
of Electrical Workers*
1125 15th Street, N.W.
Washington, D.C. 20005

National Electrical Contractor's Association
1703 Rhode Island Avenue, N.W.
Washington, D.C. 20006

*National Joint Apprenticeship
and Training Committee
for the Electrical Industry*
1703 Rhode Island Avenue, N.W.
Washington, D.C. 20036

SALARY AND EMPLOYMENT OPPORTUNITIES

The average wage for a journeyman electrician is approximately from $10 to $13 per hour for a forty-hour work week plus time and one-half for overtime. Apprentices usually receive 50 percent of the journeyman rate and increase by 5 percent in each six-month period until the journeyman's rate is reached.

Many electricians become foremen or superintendents for electrical contractors on construction jobs. These positions pay more than the average hourly rate, in some cases up to $20 per hour. Some electricians become estimators for electrical contractors, computing material requirements and labor costs.

A large number of electricians start their own contracting business. As previously mentioned, a contractor's license is required. This is obtained by passing a state-sponsored examination.

An independent electrical contractor can bill time at about $15 to $20 per hour and still stay competitive with the larger contracting outfits. Also, there is a profit to be made on the materials installed, for they are usually procured through the contractor. There is ample opportunity for the industrious self-employed contractor to solicit remodeling jobs in homes and small businesses.

Employment of electricians is expected to increase mainly because of the anticipated expansion in construction. Electricians will be required for wiring appliances, air conditioners, and electrical heating units in homes and for the extensive wiring for computers and electrical control devices in commerce and industry.

PLUMBER AND PIPE FITTER

Some people still think of plumbers as people who unplug clogged drains and toilets or fix leaky faucets—*not so.* Plumbing has become an extremely sophisticated trade with applications from the installation of plumbing facilities in private residences to the installation of intricate piping systems in space ships.

Plumbers and pipe fitters install pipe systems that carry water, steam, air, or other liquids or gases. They also alter and repair existing pipe systems and install plumbing fixtures, appliances, and heating and refrigeration units. Although plumbing and pipe fitting are sometimes considered to be a single trade, journeymen can specialize in either craft as well as practice both of them.

Plumbers install water, gas, and waste-disposal systems in homes, schools, factories, and other buildings. In new construction they initially install the pipe system as a building progresses; during the final construction stages they install the plumbing for heating and air conditioning units and connect radiators, water heaters, and plumbing fixtures for the bathtubs, sinks, and laundry facilities.

Pipe fitters install both high- and low-pressure pipes that carry hot water, steam, and other liquids and gases. For example, pipe fitters install the complex pipe systems in oil refineries and chemical processing plants.

Some plumbers and pipe fitters specialize in gas, steam, or sprinkler fittings. Gas fitters install and maintain the fittings and extensions that connect gas line mains with the lines leading to homes. Steam fitters assemble and install steam or hot water systems for commercial and industrial uses. Sprinkler fitters install and maintain the piping for fire extinguishing systems.

Plumbers and pipe fitters use wrenches, reamers, drills, braces and bits, hammers, chisels, saws, and other hand tools. Power machines are often used to cut, bend, and thread pipes. Hand-operated hydraulic pipe benders are also used. In addition, plumbers and pipe fitters use gas or acetylene torches and welding, soldering, and brazing equipment in their work.

Most plumbers and pipe fitters work for large plumbing and pipe-fitting contractors engaged in new construction activity. A substantial proportion of plumbers are self-employed, doing repair, alteration, or modernization work. Some even work on the construction of ships and aircraft. Others do maintenance work in industrial and commercial buildings. Pipe fitters, in particular, are employed as maintenance personnel in the petroleum, chemical, and food processing industries where manufacturing operations include the processing of liquids and gases through pipes.

TRAINING REQUIREMENTS

Most training authorities recommend a formal four-year union apprenticeship for plumbers and pipe fitters as the best way to learn all aspects of this trade. The apprenticeship program also includes at least 144 hours of classroom work a year.

As in other trades, a large number of plumbers and pipe fitters acquire the necessary skills by working for several years for other craftspeople, and observing and receiving instruction from them. This on-the-job training should then be supplemented by taking courses in trade schools or through correspondence courses. As in the other construction trades, after completion of a training program, the plumber is eligible to take a state-supervised exam to become a licensed plumbing contractor. This enables the licensee to contract independently for plumbing work.

Information concerning training programs can be obtained from the following organizations:

National Association of
Plumbing-Heating-Cooling Contractors
1016 20th Street, N.W.
Washington, D.C. 20036

National Automatic Sprinkler &
Fire Control Association
277 Park Avenue
New York, New York 10007

United Association of Journeymen
and Apprentices of the Plumbing
and Pipefitting Industry of the United States & Canada
901 Massachusetts Avenue, N.W.
Washington, D.C. 20001

SALARY AND EMPLOYMENT OPPORTUNITIES

The average hourly wage for plumbers and pipe fitters is from $10 to $12 per hour with time and one-half for overtime. Some plumbers and pipe fitters may become foremen for plumbing and pipe-fitting contractors, for which they receive more money.

Independent plumbing contractors may charge from $15 to $20 per hour for their services. In addition, they are able to derive a profit from the equipment installed if it is obtained through them. The remodeling of homes usually includes the installation of new plumbing facilities such as sinks, showers, and bathtubs. This can provide a great deal of business for the independent plumber.

Employment in this area is expected to grow mainly as a result of the anticipated large increase in construction activity. Furthermore, plumbing will become more important in many types of construction. For example, the trend toward more bathrooms per home is likely to continue, and many homes will routinely include air conditioning and the installation of appliances such as washing machines, gas dryers, and kitchen waste-disposal equipment. Industries such as chemical and petroleum refining, which use extensive pipe work in their processing activities, are expected to expand their facilities, thus creating additional jobs for craftspeople. Maintenance, repair, and modernization of existing plumbing or piping systems will also create employment opportunities.

ROOFER

Wherever buildings are being constructed, there is a need for a roof. In addition, roofs on long-standing buildings are periodically in need of repair. Roofs on all types of structures must withstand the elements of snow, rain, heat, and cold. When a roof gives way to wear and tear, it must be fixed immediately in order to prevent costly damage to the building's interior. Moreover, a well-constructed roof can insulate a building from penetrating heat in the summertime and help retain the building's heat in the wintertime, thus cutting down on air conditioning and heating bills. It pays for a developer to install a quality roof when constructing a new building. In fact, with the energy crisis particular attention is given to the roof construction in order to cut down on the constantly increasing air conditioning and heating costs. Likewise, owners of long-standing buildings are turning to roofing improvements in order to help remedy cooling and heating problems.

The construction and repair of roofs is the responsibility of a highly trained group of construction workers known as *roofers*. In order to provide overhead shelter to meet the new demands created by our economy, roofs have become very complex structures requiring skilled craftspeople to build and repair them.

New roofing materials are constantly being developed. This presents new challenges to today's roofers in incorporating these new materials into new building techniques.

Roofers may specialize in one type of roof construction, such as composition built-up roofing, shingle work, or slate and tile work, or they may become experienced in all of these types. It is advisable for them to become proficient in all types in order to ensure constant employment as a journeyman craftsperson or as an independent roofing contractor.

In laying a roof roofers may install roofing felt using a felt laying machine, or spread hot asphalt or coal tar pitch, or spread gravel with a gravel-spreading machine. They may cut roofing material, or apply flashing, or use caulking guns, hammer and nails, etc.

Many new materials are being used in roofing. These may require the roofer to work with rollers, brushes, spray equipment, or compression equipment. To keep up with the new developments, one must become familiar with such terms as neoprene, hypalon, butyl, and urethane foam.

As you can readily see, roofing is a craft that requires intelligence and skill and is one that a person can truly take pride in.

TRAINING REQUIREMENTS

To become competent as a roofer requires approximately a three-year apprenticeship program consisting of a minimum of 1,400 hours of on-the-job training annually plus 144 hours of classroom instruction in subjects such as blueprint reading and mathematics applicable to layout work.

If it is possible to get into a union apprenticeship program, this is ideal. However, if there are no openings, it is possible to go to a trade school or take correspondence courses and then supplement this academic training with on-the-job experience with nonunion contractors until the required number of hours are met. It is then possible to join a roofing union or take the state exam to become an independent licensed roofing contractor.

For further information, write:

National Roofing Contractor's Association
1515 North Harlem Avenue
Oak Park, Illinois 60302

SALARY AND EMPLOYMENT OPPORTUNITIES

Journeymen roofers can earn approximately $9 to $10 per hour for a forty-hour week plus time and one-half for overtime. Apprentices in training receive approximately 65 percent of this wage and increase gradually as they approach journeyman skills.

Self-employed contractors can sometimes earn one and one-half times to double this amount when contracting independently. They can even subcontract to perform the roofing requirements for general contractors.

Because of the increased awareness of the importance of well-constructed roofs, there is ample opportunity for the independent contractor to approach homeowners, small businesses, and even owners of small factories to take care of their roofing needs. If you can apply salesmanship in explaining how you can cut down on the air conditioning and heating bills of a building, you may find yourself with a long list of customers.

Employment of roofers is expected to increase rapidly through the mid-1980s. Roofing can offer an excellent financial future to the person willing to work hard and utilize some imagination.

PAINTER AND PAPERHANGER

The internal and external atmosphere of a home, office, school, or other type of building is largely dependent on the decorating materials applied to the walls.

The refurbishing of homes, offices, schools, hospitals, factories, utilities, and other facilities is a major industry. The *painter* and *paperhanger* play an important role in this industry. Pick up any home decorating magazine and observe the appearance of rooms before and after the proper paint or wallpaper patterns were applied to it; the results can be quite dramatic.

Builders are very aware of the importance of proper wall decoration to enhance the appearance of their buildings. Artistically decorated walls and ceilings can contribute greatly to the rental or sale of a structure.

Owners of businesses that depend on people patronizing a specific premise, such as a restaurant, hotel, or retail store, are constantly redecorating their establishments in order to attract customers. Paperhanging and painting play a prominent role in redecorating procedures. All this adds up to one thing—success for the hard-working and artistic person who decides to embark on these trades.

Painting and paperhanging are separate skilled trades, although many craftspeople do both types of work. Both a painter and a paperhanger apply finishes to walls and other building surfaces; however, the materials they use and the methods of application differ. The learning of both trades is recommended. Although it will require some extra training to be dually proficient, it will pay off in the long run when you consider that the employment opportunities will be doubled.

Very often the decoration of a home, office, school or other type of building requires both wallpapering and painting coordinated together to effect an aesthetic decorating scheme. If you go into business for yourself as an independent contractor in both areas, you will be better equipped to handle and coordinate both types of decorating schemes.

Painters apply paint, varnish, and other finishes to building surfaces to decorate or protect them. Paperhangers cover interior walls and ceilings of rooms with decorative wallpaper, fabric, vinyl, or similar materials. The development of new types of paint and wall-covering materials have opened up many new decorating possibilities. This can provide a challenging career to a person with a good sense for art and design. It is not unusual for a painter or paperhanger to be called upon to suggest various types of materials and color combinations to the client.

TRAINING REQUIREMENTS

Most training authorities recommend the completion of a three-year formal apprenticeship as the best way to become a journeyman painter or paperhanger. A substantial proportion of painters and paperhangers, however, learn the trade informally working as helpers to experienced craftspeople. Workers without formal apprentice training have gained acceptance as journeymen more easily in these crafts than in the other building trades. As in the other trades, a person learning this craft can always supplement this knowledge by attending classes in a vocational or trade school.

Apprentices receive instruction in subjects such as color harmony, paint chemistry, cost estimating, and paint mixing and matching. They also learn the relationship between painting and paperhanging. They learn to prepare wall and ceiling surfaces to accept either paint or wall coverings. The apprentice who wants to learn wallpapering in addition to painting will learn procedures that are applied to various types of materials and designs. He or she will learn techniques of cutting material, applying adhesive, and hanging material on walls and ceilings and will learn that these techniques vary greatly according to the materials used. Today wall coverings are made of many types of materials with variations of each type.

Additional information on training programs for painting and paperhanging may be obtained by writing:

International Brotherhood
of Painters and Allied Trades
1925 K Street, N.W.
Washington, D.C. 20006

Painting and Decorating Contractors
Association of America
2625 West Peterson Avenue
Chicago, Illinois 60605

SALARY AND EMPLOYMENT OPPORTUNITIES

The average hourly wage for a painter or paperhanger ranges approximately from $8 to $10 an hour, depending on locality. The large rise anticipated in construction activity is expected to result in a large demand for painters and paperhangers. Moreover, recently developed paints such as polyester, epoxy, and vinyl coatings, which resist heat, abrasion, and corrosion, have resulted in new uses for paints and additional job opportunities for painters. Also, a greater use of fabric, vinyl, plastic, and similar wall coverings should contribute to the demand for paperhangers.

Painting and paperhanging provide ample opportunity for the ambitious well-trained worker to go into business privately as an independent contractor. Most contractors bill their time at approximately $20 an hour when estimating a job. Also, there is a margin of profit to be made on the materials supplied for the job. Because they are part of the decorating profession, many painting and wallpapering contractors are able to purchase wall-covering materials at dealer's cost.

There are many areas from which the small independent contractor can solicit business. Owners of hotels, restaurants, and retail stores are always looking to upgrade their appearance to attract new customers. Owners of apartment houses and office buildings are constantly redecorating their units in order to rent them at the highest possible price. Sometimes the owner of an apartment house or office building will redecorate the entire structure in order to make it suitable for sale at an attractive price.

Homeowners are constantly redecorating their homes to provide a variety in the atmosphere in which they live. Schools are realizing that a well-decorated classroom can provide for an improved learning environment for the students. Likewise, hospitals are realizing that a warm internal environment can provide an atmosphere for quicker patient recovery. All of these facilities provide excellent sources of profit for the independent contractor. In addition, professional interior decorators who are hired to design the complete decorating scheme for a facility direct a lot of business to the competent person.

One of the advantages of going into the painting and wallpapering trade and becoming an independent contractor is that a business can be started with a capital investment as low as $300. As in many other trades, the necessary materials for a project are purchased after the work order has been secured.

Thus, a person considering this trade can be reasonably assured of making a comfortable living if he or she is willing to be a "go-getter."

FLOOR-COVERING INSTALLER

Floor coverings, in addition to those of walls, play an important role in adding to the warmth and beauty of all types of rooms, lobbies, and hallways of homes, office buildings, apartment houses, schools, hospitals, and other institutions.

The development of a variety of modern resilient floor-covering materials in addition to newer types of carpeting has increased the scope and opportunities offered by the floor-covering industry. Materials used include tile, mosaic wood parquet flooring, linoleum, vinyl sheet goods, marble, and terrazo. In addition, carpets containing new blends of wool, stain-resistant synthetic fibers, and combinations of natural and synthetic fibers are finding widespread use not only in homes, but also in office buildings and retail stores.

The installation of all these types of floor coverings is performed by a specialist known as a *floor-covering installer.* The installer must know how to prepare the floor for the acceptance of the floor-covering material. Different types of floor coverings require different preparations.

Some installers will specialize in either carpet or resilient floor installation, although some can install both types. It is recommended that the newcomer to this field learn to handle both types of installation. This will provide for more steady employment, and if self-employed as an independent contractor, one will be able to bid on and handle a larger number and variety of installations.

Each type of resilient floor covering has its own special characteristics. A good floor-covering installer must be familiar with these different characteristics in order to manipulate the covering for proper installation.

The floor-covering installer must be artistically inclined and be able to pay attention to small details in order to cut, fit, and glue the materials into place so that the decorating pattern is continuous and geometrically correct. Carpet installers must know how to work with the different carpet blends in order to cut, install, and stretch the carpet into place.

The work of floor-covering installers is varied. One day they may install linoleum in a two-room apartment; another day they may make a custom carpet installation in a twenty-room mansion, large office building, or retail store.

Floor-covering installers are employed by floor-covering contractors or retail establishments selling floor-covering materials, or they may be self-employed as independent contractors.

TRAINING REQUIREMENTS

Training authorities generally recommend a three-year training apprenticeship combining on-the-job training with classroom work. Many people, however, have learned the trade by observing and working with experienced installers and by attending vocational classes to supplement their work experience.

During the apprenticeship program the trainees work with skilled craftspeople on a variety of assignments. First they learn to do simple jobs. They will remove old flooring material, repair subfloors, spread adhesive, and staple material. In the classroom and on demonstration jobs they are taught blueprint reading, shop mathematics and procedures, the characteristics of adhesives, the nature of fabric and weaves, layout and setup procedures, carpet repair, and the methods of handling different kinds of materials.

It is possible in many training programs to learn both resilient floor-covering and carpet installation.

Training courses for journeymen and apprentices are also given by some manufacturers of floor-covering materials. These courses, lasting one or two weeks, provide information on new materials and review current installation methods and new or advanced practices.

For further information on career and training opportunities, write:

Carpet and Rug Institute
P.O. Box 2048
Dalton, Georgia 30720

Resilient Tile Institute
101 Park Avenue
New York, New York 10017

SALARY AND EMPLOYMENT OPPORTUNITIES

The average salary for an employee floor-covering installer is between $7.50 and $9.50 an hour plus benefits. When working as an independent contractor, it is quite common for the installer to bill the customer at a rate of from $15 to $20 per hour. Also, if the material is obtained through the contractor, there is an additional profit to be made.

After obtaining a license, the installer, with a small financial outlay for equipment, can become a self-employed businessperson and then handle various floor-covering jobs on a contract basis. You can also start a new business by devising and selling new types of flooring made from any of the new materials, such as epoxy or latex, and some of the different based fabrics.

The demand for floor-covering installers is expected to rise steadily. Also, the use of more versatile materials, newer and more colorful patterns, the demand for wall-to-wall carpeting in many homes, and the use of floor coverings alongside pools and as artificial outside "lawns" will provide increased opportunities for floor-covering installers.

Employers point to a shortage of the combination person who can install both carpeting and resilient floor covering. Floor-covering installers experienced in commercial installation, a job requiring more layout skill than residential work, are also in short supply. Hence, the employment outlook is best for the installer with all-around training and experience.

ORNAMENTAL IRONWORKER

Newer steel alloys and their increased applications to the building industry have provided opportunities to people who can learn to cut, weld, mold, and install various types of iron compounds to provide functional and decorative steel structures.

Ornamental ironworkers install metal stairways, catwalks, floor gratings, ladders, and window frames. They also install lamp posts, fences, and decorative ironwork. In addition, they work with prefabricated aluminum, brass, and bronze items. Examples are recently developed ornamental building facades that are bolted or welded to building exteriors.

In recent years there has been an increasing demand for ornamental ironworkers. Because of the increase in home burglaries, many homeowners are installing decorative steel window guards over their window frames. The increased concern over urban environment and the improving of property values has led many people to attach ornamental metal building facades to the exterior of their homes and buildings. This can give a completely new modern appearance to homes and buildings with otherwise dull-looking exteriors. New fire laws require newer and better fire escapes. Quite often a general contractor will subcontract this type of work out to an independent structural steel contractor.

Many homeowners, concerned with the external environment of their homes are having lamp posts, fences, and other decorative ironwork added to their lawns. The metal window frames that hold large glass installations is another example of ornamental ironwork.

The increased activity in these applications of iron and metal work provides excellent opportunities to the individual who can be imaginative and creative in working with steel and other metals.

TRAINING REQUIREMENTS

The average training period for an ornamental ironworker is approximately three years of on-the-job training to include 144 hours of classroom work. This will allow him or her to work in the employ of an ironwork contractor for journeymen's wages. With an extra year of experience, he or she can qualify to take the State Contractor's Exam in this craft to qualify for an independent contractor's license.

For information concerning training programs, write:

Associated General Contractors
of America, Inc.
1957 E Street, N.W.
Washington, D.C. 20006

After completion of training a journeyman ironworker can earn approximately $9 to $11 an hour working for a steel or general contractor. One may also become licensed as an independent ornamental steel contractor.

As an independent contractor, there are ample opportunities to show homeowners and owners of small buildings and factories how the appearance and property value of their dwellings can be greatly improved through the application of ornamental ironwork. This can lead to a lucrative business as the fees charged to the customer are at the rate of approximately $20-$25 per hour plus cost of materials, which can allow the contractor a profit margin of 30 percent.

Working with metal requires great skill. This skill cannot be easily developed by the weekend and fix-it-up homeowner. Therefore, the demands put upon the steel worker—not only by owners of established dwellings, but also by builders of new dwellings—can provide an attractive future for the right individual.

ELEVATOR CONSTRUCTOR

In today's modern technological society practically every new building of more than two stories contains at least one elevator. The assembly, installation, and repair of these elevators is provided by a small highly skilled group of craftspeople known as *elevator constructors* or *mechanics*.

This trade is more limited in the variety of employment opportunities than many of the other trades discussed. Moreover, the opportunities for self-employment are also small. However, it was chosen for discussion as the number of technicians trained in this trade is also very limited, and there is a constant demand by elevator companies for well-trained craftspeople.

In addition to elevators, elevator mechanics also assemble, install, and repair escalators and similar equipment. In new buildings they install equipment during construction. In older buildings they replace earlier installations with new equipment. Once the equipment is in service, they maintain and repair it. Installation or repair work is usually performed by small crews.

Alteration work on elevators is also important because of the rapid rate of innovation and improvement in elevator engineering. This work is similar to new installation because all elevator equipment except the rail, car frame, platform, and counterweight of the original elevator is generally replaced. Elevator constructors inspect elevator and escalator installations periodically and, when necessary, adjust cables and lubricate or replace worn parts.

To install and repair modern elevators, most of which are electrically controlled, elevator constructors must have a working knowledge of electricity, electronics, and hydraulics. They also must be able to repair electric motors as well as control and signal systems. Because of the variety of their work, they use many different hand tools, power tools, and testing meters and gauges.

Most elevator constructors are employed by elevator manufacturers to do installation, modernization, and repair work. Some are employed by small, local contractors who specialize in elevator maintenance and repair.

TRAINING REQUIREMENTS

Most elevator constructors begin their careers as helpers and learn their skills primarily through on-the-job training. To become a skilled elevator constructor, at least two years of continuous job experience, including six months of on-the-job training at the factory of a major elevator firm, is usually necessary. During this period the helper learns to install, maintain, and repair elevators, escalators, and similar equipment. The helper-trainee generally attends evening classes in vocational schools. Among the subjects studied are mathematics, physics, electrical and electronic theory, and safety techniques.

More information on this trade can be obtained by contacting different elevator manufacturing firms or by writing:

International Union
of Elevator Constructors
12 South 12th Street
Philadelphia, Pennsylvania 19107

SALARY AND EMPLOYMENT OPPORTUNITIES

The average hourly rate for elevator constructors varies from $9 to $11 an hour plus benefits. Elevator constructors may advance to foremen for elevator manufacturing firms, for which they receive more money. A few may establish small contracting businesses; however, as mentioned previously, opportunities in this area are generally limited.

More elevator constructors will be needed because of growth in the construction of industrial, commercial, and apartment buildings. In addition, technological developments in elevator and escalator construction will spur modernization of older installations and thus contribute to the need of skilled craftspeople. Also, installation and adjustment of automatic control systems on modern elevators require more work and higher skill levels.

SHEET METAL WORKER

In today's construction of modern equipment sheet metal has become a very popular building material. The term sheet metal is just what the name implies. It is a sheet of metal having a thickness of approximately one-eighth of an inch or less. It is a very pliable metal that can be cut, shaped, and welded or bolted to form extremely stable structures. These structures may be air conditioning and heating ducts or make make up large sections of a gigantic airplane. The men who build and install these structures are known as *sheet metal workers.*

Sheet metal workers are involved in practically everything built today, including some of the most sophisticated technology in American economic life. Where the abstract dreams of scientists are translated into the practical realities of new equipment, sheet metal workers play an extremely important role. They are involved in nuclear energy, high-voltage physics, the conquest of space, and the exploration of the ocean bottoms. Everywhere the sheet metal worker is the bridge between theoretical ideas and practical reality.

At first sheet metal workers were mainly involved with the fabrication and installation of heating and air conditioning ducts. Now the scope of their work has greatly increased due to the discovery of newer applications of sheet metal. This is mainly because sheet metal is as resistant to the elements as heavier metals and is more economical to use. It is easier to handle than the heavier metals, and if manipulated properly, it can be used to form structures possessing great strength.

Everywhere you go the thin-walled fabrications of sheet metal work are more and more in evidence—in decorative interior and exterior paneling, in chemical processes, in air conditioning and heating, in kitchen equipment, and even in space ships and satellites.

Sheet metal workers may be characterized as intelligent and highly skilled craftspeople. In performing their work, they draft and use blueprints to lay out and develop patterns. They determine the size and type of metal needed and then cut it with hand snips, power-driven shears, and other tools. After cutting the metal, they shape it with machines, hammers, and anvils. Next they bolt, solder, or weld the seams and joints together. The finished product is then fitted and joined to other components to form the completed structure.

TRAINING REQUIREMENTS

Most training authorities recommend the completion of a four-year apprenticeship program as the best way to learn the sheet metal trade. The apprenticeship program consists of classroom and on-the-job training. If unable to get into an apprenticeship program, a determined individual can attend a two-year sheet metal program in an accredited vocational school or junior college and then follow this up with on-the-job training. If unable to get into a union, one can apply for a contractor's license and go into business as an independent contractor.

In the two-year academic program workers learn drafting and blueprint reading, surface development, applied mathematics for sheet metal, tool and machine processes, sheet metal fabrication and layout, and building construction methods.

For information concerning available union apprenticeship programs, write:

Sheet Metal Workers'
International Association
1000 Connecticut Avenue, N.W.
Washington, D.C. 20036

SALARY AND EMPLOYMENT OPPORTUNITIES

The salary range of employee sheet metal workers is approximately $9 to $12 per hour plus benefits. As mentioned earlier, a sheet metal worker can become an independent contractor and earn considerably more money. An independent contractor would contract for work such as roofing and siding, air conditioning and heating ducting, fabrication of kitchen equipment, construction of architectural forms, and all other areas requiring the use of sheet metal. Sheet metal workers may even go into business for themselves building camper shells for recreational vehicles.

Employment of sheet metal workers is expected to increase due to the increase in building and remodeling plus the accelerated applications for sheet metal. The possibilities for the craftsperson with imagination and initiative are unlimited.

AIR CONDITIONING, REFRIGERATION, AND HEATING MECHANIC

Every dwelling, from the smallest home to the tallest skyscraper, has a heating unit in it; and in today's modern society it will not be long before there are almost as many air conditioning systems as heating systems. Air conditioning is one of the fields destined for rapid and continued expansion.

It takes a great deal of engineering to design and manufacture an efficient heating and air conditioning system; and it takes a highly skilled professional to install and maintain these systems.

More than 600 manufacturing plants are producing air conditioning equipment and accessories. It takes a skilled technician to decide on what type of system is best suited for each situation. A small home may require a simple unit whereas a huge skyscraper or auditorium may require an extremely complex system. It is the *air conditioning and heating mechanic* who helps in deciding on the proper equipment and then undertakes the job of installing it.

When installing new equipment, blueprint and design

specifications are followed to put motors, compressors, evaporators, and other components in place. Air conditioning and heating mechanics connect duct work, refrigeration lines, and other piping, and then connect the equipment to an electrical power source. After completing the installation, they charge the system with refrigerant and check it for proper operation.

When air conditioning and refrigeration equipment break down, mechanics diagnose the cause and make the necessary repairs. When looking for defects, they inspect components such as relays and thermostats. As you can see, a knowledge of electrical work is an absolute must in this craft.

Furnace (or heating) installers also follow blueprints or other specifications to install oil, gas, and electric heating units. After setting the heating unit in place, they install fuel supply lines, air ducts, pumps, and other components. They then connect electrical wiring and controls and check the unit for proper operation. Very often a heating unit and air conditioning unit are interconnected for reasons of economy and efficiency. Thus both systems can take advantage of the same duct and electrical system. We have given just a simple description of the work involved. Most systems are more complex. However, the more complex any type of work is, the greater the importance and the demand for the technician performing the work.

TRAINING REQUIREMENTS

New advances are constantly being made in air conditioning, refrigeration, and heating technology. The person with the best technical education will be better prepared to keep up with these advances and will be the one most sought after by air conditioning and heating firms. Many junior colleges and vocational schools conduct two-year training programs to thoroughly familiarize a student with every aspect of these fields. The training can then be backed up with one or two years of on-the-job training to produce a highly skilled and knowledgeable professional. Some of the courses learned in a good program will include heating and ventilation theory, air conditioning system installation methods, basic electrical theory, refrigeration cycle applications, air distribution principles, equipment selection, cost estimating, and design of air conditioning and heating systems.

SALARY AND EMPLOYMENT OPPORTUNITIES

The salary of a technician in an employee status is approximately from $9 to $12 per hour plus benefits. For the self-employed individual it can go much higher.

Employment of air conditioning, refrigeration, and heating mechanics is expected to increase very rapidly. This is mainly due to the fact that air conditioning units are expected to increase in offices, stores, hospitals, schools, and other buildings. Even large factories are finding that their employees are capable of increased production when working in a properly air-conditioned environment. Air conditioning mechanics are even involved in many aspects of space travel. Also, as more and more food companies are turning to freezing and storing foods for later use, their refrigeration requirements will greatly increase.

Many air conditioning mechanics are employed by the firms who manufacture the equipment, others are employed by dealers who sell and install the equipment.

There are many opportunities for the technicians who want to go into business and become self-employed. They use their skills to contract for the installation and maintenance of various sizes of air conditioning and heating units in homes, offices, and buildings. The equipment needed for a particular job can be purchased after the work order is secured. In this manner the small contractor does not have to tie up vast amounts of working capital in warehousing unsold merchandise. When mechanics are in business for themselves, their time is charged to the customer at approximately $15 to $20 per hour. Additionally, they make a profit on the unit being installed. This can all add up to a very lucrative income. The mechanic who is just starting out in business can call on stores, buildings, and restaurants, offering the repair services on a free-lance basis. There are tremendous opportunities in the repairing of industrial refrigerators found in restaurants, meat markets, and so on.

There are many ways for the small operator to get started and to grow in this field. The development of heating and cooling units utilizing solar energy is also opening up new markets for success.

WELDER

Metal is one of the most practical and widely used building materials in use today. From small electrical appliances to gigantic airplanes, most of our everyday products are made of metal. The manufacturing of these products involves the joining of several or many metal components together to form the finished product. These metal components are joined by the process of welding. This process is performed by highly skilled craftsmen known as *welders*.

Welding is the strongest and most economical method of joining metal parts. Metallurgical advancements in industry have made possible products that were undreamed of twenty years ago. In order to keep up with these metallurgical advancements, many new methods of welding have been created, thus opening the field for a greater number of welders.

Welding is a highly skilled trade, and welders have many phases in which they may specialize. Shipbuilding, bridge and building construction, and the manufacture of pipelines, refrigeration, aircraft, and automobiles are a few of the many branches of industry that depend upon welding in one form or another. More and more new industries are employing welders to help increase production and reduce costs.

Although welding is a complex science, it basically involves the melting and joining together of the edges of metal parts. Welders control the melting of the metal edges by directing heat to the edges, either from an electric arc or from a gas-welding torch. In the arc welding process, they first "strike" an arc (create an electric circuit) by touching the metal with the electrode. They guide the electrode at a suitable distance from the edges, and intense heat caused by the arc melts the edges and the tip of the electrode. The molten metal solidifies to form a solid connection.

Gas welders apply an intensely hot flame to the metal edges. After the torch is lighted, valves are adjusted to obtain the proper flame for the particular job. Gas welders heat the metal with the torch and apply a welding rod to the molten metal to supply filler for the joint. A skilled welder can perform these tasks in such a manner that the resultant weld is hardly noticeable.

Not only are there many industries in which to apply this trade, there are a variety of ways to apply it. First, there is the *manual welder* who performs his tasks generally in the manner just described. Next is the *welder-fitter*. The welder-fitter possesses the same skill as the manual welder but is also trained to read blueprints and follow specifications to perform or supervise a job completely from its inception to its completion.

With the advancement in metallurgy, many types of metals have been the result, and many of these different metals present difficulties in welding operations. In other words, it is difficult to form a good weld with certain metals. As a result, the *specialist welder* studies the metallurgical properties of the metal and experiments with various welding techniques until a suitable method is found to obtain a satisfactory bond.

Research and engineering firms will very often employ a *welding technician*. Whenever a new product has to be produced, a welding engineer may devise an experimental model. The welding technician aids the engineer in building the experimental model and then adapts the theories learned to final production techniques.

A *welding foreman* or *forelady* usually works for a large company and is completely responsible for all welding operations performed by the welders under his or her supervision. This supervisor must have a thorough knowledge of welding and must be able to supervise and motivate people.

One of the advantages of going into the welding field is that it is possible for an experienced welder to go into business as a *job shop proprietor*. An individual can maintain as small a shop as desired or turn the shop into a large operation. All types of metal products at one time or another may break. The independent operator can solicit the repair work for these products. The work can be done in the shop, or where large stationary products are involved, welding equipment can be sent to the site to perform the necessary work. Some independent operators can expand their business by contracting with manufacturing plants to perform the welding requirements of their assembly operations.

TRAINING REQUIREMENTS

To become a competent welder with the potential for advancement in the field, it is advisable to attend a two-year welding program in an accredited junior college or vocational school. This should be followed by two years of on-the-job training. Many junior colleges offer an associate's degree after compliance with the two-year training program. This education can also be applied toward a university program in becoming a full-fledged *welding engineer*. The welding engineer is involved in the development and welding techniques of newer and improved metals. This area alone can offer one a lifetime of challenge.

A list of accredited schools offering welding programs may

be obtained from a local high school guidance department or by writing:

The American Welding Society
2502 Northwest Seventh Street
Miami, Florida 33125

SALARY AND EMPLOYMENT OPPORTUNITIES

Below are the general salary ranges in the various areas of welding:

Manual welder	$7.00 to $11.00 per hour
Welder fitter	$7.50 to $12.00 per hour
Specialist welder	$7.00 to $12.50 per hour
Welding technician	$10,000 to $15,000 per year
Welding foreman	$12,000 to $20,000 per year
Job shop proprietor	Income potential almost unlimited
Welding engineer	$15,000 to $22,000 per year

The future of the welding field is excellent. Metalworking industries are continually growing, and there are increased applications of the welding process. It should also be noted that the welder is not only involved in the production of new metal products, but also in the repair of older ones.

4

Technical Services and Trades

ELECTRONIC TECHNICIAN

Practically every mechanical device used in research, industry, business, and the home operates on electronic principles. This has opened up tremendous and varied career opportunities for the person trained in electronic theory—the *electronic technician*.

The electronic technicians' knowledge of science, mathematics, industrial machinery, and electronic processes enables them to work in all phases of industry, from research and design to manufacturing, repair, sales, and customer service. These technicians use complex electronic and mechanical instruments, experimental laboratory equipment, and drafting instruments. All are able to use engineering handbooks and computing devices such as slide rules and calculating machines.

Research and development (R&D) is one of the largest areas of employment for electronic technicians. These people set up, calibrate, and operate complex instruments, analyze computations, and conduct tests. They also assist engineers and scientists in developing experimental equipment and models by making drawings, sketches, and participating in the building of such equipment. Under an engineer's direction they frequently do routine design work.

In production technicians usually follow the plans and general directions of engineers and scientists. In addition, they often work without close supervision. They may prepare specifications for materials, devise tests to insure product quality, or study ways to improve the efficiency of an operation. They often supervise production workers to make sure prescribed plans and procedures are followed. As a product is built, technicians check to see that specifications are followed and investigate production problems.

As sales or field representatives for manufacturers, electronic technicians give advice on installation and maintenance of complex machinery and may write specifications and technical manuals for machinery.

An electronic technician may work with radio, radar, sonar, television, and other communications equipment, industrial and medical measuring or control devices, navigational equipment for ships and airplanes, electronic computers, and many other types of electronic equipment. The servicing and repair of vending machines (also discussed in this book) is another prosperous endeavor that the electronic technician is qualified to undertake.

Because the field of electronics is so broad, technicians often specialize in one area such as automatic control devices or electronic amplifiers. Furthermore, technological advancement is constantly opening up new areas of work. For example, the development of printed circuits stimulated the growth of microminiaturized electronic systems.

TRAINING REQUIREMENTS

Probably the best preparation enabling someone to take advantage of all of the opportunities in this field, is in the obtaining of an associate's degree in electronic technology. This can usually be accomplished through a two-year training program at an accredited vocational or technical school or junior college.

Among the courses taught in a good electronic's program are electronics mathematics, alternating and direct circuitry fundamentals, physics, electron tube theory, semiconductor principles, time base circuits, computer circuit analysis, radio frequency lines and antenna theory, wave guides and cavity resonator theory, UHF and microwave oscillator principles, and an advancing series of electronics systems laboratories.

For information concerning training programs in electronic technology, write:

Engineer's Council
for Professional Development
345 East 47th Street
New York, New York 10017

National Council
of Technical Schools
1835 K Street, N.W.
Room 907
Washington, D.C. 20006

National Association of Trade
and Technical Schools
2021 L Street, N.W.
Washington, D.C. 20036

U.S. Department of Health,
Education and Welfare
Office of Education
Washington, D.C. 20202

SALARY AND EMPLOYMENT OPPORTUNITIES

The opportunities for someone trained in electronic technology are almost unlimited. There are many employment opportunities in research and development, production, customer servicing, or sales with manufacturing firms involved in electronics that pay an experienced technician approximately $17,000 a year.

An electronic technician with journalistic talents can become a technical writer (also discussed in this book), and one with artistic talent may even become a technical illustrator, drawing detailed pictures and diagrams of technical products for scientific journals and manufacturers' brochures. A technical writer or illustrator can earn salaries of up to $20,000 a year, and even more.

The radio and television industry offers vast opportunities to the electronic technician, not only in the manufacture of radio and television products, but also in television and radio broadcasting stations. There are also great financial opportunities for an electronics technician who operates an independent radio and television repair service.

Today practically every instrument used in research, industry, business, and medicine operates on electronic principles. These instruments are very complex, and they all have one thing in common—they break down. This offers excellent income opportunities to individuals trained in repairing these instruments.

The training and background of an electronics technician is a tremendous asset in learning instrument repairing. An instrument repairer can work in the employ of a manufacturer of instruments, or can open a business servicing instruments used in business, industry, and medicine. As an independent, a technician can earn well over $25,000 a year. This field is treated separately in this book. The same principles and opportunities apply for vending machine repair.

We are living in an electronic society; this society offers tremendous opportunities to the individual trained to meet its needs.

ELECTRONIC SERVICE
TECHNICIAN

Since 1965 factory sales of consumer electronic products have grown at an average rate of 25 percent each year. Factory sales of consumer electronic products in 1976 amounted to $5.3 billion in the United States alone. Growth will continue through the introduction of reasonably priced products such as videotape records, pocket-sized and three-dimensional television, autotape players, compact stereo phonographs, etc. Over 500 million consumer electronic devices are still in use today. Over 80 million new units are produced annually.

But this is only the beginning! In the next few years consumer electronics, through the introduction of new products and radical changes in the now familiar ones, is likely to become the largest and most important business in the world.

The above facts, together with more complicated products, will place heavy demands on available *electronic service technicians* to provide necessary installation and maintenance services. There is a current need for 30,000 additional technicians. The United States Department of Labor estimates that the number of service technicians is increasing by 2 percent per year, while the number of consumer electronic products is increasing at an average rate of 25 percent per year. A service technician shortage becomes immediately apparent from these figures, and where there is a shortage, there is opportunity.

TRAINING REQUIREMENTS

The field of electronic servicing offers many advantages and opportunities to the person who is at the point of choosing or changing a career. The knowledge and skill required to be a successful service technician is well within the ability of the average man or woman. It is recommended, however, that the prospective technician have reasonable mathematical and mechanical ability.

The work performed ranges widely, from those tasks requiring only an elementary knowledge of electronics to those demanding a comprehensive understanding of electronic theory, an understanding that can be gained only by technical education and considerable work experience. We recommend that a prospective service technician attend a recognized and accredited trade school for training. Many junior colleges offer excellent two-year training programs in electronics at very little financial cost. In fact, many junior colleges now award associate in science degrees in television and electronic work. We highly recommend these courses to get the best possible start in this field. Many manufacturing companies offer free training in repairing their particular line of equipment. If you are just out of high school and are thinking of entering the military, most branches of the armed services offer an excellent program in electronic servicing.

SALARY AND EMPLOYMENT OPPORTUNITIES

A good technician with experience can earn over $300 per week. The pay scale is approximately $9 per hour and better for a technician in an employee status. With a reasonable cash outlay, a technician can go into business, and then the opportunities for financial success are excellent.

If a good technician can combine technical abilities with abilities to sell and promote, the income possibilities are almost infinite. What is more, he or she can build up a large clientele while working out of a small shop with relatively little overhead. Therefore, a technician with a self-owned shop can program the labor at about $20 per hour and receive about 40 percent profit on the repair parts. Remember, technicians do not have to limit themselves to just television sets. They can also work on recording and videotape equipment, radios, short-wave receivers, and just about anything that falls into the consumer electronic field. The following are just five suggestions of the many ways a technician can start and build a business:

1. Obtaining a repair concession in a store that sells appliances.

2. Making arrangements with manufacturers to do their warranty work.

3. Arranging with stores without service departments to do their servicing for them, thus allowing them to offer more to the public.

4. Advertising in the yellow pages of the telephone directory and local neighborhood newspapers.

5. Arranging with hotels and motels to service all of their television sets.

For the serviceperson who desires to work for someone else, it is possible to obtain jobs as electronic "trouble shooters" or technicians in manufacturing industries or government agencies. A small number of highly qualified technicians who are employed by manufacturers can advance to higher paying occupations, such as technical writer, sales engineer, design engineer, or service training instructor.

As you can see, the future in consumer electronic servicing is unlimited.

COMPUTER SERVICE TECHNICIAN

The widespread use of computers in business, industry, science, and government has created a market for the individual who is trained and qualified in the installation, servicing, and repair of electronic data-processing machines and allied equipment. Each new installation brings with it requirements for testing, check out, repair, adjustment, and upkeep.

The computer industry is embarking on an expansion program. The price of medium and small systems has dropped to a point where they are now financially within reach of many more small companies. In addition, electronic research has created newer and more sophisticated computer systems plus new adaptations for existing systems.

A computer system is the combination of a computer and computer-related machine, such as magnetic tape readers and high-speed printers. Keeping this intricate set of machines in proper working order is the job of a highly trained group of individuals known as *computer service technicians*.

The more sophisticated a machine is, the greater the chance for mechanical breakdown. The working time lost during a computer breakdown may cost a customer several hundred dollars or even thousands of dollars an hour. This has led to the increased importance of the role that the service technicians play in the computer field.

Computer technicians often help install new equipment; they lay cables, hook up electrical connections between machines, thoroughly test the new equipment, and correct problems before the customer uses the machine. To diagnose electronic failures, technicians must use several kinds of test equipment, including voltmeters, ohmeters, and oscilloscopes. They also run special computer programs that help pinpoint some kinds of malfunctions.

Besides knowing how to use specialized tools and test equipment, computer technicians must be familiar with technical and repair manuals for each piece of equipment. They must also keep up with the technical information and revised maintenance procedures issued periodically by computer manufacturers.

Although technicians spend most of their time working on machines, they work with people also. They listen to customers' complaints, answer questions, and sometimes offer technical advice on machine operation and maintenance.

Most technicians work for computer manufacturing firms. They may be involved in the actual research and manufacture of the computer, the installation of the computer on the customer's premises, or the repair of the computer, or they may participate in all three of these functions. A small number of technicians work for companies that sell computer maintenance services. Others work for firms who maintain their own service departments, such as government agencies, banks, insurance companies, and other organizations that have large computer installations.

TRAINING REQUIREMENTS

Most employers require applicants for technician trainee jobs to have one to two years' post high school training in basic electronics. This training may have been acquired at a computer school, a technical institute, or a junior college. Basic electronics training offered by the armed forces is excellent preparation for technician trainees. After completion of a basic electronic program, trainees usually attend company training centers for three to six months to learn elementary computer theory, math and circuitry theory, and additional electronics.

Because manufacturers continually redesign equipment and develop new uses for computers, experienced technicians frequently attend retraining sessions to keep up with these changes and to broaden their technical skills. Many technicians take advanced training to specialize in a particular computer system or type of repair. Instruction may also include programming, systems analysis, and other subjects that improve the technician's general knowledge of the computer field.

Experienced technicians with advanced training may become technical specialists making difficult repairs and working with engineers in designing new equipment and developing maintenance procedures. Those with leadership ability may become supervisors or service managers.

It is possible for a computer service technician to supplement his or her training with advanced courses leading to a bachelor's degree in electrical engineering. Many computer companies will pay the advanced education costs for technicians who show promise in becoming valuable assets to the company.

For more information concerning training programs, write:

American Federation of Information
Processing Societies, Inc.
210 Summit Avenue
Montvale, New Jersey 07645

Institute of Electrical
and Electronic Engineers
345 East 47th Street
New York, New York 10017

The personnel and service departments of computer manufacturers and other firms employing computer technicians can also provide more details on training and job opportunities.

The nearest local office of your state employment service can provide details on training programs in electronic mechanics operated under the Manpower Development and Training Act.

SALARY AND EMPLOYMENT OPPORTUNITIES

The average salary for an experienced computer service technician is approximately $325 a week plus benefits. This may increase as the technician advances in training and experience.

Training and experience in computer maintenance may also qualify a technician for jobs in programming, systems analysis, management, and equipment sales.

Computers are here to stay. Business, government, and

other organizations will be buying or leasing additional equipment to manage vast amounts of information, control manufacturing processes, and aid in scientific research. The development of new uses for computers will also spur demand. The demand for service technicians will increase with these new developments.

BIOMEDICAL EQUIPMENT REPAIR TECHNICIAN

Go into any hospital, clinic, or well-equipped physician's office; you will see a vast array of sophisticated electronic equipment used in the diagnosis and treatment of disease. Medical practitioners are depending more and more on this equipment in the performance of their duties. Moreover, this is just the beginning. There is more new equipment on the way. The procession of new and advanced equipment will never cease. Who maintains and repairs this equipment? The answer is the *biomedical equipment technician,* one of the newest members of the nation's large and very diversified work force.

The more sophisticated and complex medical equipment becomes, the more subject it is to mechanical failure—consequently, the increased importance of the technicians who can repair this equipment quickly and efficiently. And as stressed throughout this book, the more important your work is to society, the more money you can command.

Some of the equipment the biomedical equipment repair technicians work on are heart-lung machines, electrocardiographs, dialysis machines, artificial kidneys, chemical analyzers, radiation meters, X-ray machines, blood pressure monitoring equipment, diathermy machines, and a host of other sophisticated medical devices too numerous to mention here.

The biomedical repair technicians use schematic diagrams,

hand tools, and test meters to test electrical circuits and components in order to locate short circuits, faulty connections, and defective parts. They solder loose connections with a soldering iron and use hand tools to replace tubes, transformers, resistors, condensers, and switches. They disassemble equipment and repair or replace faulty mechanical parts and adjust and repair styluses, graphs, and other recording devices. They also may be called on to operate engine lathes in order to shape replacement parts.

The biomedical repairperson not only must have a knowledge of the fundamentals of medical equipment repair, but must also be familiar with the individual mechanics of each major medical equipment manufacturer's products. This can be attained by attending company-sponsored training programs and by reading professional journals and literature from the equipment manufacturers.

TRAINING REQUIREMENTS

Qualifications for this field can be achieved in many ways. Since practically all medical equipment operates on electronic principles, a two-year junior college program leading to an associate's degree in electronics is especially helpful. It should be supplemented by some courses in the life sciences, such as chemistry, biology, and physiology, in order to allow the repair technician to adapt electronic training to medical applications. In recent years some community and junior colleges have developed two-year courses in biomedical technology. These programs combine electronic theory along with the biological sciences. Many branches of the armed forces have excellent training programs in biomedical equipment repair. These programs can be investigated by contacting the recruiting offices of the various branches of the military.

After a basic knowledge of electronic equipment repair is achieved, it is often possible for technicians to enter training programs sponsored by the different medical equipment manufacturers in order to fill technical gaps in their backgrounds. These programs usually last from six to eight weeks. Information on these programs may be obtained by writing the various manufacturers. The purchasing office of a hospital can furnish their addresses.

Information on general training programs may be obtained from a high school guidance officer or by writing:

Division of Career Information
American Hospital Association
840 North Lake Shore Drive
Chicago, Illinois 60611

*American Association of Community
and Junior Colleges*
One Dupont Circle, N.W.
Suite 410
Washington, D.C. 20036

*National Association of Trade
and Technical Schools*
2021 L Street, N.W.
Washington, D.C. 20036

Los Angeles City College
855 North Vermont Avenue
Los Angeles, California 90029

Los Angeles Valley College
5800 Fulton Avenue
Van Nuys, California 91401

SALARY AND EMPLOYMENT OPPORTUNITIES

Because of the increased use of biomedical equipment in diagnosing and treatment of disease, there will be a definite demand for the biomedical equipment repair technician. Moreover, there are many career paths to be followed.

Biomedical repair technicians may be employed by a hospital where their main function will be to inspect, maintain, and repair all of the facility's electronic equipment. In this area they will usually work independently and be somewhat their own bosses. They may even be called upon at times to show the hospital staff the proper operation of various equipment.

Medical equipment manufacturers require full-time technicians on their staff to install, maintain, and repair the equipment that they manufacture and sell to the various medical institutions. Those technicians may have to travel considerable distances in order to serve the employer's customers.

Repair technicians may also work for a medical supply house or a contract maintenance company. A supply house functions as a wholesaler of a vast array of medical equipment from many companies. It is to the organization's advantage to have repairpeople on its staff to service customers properly. A medical contract maintenance company functions primarily as a repair service, taking care of the repair needs of hospitals, clinics, institutions, and doctor's offices.

Medical equipment repair technicians employed in the mentioned areas can usually earn an annual salary of from $17,000 to $20,000 a year.

There is one other area in which the well-trained and experienced repairperson may function: this is as an independent technician who services under contract various medical institutions, such as hospitals and doctor's offices. The technician is responsible for periodic inspection and maintenance of equipment as well as emergency service when required. Advertising in local medical journals and the yellow pages of the telephone directory can aid in making repair services known to the medical community.

A technician may even contact medical equipment manufacturers to take care of their warranty work in areas where it is not feasible for them to maintain or send their own technicians. In this capacity the repair technician not only is one's own boss, but also can earn an income of over $25,000 a year. As the business grows, other technicians may be hired. An experienced independent contractor can usually charge from $20 to $50 an hour for services rendered.

It should be noted that this type of work is very clean and does not require a great deal of physical strength.

INSTRUMENT REPAIR
TECHNICIAN

Manufacturing plants, public utilities, and certain government installations use sensitive and often intricate instruments to measure, record, and control the volume, flow, weight, temperature, and pressures of fluids and gases. Other instruments control and activate machinery. Industries using large numbers of instruments include oil refineries, food processors, wineries, and chemical firms. Technological developments in control instruments have enabled many plants to increase production with less labor and more safety.

A faulty instrument can be costly to a manufacturer in wasted material, below standard products, and possible damage to plant and machinery. The *instrument repair technician* is the employee responsible for the continuous, efficient, and trouble-free performance of instruments.

Most instrument repair technicians service a variety of instruments; others specialize in electronic, hydraulic, or pneumatic instruments. Some install and test new instruments and advise operators on how to use and care for them.

When an instrument-controlled system is not working correctly, these service people determine whether the trouble is caused by the instrument or by other equipment. They may take apart faulty instruments and examine and test the parts for defects. They use test equipment, such as pressure and vacuum gauges, speed counters, voltmeters, ammeters, and oscilloscopes. Readings shown on test equipment are compared with readings that would be shown if the instrument were operating properly.

Repairers work at the site of the trouble or in repair shops. They may perform major overhauls, replace worn or damaged parts, or make minor repairs, such as soldering loose connections. They use hand tools, such as screwdrivers and wrenches, and bench tools, such as jeweler's lathes, pin vices, and ultrasonic cleaners for small metal parts. In some companies they operate drill presses, polishers, and other machine tools to make new parts or to change standard parts to fit particular instruments. When an instrument must be set very precisely, they may use jeweler's loupes, micrometers, or microscopes. They frequently use instruction books, maintenance manuals, diagrams, and blueprints in making repairs.

TRAINING REQUIREMENTS

The best way to prepare for a career in instrument repair is to attend a one- or two-year program at a junior college or technical school taking courses directed toward instrumentation. These courses should include electronics, physics, machine shop, blueprint reading, and mechanical drawing.

Military experience in mechanical or electronic fields is considered qualifying by most employers. Correspondence courses supplemented by on-the-job training are also a suitable method of learning this craft.

Several instrument manufacturers offer specialized training to experienced people. This training generally lasts from one week to nine months, depending upon the number and complexity of instruments studied. Courses are given in theory, maintenance, and operation of the instruments produced by these manufacturers. Repair technicians also keep up with new developments in their field by reading trade magazines and manufacturers' service manuals.

Once an individual learns the fundamentals of instrument repair, the remainder of the knowledge necessary in becoming a full-fledged repair technician is gained through on-the-job experience.

Additional information about training and employment opportunities is available from:

Instrument Society of America
400 Stanwix Street
Pittsburgh, Pennsylvania 15222

Scientific Apparatus Makers Association
1140 Connecticut Avenue, N.W.
Washington, D.C. 20036

SALARY AND EMPLOYMENT OPPORTUNITIES

The experienced instrument repair technician earns approximately $9 to $10 an hour plus vacation, medical, and retirement benefits. An employee may be called upon to make emergency repairs at night, on Sundays, and on holidays. For this, premium pay is received.

Service technicians are employed by instrument manufacturers, industries that use instruments (practically all do), government agencies, and private instrument repair firms that service industry. Utility companies hire instrument service people in generating plants, power houses, and similar installations. Defense plants, water supply systems, and sewage disposal systems are among the other organizations that employ instrument repairers.

A person experienced in instrument repair may also go into business doing free-lance repair and maintenance service for small organizations who do not find it feasible to hire a full-time service technician. For such service the fee is usually $20 per hour plus parts and travel time. Many independent service people charge a $20 minimum fee for service work even if the job requires only a few minutes to perform. Very often an experienced technician will contract with an instrument manufacturer to perform that company's warranty work in areas where it is impractical for the company to maintain a field representative.

Employment of instrument repairpeople is expected to increase rapidly. Additional repair technicians will be needed because the use of instruments is expected to increase, particularly in areas such as oceanography, pollution monitoring, and medical diagnosis. Industrial instruments for process control in industries such as petroleum, steel, chemicals, food, and rubber are also expected to increase substantially. In addition, more instruments will be needed for research laboratories, aircraft and missiles, automotive repair shops, and optical applications. The anticipated United States conversion to international units of measure will require altering and recalibrating many existing instruments to the metric system. This conversion will largely be done by instrument repair technicians.

As new firms are created and older plants are modernized, employment opportunities will expand for the instrument specialist. The field is wide open.

TYPEWRITER REPAIR MECHANIC

Typewriters are used as one of the main means of communication in business, industry, science, and personal communication. They are the most widely used business machine and are found in almost every business office, as well as in many homes. As businesses and their paper work continue to grow, typewriters are becoming more complex, thus creating a greater need for more and better trained service people.

Typewriter repair mechanics inspect, adjust, and repair manual and electric typewriters. Repair work may involve replacing worn or broken parts, aligning type to print evenly, fixing the spacer bar, and adjusting the shift mechanism, ribbon movement, and other mechanisms. These repairpeople also clean and lubricate machines and fix typewriter motors.

Because of the dependence on the typewriter by so many businesses, whenever a mechanical failure occurs, it must be fixed immediately. This prevents a lot of haggling over price.

A good typewriter mechanic should be able to repair both manual and electric typewriters and may be employed by a typewriter manufacturing firm servicing only one company's products or by a local dealer or repair shop servicing many different makes. A typewriter mechanic may even go into business for him or herself.

TRAINING REQUIREMENTS

There are various ways of becoming accomplished in this field. Many vocational and technical schools offer one-year training programs in typewriter repair. Because of the widespread use of electric typewriters, service people should have a basic knowledge of electricity. With the advent of magnetic tape electronic typewriters, they must have an electronic technology background to be able to repair these machines.

After a student has received a basic education in general typewriter repair or electronics, he or she is suitable for employment by either a typewriter manufacturing firm or general repair shop. After being hired, an employee usually is given a one- to two-year on-the-job training program to supplement the academic training in becoming skilled. A typewriter mechanic can also take additional training in becoming a general office machine repairperson, repairing adding machines, calculators, and other types of office equipment discussed in the next chapter.

SALARY AND EMPLOYMENT OPPORTUNITIES

Many typewriter repair mechanics are employed by manufacturers as customer service representatives. In this capacity they will work on machines sent to the factory for repair or visit customers to service their products on their own premises. A customer service person usually makes approximately $8.50 an hour plus vacation, medical, and retirement benefits. A repair mechanic may also work for a typewriter dealership or repair shop. In this capacity the pay, in many parts of the country, will be approximately $9 an hour. The reason the pay is more in a general repair shop is because the mechanic must be familiar with the servicing and repair of all types of makes and models. It should be noted, however, that the small repair shop does not usually offer the fringe benefits that the large manufacturer does.

The area offering the greatest potential for independence and financial growth is in the ownership of a private repair shop. When most people need a typewriter repaired, they don't know where to go. The individual who lets it be known that he or she is a typewriter expert and will give fast service can build a large clientele.

The average repair shop usually bills a mechanic's services at approximately $20 an hour and makes an approximate 50 percent markup on repair parts used. The average fee to clean, oil, and adjust a manual typewriter is $25; for an electric typewriter it is $30. The time required to complete this operation is usually about forty-five minutes. Since a repair shop requires very little commercial space, overhead can be kept to a minimum. Moreover, the tools and equipment necessary for the most sophisticated shop can usually be purchased for under $2,000. Thus, the independent owner-operator "pockets" most of the fee charged.

It is easier to build up a loyal clientele if a shop owner can provide customers with a "loaner" typewriter while a typewriter is being repaired. One can provide a reasonable inventory of loaner typewriters at a modest cost by purchasing government surplus typewriters, or typewriters sold at auctions from bankrupt firms, or typewriters being replaced in business offices. If the typewriters are in need of repair, they can usually be purchased for a fraction of their original worth. The technician can then fix them. A good worker can even operate a sideline business of purchasing surplus or bankrupt stock typewriters and reconditioning them for resale. In many cases the profit can be quite high.

For information on obtaining government surplus typewriters, contact your local office of the Small Business Administration for names and addresses of local defense and civilian surplus sales offices.

When soliciting business, the independent repair mechanic can obtain large repair contracts by contacting large offices, business firms, government agencies, and school systems. A repairperson who is experienced in repairing different makes of typewriters may be able to make arrangements with various manufacturers designating his or her shop as an official repair shop for the warranty work of that company.

A good repair mechanic with an aptitude for business may obtain a "dealership" for one or more of the many typewriters on the market. As a dealer, one can sell these machines or rent them out on annual leases at highly profitable rates. The mechanic who is a dealer is in a favorable position because service on the machines sold or rented can be guaranteed. As business grows, the owner can hire other technicians to perform the repair work.

The public thinks of the typewriter merely as a writing machine. For the mechanically minded person it can be the door that opens up an unlimited opportunity for prosperity.

There are millions of office machines used daily throughout America to speed the paperwork and bookkeeping procedures in all fields of endeavor. They include typewriters, adding and calculating machines, cash registers, accounting and bookkeeping machines, dictating machines, duplicating machines, and mailing equipment. It takes an expert *office machine repair mechanic* to keep each of them operating.

Many mechanics repair a variety of machines; others specialize in one or a few types. For example, one specialist may service just duplicators, copiers, postage meters, and mailing equipment. Some restrict their repair work to cash registers; others work only on adding and calculating machines.

Whether the entire spectrum of office machines or just one category is serviced, office machine servicing offers considerable variety in work assignments. People who have analytical ability find considerable satisfaction in finding and correcting the cause of trouble in a faulty machine. Some of them may work for a business machine manufacturer, retail dealer, or repair shop; others may open their own repair shops.

In a manufacturer's branch office the technicians usually work exclusively on the manufacturer's products. They may specialize in one or two machines or service the full line of equipment. Those working in a full-line dealership or repair shop will have to be familiar with the mechanics of the products of a variety of manufacturers. This can be accomplished by reading the service manuals published by various manufacturers and attending their workshop seminars.

TRAINING REQUIREMENTS

The "bottom line" in this field is mechanical and electronic ability, as practically all business and office machines operate on mechanical and electronic principles. Most business machine manufacturers and repair shops will give a technician on-the-job training. This is especially true with manufacturing firms who have specific procedures that they want followed in the servicing of their machines.

To be given preferential treatment when applying for trainee jobs, it is advisable for an individual to have a background education in business machine repair or basic electronics. There are many vocational schools, junior colleges, night school programs, and correspondence courses offering these programs. Electronic training obtained in the Armed Forces provides an excellent background for on-the-job training. The length of the program is usually determined by the natural aptitude of the student and his or her background training. The more sophisticated and complicated machines require extra training. However, the additional training will result in more secure employment and a better financial future. Once a technician is in the field as a full-time mechanic, he or she can always attend short company-sponsored training programs to keep abreast of new developments. In addition, many companies pay their technician's tuition for work-related courses in college and technical schools.

SALARY AND EMPLOYMENT OPPORTUNITIES

A new trainee earns from $175 to $200 a week. As the trainee becomes more skilled, the pay will most certainly increase. A person who has had previous electronic training in the armed forces or has had technical school training generally receives somewhat higher wages in the beginning. Once the trainee becomes a full-fledged service technician, his or her wages can go as high as $350 a week.

Business machine mechanics may move into sales positions for even higher earnings. Those who show exceptional abilities may advance to foremen or foreladies. Experienced mechanics can even open their own sales and repair shops. Those who work in a manufacturer's branch office can sometimes become independent dealers or purchase sales franchises from the company.

An independent technician owning his or her own repair shop can bill the customers at the rate of $20 an hour plus parts for repair services and can even contract large manufacturing firms to perform some of their warranty work for them. This practice is especially common in small towns where it is not practical for manufacturers to operate branch offices.

An independent mechanic can build up business by personally contacting large organizations to solicit their repair needs. Since most organizations use business machines, practically any facility that the mechanic contacts can be a potential customer. Advertising in the telephone book's yellow pages is an excellent way of making services known throughout the business community.

A business machine mechanic also trained in typewriter repair can combine both talents to offer a complete all-around office repair service.

Many government agencies periodically offer surplus and worn-out business machines for sale at a fraction of their original cost. These machines can be purchased by an independent person, reconditioned economically at cost, and then resold to private businesses at a handsome profit. The same can be done with machines obtained through bankruptcy auctions.

For information on obtaining government surplus business machines, contact your local office of the Small Business Administration. It can furnish you with names and addresses of local defense and civilian surplus sales offices. Information on bankruptcy auctions can be obtained through your local newspaper or by contacting city hall.

Business machine technicians work year-round and have steadier employment than many other skilled workers. Office machines must be maintained, even when business slackens, as records must be kept, correspondence carried on, and statistical reports prepared.

VENDING MACHINE
MECHANIC

Vending machines have become a familiar part of the everyday lives of most people. You find them wherever you go. They are used to dispense all types of merchandise from cigarettes and candy to hot and cold foods and beverages. They provide a variety of services, such as change making, tube testing, and even car washing. They provide entertainment in the form of video pong machines, game machines, juke boxes, and pinball machines. The volume of business done through vending machines is almost $10 billion annually.

Vending machines are becoming more and more sophisticated. Most have complex electrical circuitry. Many contain refrigeration and heating units. The complex construction of the modern vending machine means one thing—there is certain to be mechanical breakdown. Since service and trouble-free operation are the foundation of a vending business, the success of a company's automatic vending operations depends on the talents of those who repair its machines—the *vending machine mechanics.* As the numbers and kinds of machines in operation continue to increase, employers will need more skilled mechanics to solve repair and maintenance problems.

When a machine breaks down, the repair mechanic first diagnoses the problem with such equipment as test lamps, ammeters, and ohmeters to check the electrical system for possible short circuits or other electrical troubles. Pressure gauges and thermometers are used to test refrigeration and heating systems.

To repair a machine, it is necessary to disassemble parts of the vending machine, adjust the mechanical parts, and repair electrical circuits and liquid piping systems.

The skilled vending machine mechanic has some of the skills of the plumber, electrician, and machinist. A must is the ability to read blueprints and understand technical illustrations.

A trainee can learn this trade on the job through observing, working with, and receiving instruction from experienced mechanics. Sometimes the trainee attends manufacturer-sponsored training sessions that emphasize the repair of new and complex machines. Correspondence or night school courses in related technical subjects are important for information not usually learned during on-the-job training.

A few vocational schools and junior colleges offer one-year and two-year programs in automatic vending machine repair. These programs can provide a student with a thorough understanding of all phases of vending machine operation and repair. Included in most vocational programs are the following courses: hand and machine tool principles, vending machine tool principles, soldering and brazing theory, vending machine circuitry, principles of timers and controls, vending machine plumbing principles, food and beverage heating and refrigeration methods, principles of carbon dioxide systems, principles of coin and currency devices and cup-dispensing components, and repair cost estimating. A good program can accelerate becoming a first-class mechanic with top wage-earning potential.

For information concerning training programs, contact:

The National Automatic
Merchandising Association
7 South Dearborn Street
Chicago, Illinois 60603

SALARY AND EMPLOYMENT OPPORTUNITIES

A vending machine repair mechanic usually makes from $8 to $11 an hour. The widespread use of vending machines to provide automatic food services for employees in factories, offices, hospitals, military camps, and other institutions has increased the need for experienced mechanics to keep these machines functioning properly.

It is not difficult for a vending machine mechanic to operate an independent repair service. There are many machines to be repaired for organizations who own their own machines. Vending service firms also need repair work done for them and will contract independent technicians to perform their service calls.

A machine repair firm will usually charge its customers from $20 to $25 an hour for services performed. An independent repair mechanic may charge the same fee or less. Since a technician depends mainly on knowledge and skills in the performance of the repair work, the independent does not have to pay out large sums of money for equipment. Usually a few hundred dollars for testing and repairing equipment will suffice the beginning technician.

It may be advantageous to start a vending route. Once in the business as a repair technician, a vending machine mechanic can easily ascertain the best prices vending machines may be purchased at. This is mentioned because many novices going into the vending machine business pay inflated prices for equipment that can be purchased more cheaply by experienced personnel in the field. Vending machine mechanics who are able to purchase and install their own machines can do very well financially. By combining these two services, these enterprising people will have eliminated the single biggest overhead expense faced by vending machine operators.

The widespread use of sophisticated vending machines to dispense many products and services can provide a good financial future to the ambitious mechanic who keeps up with the latest advancements in this field.

WATCHMAKER

For the man or woman with an aptitude for mechanical operations plus finger dexterity, the repair of watches, clocks, and other time measuring devices offers a rewarding future as a member of a widely respected craft. In today's technological age the skills and services of the competent, fully trained watch repair technician (known professionally as a *watchmaker*) are in broad demand.

Approximately nine out of ten adults own watches with almost half of them owning more than one timepiece. Trends in the kinds of watches in use also serve to increase the need for watch repair services. For instance, women's preference for small watches require more frequent servicing. The growing popularity of more complicated watches, such as calendar, self-winding, chronograph, and electric watches will call for a growing volume of repair work. Futhermore, the advent of digital watches in the marketplace is creating an entirely new field in watch repair. Their repair requires knowledge and skills different from those involved in fixing conventional watches. At present there are very few people qualified to repair digital watches. This opens a completely new avenue of opportunities to the watchmaker willing to undertake extra training in digital watch repair.

Today's qualified watch repair technician is prepared to service and repair the many different kinds of timepieces in popular usage. He or she understands and is familiar with the functioning not only of the basic timing mechanism, but also of the calendar, automatic, alarm, and other features of the modern timepiece.

While the sophistication of parts standardization relieves the technician largely of the production of new parts, a person considering watchmaking as a career should possess adequate skills in this area so that if the need arises he or she can manufacture or alter a part and finish it to factory specifications. This is especially true if one is to qualify for the repairing of complicated watches and clocks and special timing devices.

TRAINING REQUIREMENTS

Before you enter the field of watchmaking you must ask yourself these questions:

1. Do you enjoy working with small mechanical devices?

2. Are you inquisitive? Can you analyze and diagnose mechanical failure?

3. Do you enjoy working with instruments?

4. Are you mechanically inclined?

If you can answer "yes" to these questions, you may enjoy watch repairing.

There are a number of watchmaking schools located throughout the country that provide the training necessary for one to enter this craft. However, it is beneficial to the new trainee if he or she has a high school background in mathematics, physics, chemistry, electricity, mechanical drawing, and machine shop.

Most watchmakers are trained in private watch repair schools and public vocational schools. The technical course progresses from simple to complex, with particular stress on the practical. In most schools emphasis is placed on disassembling and assembling watch movements, truing hairsprings, truing and poising balance wheels, removing and replacing balance staffs, adjusting escapements, setting friction jewels, operating a watchmaker's lathe, and overhauling watches.

To complete the fundamental requirements for holding a job, a training period of from twelve to twenty-four months is required, the duration of the training depending largely on individual ability. To obtain a national roster of watchmaking schools, write:

American Watchmaker's Institute
P.O. Box 11011
Cincinnati, Ohio 45211

Some states require watch repair technicians to obtain a license, which is issued upon passing an examination designed to test the technician's skill with tools and to test the knowledge of watch construction and repair.

In addition, voluntary proficiency examinations are offered by the American Watchmaker's Institute to graduates of watchmaker's schools and to practicing watchmakers who wish to demonstrate their ability. Through these examinations watchmakers in all states can demonstrate their degree of competence by passing one or two certification examinations. Successful examinees receive the title of either Certified Watchmaker or Certified Master Watchmaker, depending on their proficiency. Annual voluntary examinations covering new phases of watchmaking are also offered, and those who pass are given a plaque of recognition. These certificates and plaques can increase the employment opportunities and starting salaries for technicians. Furthermore, the watchmaker who owns a shop can display the certificates in the shop to help create a professional image, which can also increase business.

SALARY AND EMPLOYMENT OPPORTUNITIES

The new technician is well advised to seek his or her first job with an experienced watch repair technician in order to continue to learn and train for more responsibility. A newly graduated watchmaker can find employment opportunities in specialized shops that only do watch repair work or in retail jewelry stores taking care of all of the watch repair needs of an individual store. An experienced watch repair technician can earn approximately $8.50 an hour, even more if able to handle some of the more complicated watches such as the digital watches.

Some graduates who have completed courses in all phases of watch repairing choose to open their own businesses. In addition to building a retail clientele of their own, they frequently enter into agreements to do watch repairs for retail jewelry stores. They may even solicit the repair requirements for a small chain of jewelry stores. Some shop owners may take special factory-sponsored courses that teach the repair techniques of a certain watch manufacturer. In this manner their shops may become designated as official repair stations for the repair work of a particular watch manufacturer.

The owner of a good watch repair shop can eventually obtain franchised dealerships from several watch manufacturers not only to repair their watches, but also to sell them. Some watch repair shops also do a good business in purchasing damaged watches for very little money, repairing them, and then reselling them for considerable profit.

The owner of a watch repair shop usually charges for work at the rate of from $14 to $18 an hour. To obtain a large service contract from a busy jewelry store or chain of stores, one may alter this fee slightly. Once a large volume of business has been developed, the shop owner can hire other competent watch repair technicians; and even though it may be necessary to pay them $8.50 an hour, the store owner can still profit by about $7 an hour from the work of such employees. For the owner of a busy shop who also sells watches, this can add up to quite a sum of money at the end of the year. Another plus about watch repair is that for about $5,000 you can set up a sophisticated attractive shop capable of handling many types of work orders.

A variety of positions in industry, in addition to the watch manufacturing industry itself, require skills possessed by the watchmaker as a basis for specialized adaptation. Manufacturers of tiny electronic components for space, computer, and other applications need technicians who can work to precise specifications and are able to assemble small parts. Precision instrument manufacturers also seek to hire watch repair technicians. Some added specialized training will qualify the watchmaker to work as an instrument maker, instrument repair technician, camera repairperson, assembler, and aviation and meteorological instrument technician. The opportunities are there.

CAMERA
REPAIR TECHNICIAN

Modern cameras, along with their accessory equipment, are extremely complex, and they frequently break down. This has opened up unprecedented opportunities for technicians skilled in camera repair. The critical need for men and women to service photo equipment occurred when the photo industry began its rapid growth in the 1950s. Since then more and more highly sophisticated cameras, projectors, light meters, and flash units are constantly being produced and marketed. Technicians to service this equipment have not been trained in large enough numbers. Consequently, the average person might wait months to get a camera serviced.

If you like photography, are mechanically inclined, enjoy problem solving, and can work with tiny, precise mechanisms, there may be a bright future for you in camera repair. Some of the greatest, most available jobs in the photographic industry today are related not to taking pictures, but to the ever growing technology that supports today's photography. Photo equipment technology offers unique opportunities. It is varied and challenging and brings satisfaction with every project completed.

The *camera repair technicians* find causes of malfunctions and then repair them, having at their disposal a complete array of highly sophisticated electronic equipment to aid in testing shutter speeds, shutter and flash synchronizatlons, light meters, and range finders.

TRAINING REQUIREMENTS

It is necessary for the successful camera repair technician to have a good knowledge of electronic and mechanical principles. Various instrument technology courses may be helpful in this field. To the person with some electronic and mechanical training, an on-the-job training apprenticeship in a good all-around camera repair shop may prove extremely valuable. Some large camera manufacturing firms offer factory training programs in repairing their equipment. Several technical schools in the country offer resident and correspondence courses in camera repair. One such school is:

The National Camera
Technical Training School
2000 West Union Avenue
Englewood, Colorado 80110.

Once you learn the basics of camera repair, you must always keep up with the latest developments in the field. This can be accomplished through factory-sponsored training seminars, camera repair journals, manufacturer's repair booklets, and correspondence programs. It is estimated that in order to stay current with the new inventions in photographic equipment, an individual must completely relearn the field every seven years. Although this may be time-consuming at times, it also makes camera repair a very exciting, unique, and challenging field and offers the up-to-date repair technician a somewhat exclusive franchise in the camera repair field.

For information concerning training programs in camera repair, write:

*National Association of Trade
and Technical Schools*
2021 L Street, N.W.
Washington, D.C. 20036

National Home Study Council
1601 Eighteenth Street, N.W.
Washington, D.C. 20009

SALARY AND EMPLOYMENT OPPORTUNITIES

The skilled camera repair technician can go into business for him or herself, work for a manufacturer, sales organization, photo laboratory, a photo dealer, industry, or a government agency. Trained camera technicians are skilled in the needs of photography and sometimes branch out into manufacturing, photographic instrumentation, instrument servicing, or other photographic sidelines.

A good repair technician can earn approximately $8 to $10 an hour working for someone else. The work is not strenuous. Skilled technicians can go into business for themselves in their own repair shops.

The independent operator usually charges on the basis of $20 an hour for his or her services. A good shop can be opened with approximately $6,000 worth of equipment. The beginner can start at home or as a concessionaire in an existing photographic supply store.

To get a business started, in addition to advertising in local newspapers and the yellow pages of the telephone directory, the aggressive entrepreneur can call on camera supply stores and camera manufacturers and offer to handle their general repair and warranty work.

Camera repair can provide an individual a secure financial future plus prestige approaching professional status.

ELECTRIC SIGN
SERVICE MECHANIC

Wherever you go, there are electric signs. Such signs are used to advertise and make known the presence of every type of business from the corner drugstore to the largest department stores to an amusement park. As businesses modernize, so do the signs that announce and advertise them, and they become the hallmark of the businesses they advertise.

Electric signs also break down. Whenever they undergo mechanical and electrical failure, they must be fixed immediately in order to preserve the identity of the store or building they advertise. *Electric sign service mechanics* maintain and repair hundreds of thousands of neon and illuminated plastic signs. Some even assemble and install the signs.

Service mechanics diagnose trouble in faulty signs. They repair defective wiring and replace neon tubing and burned out lamps. For revolving signs, they repair and overhaul motors, gears, bearings and other parts necessary for the proper operation of the sign. Sometimes they can suggest ways to increase the attractiveness and visibility of signs, such as changing the color of the tubing or redesigning the face of the sign. To make the adjustments, they might use hand tools and power tools, such as screwdrivers and electric drills, and testing devices, such as voltmeters. Their trucks are equipped with ladders and boom cranes so that they can reach the signs they service.

TRAINING REQUIREMENTS

Most electric sign mechanics are hired as trainees and learn their trade informally on the job. They rotate through the various phases of sign making to obtain a general knowledge of tasks—such as cutting and assembling metal and plastic signs, mounting neon tubing, wiring signs, and installing electric parts. Approximately three years of on-the-job training is required to become fully qualified. A trainee can supplement this training with night school classes in electrical theory, blueprint reading, mechanical drawing, and plastic technology.

All electric sign mechanics must be familiar with the national electric codes. Where local electrical codes exist, they must know these too. Many cities require that sign mechanics be licensed. Licenses can be obtained by passing an examination in electrical theory and its applications.

SALARY AND EMPLOYMENT OPPORTUNITIES

The salary of a fully trained electric sign service mechanic is approximately $8 to $10 an hour with time and one-half for overtime. It is relatively easy for a mechanic to open a repair shop. All types of businesses need to have their electric signs serviced and repaired. Mechanics in business for themselves usually charge clients approximately $20–$25 an hour for labor, plus parts, which allows them a profit.

To go into business for oneself, an electrical sign contractor's license is usually required. A person who has gone through a thorough on-the-job training program will usually have no trouble passing the licensing exam. As for equipment, a worker will need a truck outfitted with a boom crane. If the beginning service mechanic does not have the initial capital for this investment, it may be possible to lease or rent the equipment. In fact, if it is possible to get written maintenance contracts from the businesses and firms solicited, the new businessperson may be able to borrow the money from a bank or another lending institution on the strength of the contracts alone.

A service mechanic with some artistic ability can even open a sign manufacturing shop. The material necessary for the construction of each sign can be purchased after a work order has been procured, thus eliminating the need to tie up large sums of money in inventory. A sign manufacturer will usually calculate the selling price of a sign at triple the actual cost of manufacturing. As you can see, there is money to be made in this business.

One way to promote a new sign business is to find out about new construction and remodeling plans of various businesses. This can be done by contacting real estate agencies, reading the real estate section of the local Sunday newspaper, and contacting the appropriate town department that receives applications for building and remodeling permits. Whenever a business structure is newly built or remodeled, the electric sign requirements are contracted out to private sign manufacturing shops.

Employment of electric sign service mechanics is expected to increase very rapidly through the mid-1980s. More signs will be needed as new businesses open and as old ones expand and modernize their facilities. Signs already in use will also continue to require maintenance.

For additional information on opportunities in electrical sign servicing, write:

National Electric Sign Association
600 Hunter Drive
Oak Brook, Illinois 60521

LOCKSMITH

Wherever you have a door or other opening whose access you want restricted to only certain people, you have a lock. Consequently, wherever you have a lock, at one time or another the services of a *locksmith* will be required.

A locksmith is a skilled craftsperson who is paid for knowledge and skill in installing new locks, repairing broken ones, making new keys to replace lost ones, changing combinations on safes, and rekeying locks to accept new keys. A locksmith may be called upon to advise various businesses and industrial firms on the best types of locks to install in fulfilling their security requirements.

A key cutter is able to make duplicate keys by tracing the outline of the original. But it is the locksmith who is able to make a new key without the original because of the knowledge of the inner workings of that particular lock. Naturally, this is of particular importance when the original key has been lost. It is usually done by knowing how to interpret the various code numbers assigned to the lock.

Locksmiths can determine the cause of a malfunctioning lock by removing the entire lock or cylinder. Afterward it can be fixed by making certain adjustments or in some cases by fashioning new parts. To fix a lock, the smith may use welding and soldering equipment as well as such other tools and equipment as tweezers, files, calipers, clamps, vices, spacers, feeler gauges, extractors, lockpicks, hacksaws, chisels, and rules.

Combination locks offer a special challenge. The experienced locksmith quite often will open them by touch, that is, by rotating the dial and feeling the vibrations when the wheel comes into place. Occasionally a bank will call upon a locksmith to change the combination of a safe. To do this, one must have a thorough knowledge of the intricate mechanisms of a particular lock and then make a series of adjustments so that the lock will open when a predetermined combination of numbers are dialed.

Whenever a retail store or home is purchased, the new owners will immediately have the locks changed to prevent any former inhabitants from reentering at a later date.

As a security measure, many firms periodically have their locks rekeyed to accept new keys and make old keys useless. To do this, locksmiths change the locking mechanism to fit new key codes. Rekeying a master system is one of the most complicated and time-consuming jobs handled by a locksmith. In a master system some keys must open all doors, while others are required to open only certain doors.

Some locksmiths install and repair electronic burglar alarms and surveillance systems. A basic knowledge of electricity and electronics is needed to install and repair these systems. If a master locksmith does learn this extra skill, that person is in an opportune position to solicit the security business from large firms. Unfortunately, crime is continually increasing, and many firms, both large and small, are giving their security requirements top priority. This bodes well for the locksmith proficient in the installation of electrical surveillance equipment.

TRAINING REQUIREMENTS

The skills of this trade can be learned on the job in a three- or four-year apprenticeship program. The future locksmith will start out as an apprentice, then advance to journeyman, and finally to master locksmith. Included in the training are 144 hours of classroom work. Either formal classroom instruction or supervised correspondence courses are acceptable. A candidate should have mechanical aptitude, good eye–hand coordination, and manual dexterity. In high school it is advisable to take courses in machine shop, mechanical drawing, and mathematics. Training on the job starts with the more elementary tasks, such as identifying key blanks, duplicating keys, and learning how to fit keys to locks.

As the trainee becomes more proficient, he or she will learn to make parts for locks, change combinations, and fit keys by impressions. All through one's career, however, it will be necessary to keep up with new lock systems and other new developments. This can be accomplished by reading monthly technical journals, attending training classes given by lock manufacturers, and attending various lock conventions.

Several schools offering correspondence courses in locksmithing are:

Belsaw Institute
315 Westport Road
Kansas City, Missouri 64111

Locksmith Institute
Little Falls, New Jersey 07424

Other information concerning training programs may be obtained by writing:

Associated Locksmiths of America
11 Elmendorf Street
Kingston, New York 12401

SALARY AND EMPLOYMENT OPPORTUNITIES

An experienced locksmith can earn approximately $8 to $11 per hour working for someone else. The appeal of becoming a locksmith, however, is that it is very practical and feasible to go into business for yourself since the locksmith depends upon the knowledge and skills in performing the job rather than on expensive equipment. One does not need a large work area; therefore, the rental of a small workshop will usually suffice. Sometimes a locksmith can work from home and keep the equipment needed in a mobile van in which to drive from job to job. The rental of a small concession in a busy shopping center or department store will expose a locksmith to the customers requiring services.

A self-employed locksmith can make from $20,000 to $40,000 a year, and possibly even more. It depends on how much you, the locksmith, want to go out and promote yourself. You can contract for the permanent business of hotels and motels, local school systems, office buildings, automobile dealers and garages, banks, real estate developers, retail businesses and government installations and industries that require tight security measures. In fact, any type of structure that requires doors and locks means potential business to the locksmith who is willing to seek the business.

The locksmith profession will always be a stable one since during good economic times increased building requires the installation of new locks and during poor economic conditions (when crime increases) people tend to be more protective of their possessions and thus need the services of a locksmith.

Over half the people in this country wear glasses and contact lenses to correct irregularities of vision. This creates not only professional opportunities for ophthalmologists and optometrists, who diagnose and prescribe corrective lenses, but also career and business opportunities for people who fabricate and dispense these lenses—the *opticians.* Moreover, eyeglasses have entered the world of high fashion. Not only have people become clothes conscious to improve their appearance, but now they may also change the style of their eyeglasses to enhance their appearance. This alone has created many job and business opportunities for opticians, both as employees of others and as proprietors of their own optical shops.

Dispensing opticians and optical mechanics (also called optical laboratory technicians) make and fit eyeglasses prescribed by ophthalmologists and optometrists. *Dispensing opticians* adjust finished glasses to fit the customer. In some states they are also permitted to fit contact lenses. *Optical mechanics* grind and polish lenses according to prescription and assemble lenses in frames. Occasionally, the jobs of dispensing optician and optical mechanic are combined.

Dispensing opticians determine where lenses should be placed in relation to the customer's eyes by measuring the distance between the centers of the pupils. They also assist the customer in selecting the proper eyeglass frame by measuring the customer's facial features and showing the various styles and colors of frames.

Dispensing opticians prepare work orders that give optical mechanics the information they need to interpret prescriptions properly, grind the lenses, and insert them in a frame. The work orders include lens prescriptions, information on lens size, tint, and optical centering as well as frame size, color, and style. Sometimes dispensing opticians stock large quantities of lenses with the more common prescriptions already ground into them. They shape the lenses to fit the frames and then insert them into the frames. This allows them to eliminate sending some work orders to the optical laboratory, thus providing quicker service for their customers.

After glasses are made, dispensing opticians adjust the frame to the contours of the customer's face and head so they fit properly. Adjustments are made with hand tools such as optical pliers, files, and screwdrivers. A special instrument is used to check the power and surface quality of the lenses. In some shops dispensing opticians grind and finish lenses and sell other optical goods, such as binoculars and nonprescription sunglasses.

In fitting contact lenses, dispensing opticians follow ophthalmologists' or optometrists' prescriptions, measure the corneas of the customer's eyes, and then prepare specifications to be followed by the lens manufacturers. They also instruct customers on how to insert, remove, and care for contact lenses.

Optical mechanics use precision tools to grind and polish lenses to meet the specifications of ophthalmologists and optometrists and then shape the lens for insertion into the selected frame. They usually work in wholesale optical laboratories that supply optical shops with work orders submitted by them. Occasionally an optician with his or her own optical shop will perform both the dispensing and grinding work.

TRAINING REQUIREMENTS

Dispensing opticians and mechanics can learn their specialties through four-year, on-the-job training programs in dispensing optical shops and manufacturing firms. However, formal institutional training for the optician and optical mechanic is becoming more common. There are a number of two-year academic programs in the United States leading to an associate's degree in optical technology. Large manufacturers of contact lenses offer nondegree courses in contact lens fitting that usually last a few weeks. A number of opticians and mechanics learn their trades in the armed forces. Anyone wanting to pursue a career in the optical field should take physics, algebra, geometry, and mechanical drawing courses in high school.

A list of schools offering courses for people who wish to become dispensing opticians or optical mechanics may be obtained from:

Associated Opticians of America
1250 Connecticut Avenue, N.W.
Washington, D.C. 20036

SALARY AND EMPLOYMENT OPPORTUNITIES

Dispensing opticians generally earn a salary of $10,000 to $15,000 a year, depending on experience and position held. They are usually employed in commercial optical shops, government facilities such as Veterans Administration hospitals, and optometrists' and ophthalmologists' offices.

Those employed in ophthalmologists' offices sometimes are paid a percentage of the profit on the work they perform in addition to a base salary. In some cases this can add up to a salary of $20,000 a year. A dispensing optician with a capital investment of approximately $15,000 can open an optical shop dispensing prescription glasses. With a good location and a good selection of frames, the owner can earn well over $25,000 a year.

In building up an optical business, an optician can call on busy ophthalmologists who do not employ their own optician to solicit their patronage in servicing their patients' eyeglass needs. In addition, joining civic groups can greatly increase the opportunities of making an optician's services known throughout the community. Also, offering specialized services can add to a shop's clientele. An example of such a service is the personalizing of frames and lenses by inscribing the customer's names or initials on the temples of the frame or in a corner of the lenses.

The salary of an optical mechanic is generally in the neighborhood of $12,000 a year. This can increase by 20 percent if the mechanic is promoted to a supervisory position. Mechanics are usually employed by large manufacturing laboratories. They also have the opportunity of opening their own laboratory and soliciting work orders from dispensing opticians.

Employment of dispensing opticians and optical mechanics is expected to increase very rapidly, for demand for prescription lenses is expected to increase as a result of population growth, rising literacy and educational levels, and a large increase in the number of older persons (a group most likely to need glasses). State programs to provide eye care for low-income families, union health insurance plans, and Medicare will also stimulate demand. Moreover, the growing variety of frame styles and colors are encouraging individuals to buy more than one pair of glasses.

While the eyeglass business employs a large number of optical technicians, new developments in optics have brought opportunities for these skilled workers in a variety of industries. These include the photographic industry, missile industry, copying industry, space exploration, and many other industries requiring precision optical instruments.

General information about these occupations may be obtained from:

American Board of Opticianry
821 Eggert Road
Buffalo, New York 14226

Optical Wholesalers Association
6935 Wisconsin Avenue
Washington, D.C. 20015

DENTAL LABORATORY TECHNICIAN

Many of the beautiful smiles you see people flashing are the result of the expert dental work performed by skilled dental technicians. Adults have just one set of teeth. When something happens to them as a result of tooth decay, infection, or accident, fortunately they are able to be restored or replaced through artificial methods performed by the dentist and the dental laboratory technicians.

A *dental laboratory technician* is defined as one who, qualified by education, training, and experience, may assist in the design, fabrication, and production of artificial dental devices. All work is done under the direction and orders of a dentist.

Some of the work requirements performed by the technician are the making of crowns, inlays, bridges, and complete dentures. Some of the skills employed in the execution of the preceding requirements are the following: pouring of impressions, model making and trimming; the routine setup and arranging of artificial teeth for dentures; waxing and contouring; working with porcelain or plastic in making crowns; making the metal framework for complete and partial dentures; tooth staining and the individualization of teeth; adapting and carving of patterns; investing, burning out, and casting of precious metals such as gold in the making of inlays; and sometimes making braces to correct faulty positioning of teeth.

In a typical dental laboratory the technician, working from the impressions and written directions supplied by the dentist, fashions a model of the dental appliance in wax, checks it, makes final adjustments, and then recasts the dental replacement in one of a number of suitable substances.

Typically, the materials used by the dental technician are wax, plaster, acrylic resin, porcelain, and a number of precious metals. To perform their work, technicians use small hand tools as well as special electric lathes and drills, high-heat furnaces, and other kinds of specialized laboratory equipment.

TRAINING REQUIREMENTS

The prospective dental laboratory technician must be mechanically and artistically inclined and possess manual and digital dexterity.

This craft may be learned through on-the-job experience in a commercial dental laboratory or in a dental laboratory technology program accredited by the Council on Dental Education of the American Dental Association. These accredited programs last approximately eighteen months. Dental laboratory technology is taught in a variety of educational institutions, such as a department of a dental school, vocational and technical schools, or a military training center.

After completion of a thorough on-the-job training program or an academic program in dental laboratory technology, the dental laboratory technician is eligible for certification by the National Association of Dental Laboratories as a Certified Dental Technician (CDT).

For information concerning training programs in dental technology, write:

National Association of Trade
and Technical Schools
2021 L Street, N.W.
Washington, D.C. 20036

American Dental Association
Council on Dental Education
211 East Chicago Avenue
Chicago, Illinois 60611

National Association
of Dental Laboratories, Inc.
3801 Mt. Vernon Avenue
Alexandria, Virginia 22305

For scholarship information, write:

The American Fund
for Dental Education
211 East Chicago Avenue
Chicago, Illinois 60611

An experienced dental laboratory technician can earn approximately $250 to $350 a week in a commercial dental laboratory, large group-practice dental office, and government agencies such as Veterans Administration hospitals.

Once a technician acquires a great deal of proficiency through experience and becomes known in the dental community for expert work, it is quite feasible for that individual to open a dental laboratory. A small laboratory can be set up with just a few thousand dollars worth of equipment, and the earning potential is over $25,000 a year for the technician-proprietor.

Employment of dental laboratory technicians is expected to grow rapidly due to the expansion of prepayment dental plans and the increasing number of older people who require artificial dentures. In addition, the number of dentists is not expected to keep pace with the demand for their services. Therefore, to devote more time to treatment of patients, dentists will send more and more of their laboratory work to commercial firms or hire dental laboratory technicians to work directly for them.

ANTIQUE RESTORER

Antique collecting has always been a favorite pastime of many people, and today, it is becoming more popular than ever before. People collect antiques for reasons: some for nostalgic purposes, some for financial investment, some to complement an interior decorating scheme, some because the old designs are attractive to them, and many for all of these reasons. Most people want their antiques to be more than just conversation pieces and items of interest; they want them to be functional and add to the appearance of their surroundings as well. This has opened up a fairly new field known as antique restoring. A good *antique restorer* who can take a heavily worn and dull-looking antique and return it to its original luster and beauty can profit handsomely from doing so.

TRAINING REQUIREMENTS

Learning antique restoring does not require a lengthy training program. People desiring to go into this business should possess artistic and mechanical aptitude and like working with their hands. Many antiques are made of wood. To restore these items involves the treating and refinishing of the wood to return it to its original color and luster. A single piece of old furniture is usually made up of several antique items. It is often necessary to remove old padding and coverings and replace them with new padding and coverings that have the same color tones and texture of the original item. Therefore, a knowledge of basic reupholstering is helpful. A knowledge of woodworking is a must since very often an antique may have become broken or weakened with age and will require minor repairs that must blend in with the original design.

There are antiques that contain metal work that may have become tarnished or broken through the ages. Some courses in basic welding can be very useful in this area. A good hardware store can give advice on what chemicals and polishes can be used to restore metal parts to their original luster. Some antiques have mechanical devices that no longer work. Very old sewing machines, washing machines, or phonographs, for example, are popular collector items. The ability to make mechanical repairs on such items can put a good antique restorer way out in front of his or her competition.

Because antiques comprise so many different types of items from the past, there are no set requirements or credentials that one must have to become a restorer. The exciting thing about this type of business is that it allows someone to use imagination and ingenuity in restoring an item. Each antique can present a new and exciting challenge to the innovative craftsperson. An ambitious person with business ability can keep experimenting with new methods and techniques in solving all kinds of restoration problems. Many people who have had experience working with wood and metal objects may not need any formal training to practice this craft. They can always find new ways of doing things by reading various mechanical and wood-working journals.

To the beginner in this field, it is advisable to take night school courses in subjects such as wood and metal finishing, machine shop, cabinet making, carpentry, soldering, and reupholstery. Some schools offer antique restoration classes; these combine most of the fundamental techniques needed in antique restoring.

SALARY AND EMPLOYMENT OPPORTUNITIES

There is no one basic salary for an antique restorer. Usually an individual with some training and experience in this field can go directly into business as the cost of the necessary tools required is very low. Antiques are repaired and restored by the skill of the person's hands, not by expensive machinery. The work can be done in a garage or small shop.

People spend a lot of money on antiques today. They are also willing to spend more money to restore their purchases to the original condition. Therefore, the price that can be charged for a restoration job is usually "wide open." A good crafter can charge $20 an hour or more for the service. The purchaser of an antique buys the item to recapture a time in history and very often as an investment for resale at a later date. Therefore, the cost of restoring an item, as long as it is not outrageous, is not of prime concern to the purchaser.

There are many ways an antique restorer can advertise. Small ads in local newspapers are helpful. Many supermarkets and laundromats have neighborhood bulletin boards where a craftsperson can put an advertisement advising the community of the talents and services offered.

Keep one thing in mind: when an individual purchases an

antique, he or she usually does not know where to go for restoration services. What is more, the people specializing in this type of work are few in number. Therefore, you are doing the antique purchaser a service by making him aware of your services. It is a good idea to go to all of the antique shops in your area advising the owners of your services and leaving them your business cards to pass out to their customers. Very often a shop's owner can make an otherwise difficult sale on a badly worn piece of merchandise by directing the customer to a good restorer. In fact, the owner of the shop may even use the services of the restorer to improve upon some items to increase their chances for sale.

Practically every week, in many cities, there are antique auctions. It is a good practice to frequent these auctions, passing out your business cards to the crowd, especially to the people who have just purchased an item. In most cases they will be grateful to you for doing so.

Interior decorators are another valuable source of customers. Very often they will advise their clients to purchase certain types of antique items to add to and complete a decorating scheme. To make your services known, write or personally call upon those listed under Interior Decorators in the telephone directory's yellow pages. In fact, list yourself in the yellow pages under Antique Restoring. You may find that you will be the only one listed.

There are many ways for both men and women to make an excellent income on either a full-time or part-time basis in this exciting craft. If this be your forte—good luck!

FIBERGLASS REPAIR
MECHANIC

When people speak of certain products being made out of fiberglass, in most cases they are actually speaking of fiberglass-reinforced plastic. Fiberglass is glass that has been drawn or blown into fine, flexible fibers or filaments. These fibers are then imbedded in a thermosetting plastic resin and subjected to heat and pressure. The resulting product is called a fiberglass-reinforced plastic, commonly referred to as fiberglass. Laminates of this kind, in which parallel glass strands are employed, are stronger per unit weight than any of the other common structural building materials including steel, magnesium, and aluminum. Fiberglass is nonreactive and provides for a noncorrosive and easily maintained attractive finish. Laminated sheets of fiberglass-reinforced plastic are used in the construction of many products including the following: truck and car bodies; corrugated paneling for use as partitions and as roofing for carports, patios, and swimming pools; bodies of pleasure boats, recreational vehicles, motor homes, and dune buggies; outdoor recreation equipment; bathtubs; swimming pools; shower stalls; and chemical storage tanks.

As strong as it is, fiberglass, like all other products, is subject to cracking and breaking due to naturally occurring wear and tear or damage due to impact. When this happens, there are relatively few people with the knowledge and skill to repair fiberglass. Therefore, the opportunities for someone in this field are tremendous. The process is easy to learn, and with some experience an individual can become highly skilled and build up a profitable reputation in the performance of fiberglass repair. We will call this repairperson a *fiberglass repair mechanic*.

TRAINING REQUIREMENTS

A three-month training program in a good trade or technical school can provide an individual with the essential knowledge and skills necessary to perform fiberglass repair operations. Any school offering a plastics technology program will usually provide a short training program in this field.

When a piece of fiberglass is broken, the jagged edges are filed away and a piece of fabric is placed in the area of the hole. Next, the repair mechanic applies various plastic resins over the fabric and blends it in with the solid fiberglass left intact. After the resin sets, it is sanded down to provide a smooth finish, after which it is painted to match the rest of the structure. When there is only a crack in a piece of fiberglass, the fabric is eliminated and the resins are skillfully applied to penetrate and cover the crack. After setting, it is also sanded and painted.

SALARY AND EMPLOYMENT OPPORTUNITIES

The best way to make money in this field is to be in business for yourself. All you need are your hands, your ingenuity, and a few dollars worth of tools. When someone needs an important product fixed, they are not about to quibble over price. Therefore, it is common for a good mechanic to charge $20 an hour and even more for services. It is also a common practice to charge a fee for travel time to and from a job.

The first step in starting a repair business is to advertise in the telephone book's yellow pages under Fiberglass Repair. You may be the only one listed. Next, every person or firm that may eventually be in need of fiberglass repair services should be contacted. If there is a marina in your area, every boat owner should be informed of your services, via boating newspapers and listings in marine supply shops. Since most pleasure boats today are constructed totally of fiberglass, a fiberglass mechanic may work full time specializing in just boat repair.

Diesel truck dealers are another possible source of income. The cabs of most large diesel trucks are now constructed from fiberglass. Furthermore, most body shops do not handle fiberglass repairs. Essentially, a beginning repairer should go through every listing in the phone directory's yellow pages, and whenever a business organization that might possibly sell or utilize fiberglass products in its operations is found, the personnel should be contacted to advise them of the services offered. In a heavily populated industrial area the repair mechanic who gets out and hustles may eventually have more business than one person can handle.

For additional information, write:

Owens-Corning Fiberglass Corporation
5933 Telegraph Road
Los Angeles, California 90040

UPHOLSTERER

We live in a comfort- and style-conscious society. We are very aware of the internal environment in homes, hotels, offices, restaurants, travel facilities (such as cars, buses, and airplanes), and any other place where people congregate and relax for a period of time. The style and comfort of sofas and chairs add a great deal to the warmth and beauty of any of the facilities.

Sofas and chairs have to be built, and when they wear out and their style becomes passé, some people buy new ones, but many others have the old ones rebuilt and reconditioned. It is the *upholsterer* who performs these skills.

An upholsterer can work in a furniture factory participating in the original construction of furniture or in a shop concerned with the rebuilding and restyling of furniture. The latter description can be termed the *reupholstering* of furniture. We will restrict our discussion to the craftsperson engaged in the reupholstering of furniture in custom repair shops. The reason for this is that most factories use assembly-line production methods whereas in a custom repair shop the upholsterer is usually responsible for the entire rebuilding of a piece of furniture and can, therefore, best express individual talent and craftsmanship in this type of facility. Also, the craftsperson specializing in reupholstering can easily open up a custom repair shop and advance more rapidly monetarily than a worker in a furniture factory.

An upholsterer may completely rebuild a piece of furniture or just rebuild and replace certain worn-out parts. In a complete rebuilding of a chair or sofa it is usually necessary to remove the old fabric, padding, and burlap that cover the springs. The springs, frames, webbing, burlap filling, and padding will be replaced, and next the padding will be covered with muslin. Finally, new fabric and finishing materials are placed on the piece of furniture. In the process the upholsterer will have to stitch the covers, usually both by hand and by sewing machine.

TRAINING REQUIREMENTS

The best way to become skilled in this trade is to attend a good vocational school to learn the fundamentals of the craft and then get about three years of on-the-job training in a good repair shop. Most large cities have excellent vocational schools for upholstering.

SALARY AND EMPLOYMENT OPPORTUNITIES

A highly skilled and creative craftsperson can earn approximately $9 an hour as an employee in a repair shop. However, it is extremely feasible for good craftspeople to open their own shops. In fact, one out of every three upholsterers is self-employed. This is largely due to the fact that an upholsterer depends mainly on personal skills in executing the craft rather than on expensive equipment. An upholstery shop with all the necessary tools and materials of the trade can be furnished for under $2,000.

Whereas an employee upholsterer receives about $9 per hour, the work done for the employer is usually billed to the customer at the rate of $20 or more per hour. Therefore, to be self-employed means a substantially higher income for the upholsterer. Also the shop owner charges the customer additionally for the various parts and fabric covering applied to the furniture. The materials charge usually includes a markup of approximately 40 percent. As you can see, the successful shop owner can build a very lucrative business.

We feel that the future of a highly skilled upholsterer is extremely bright. There are several reasons for this. The price of new furniture, like most other commodities, is soaring. As a result, many people in need of new furniture are having their old furniture reupholstered rather than buy new pieces. This is extremely practical as a reupholstered piece of furniture will be in as good a condition as a new piece—and at a considerably lesser price. By the same token many people whose furniture is in good condition, but who wish to redecorate their homes, are turning to upholsterers to recover their present furniture with newer and more modern fabrics. Thus, a home may assume a new appearance without the owner spending huge sums of money on new furniture.

There are many ways an upholsterer can build up a business. First, one can call on interior decorators and offer to do their clients' work. This type of arrangement usually allows a margin of profit for the interior decorator in addition to the upholsterer; so everyone is happy. Second, the upholsterer may solicit the work of restaurants, airlines, bus companies, hotels, large offices, and just about any institution that utilizes seating. A large work order from one such organization can add considerably to an upholsterer's income. Third, and most important, soliciting the business of the home or apartment dweller via various advertising media can insure a bright future to the qualified upholsterer.

Skilled tailors are true craftspeople. Not only do they mend and alter clothes to make them fit properly, but are also capable of designing and custom making exquisite clothes for the discriminating individual. A good tailor can profit from the needs of people in different income groups. As the economy tightens and inflation increases, many people cannot afford to purchase new clothes. Nevertheless, they still desire to remain stylish and project that well-tailored look. To solve their dilemma, many people are turning to tailors to alter and restyle their old clothing to match the latest fashion trends. This can be done for less money than required for the purchase of new clothes.

Besides the people who have to watch their money closely, there is the other end of the spectrum—the affluent who can afford to have their clothes custom tailored. Here, also, the well-trained tailor can profit. A good tailor can take a bolt of fabric and perform every step needed to turn it into a fine suit, dress, or other piece of wearing apparel. The tailor can have the best of both worlds.

TRAINING REQUIREMENTS

The aspiring tailor should enjoy working with his or her hands, have good depth perception, be artisically inclined, and be imaginative. There are many vocational and trade schools that give excellent training in the fine art of tailoring.

Included in a good program should be the following: clothing design, pattern making, cutting, construction of each part of a garment, stitching, and remodeling techniques. Academic training followed by on-the-job training in a fine tailoring shop can prepare an individual to become a talented and successful tailor.

A tailor working as an employee in someone else's shop is not going to make a high salary. On an employee basis, a tailor earns approximately $6 to $7 an hour. However, it is very practical for a skilled tailor to open his or her own shop. The overhead is low and the initial investment minimal. The self-employed tailor charges for alteration work at the rate of $12 to $15 an hour. For custom work the rate may go higher.

A good tailor shop requires three basic machines.

1. A single-stitch sewing machine

2. A blind-stitch sewing machine

3. An overlock-stitch sewing machine

Each machine costs approximately $400 new or $255 used. Therefore, a shop can be equipped for anywhere from $765 to $1,200. This is a relatively small sum of money to start a business.

In addition to alteration and custom tailoring work, a tailor may also do "Contract Work." This involves contracting clothing manufacturers to perform their sewing requirements. It is a common practice in the garment industry for a manufacturer to cut the cloth for each component of a garment and then subcontract a tailoring establishment to sew each piece together, thus forming the finished product. This type of work requires extra equipment. There are firms that specialize in renting such equipment to tailoring concerns on a month-to-month basis. Therefore, a tailor can obtain a sewing contract, rent the necessary machines, perform the work, and then return the machines. In this manner the tailor pays for the machines only when needed, and thus obtains maximum utilization of capital. A good tailor shop can handle from 500 to 1,000 contract garments a week.

It is also possible for an independent tailor to sign a contract with clothing stores to handle their alteration requirements on new sales.

In custom tailoring, the tailor usually provides the material for the client. Thus the tailor realizes an extra profit of approximately 50 percent or more above the hourly fee for the tailoring skills. Many tailors specialize in custom tailoring one type of garment, such as shirts only or slacks only. Tailors who do this often build up an area reputation for their specialty.

There are several ways for a custom tailor to attract the clientele who would be most interested in the services and who could best afford them. Business executives can be attracted by placing small ads in the business section of local newspapers and in business journals. Likewise, professional people can be attracted by placing the same type of ads in various medical and legal journals. Direct-mail advertising to professionals and executives can also be very effective.

To attract alteration and remodeling work, ads in dry cleaning stores, in local newspapers, and on bulletin boards in laundromats and supermarkets can be effective.

There are many ways the skilled tailor can sell and promote talent to success.

LITHOGRAPHY

Printed material is one of the main means of communication in today's world. It always has been and always will be. The publishing of textbooks, novels, newspapers, magazines, brochures, and catalogues all require the expert attention of the printing profession.

Printing is an involved process involving the skills of many experts in its operation. In a small print shop one person may perform several operations. In a larger shop each worker usually performs just one operation.

Lithography, also called *offset printing*, is one of the most rapidly growing methods of printing. It is a process of photographing the materials to be printed, making a printing plate from the photograph, treating the plate to accept the ink only in the areas to be transferred to the paper, and pressing the inked plate against a rubber plate which, in turn, is pressed against the paper.

Each operation is performed by a specialized group of workers. There are typesetters, paste-up personnel, camera persons, touch-up artists, strippers, platemakers, and press operators, to mention only the most important groups.

In printing operations involving the reproduction of color photographs, a procedure known as color separation is required. This complex procedure is performed by a specialist known as a color separator.

The following are job descriptions of the various specialists concerned with the printing operation.

Typesetter

The first step in any printing operation requires the transferring of the material to be printed from the writer's manuscript to the type style and format to be used on each page of the publication. This is done by a worker called a *typesetter* who uses a special typesetting machine. Usually the editors or art director of the publication choose a type style most suitable for the nature of the material being printed. For example, you have probably noticed that a Bible has one type of print, a brochure another style, and a novel even another type. All together, there are approximately twenty-two different printing faces, each specifically suitable for a particular type of text. In addition to the type face to be used, the editor or art director will decide on how each letter and each line should be spaced. They also determine where the photographs or other illustrations should be placed.

All of this information is given to the typesetter. He or she usually uses a computerized typesetting machine in which the desired type style is inserted. The typesetter must program the machine so that all right-hand margins are even. Naturally, the left-hand margins are identical. The evening of the right margins can become a complex procedure, especially when typing around an area where a photograph or other type of illustration is to appear.

The typesetter's job is basically that of a typist. The worker types out the complete text of the publication, changing type styles where indicated by the editor or art director and always making sure that all margins are even and that everything is properly spaced. When this operation is completed, the material is then ready for "layout" or "pasteup."

Layout or Paste-up Artist

The second step is to "lay out" the job. This is also known as the "paste-up" operation. Here the *paste-up* (or *layout*) artist determines how the finished product should look, arranges the copy (text or reading matter), and proportions or scales photographs and artwork for the desired positions. After the copy and artwork have been properly positioned, they are literally pasted up on a hard board, ready to be photographed by the camera person.

Camera Person

The *camera person* starts the process of making a lithographic plate by photographing and developing negatives of both line copy and continuous-tone copy. Each has to be done separately.

Typewritten material or material consisting of solid lines or areas with no graduation of tone, such as pen-and-ink drawings, are known as line copy. Material containing various degrees of black-and-white shading or any type of artwork containing a range of grays, such as black-and-white photographs or shaded drawings, is known as continuous-tone copy.

Line and continuous-tone copy are photographed separately because different techniques must be used. The lithographic camera breaks up the tone values of a photograph or shaded drawing into tiny dot formations by using a halftone screen between the copy and film during exposure. These dots are arranged on the negative to form an image of the original picture or drawing. In the dark areas the dots are larger and in the lighter areas they are smaller.

After the pictures of both types of copy are taken, the negatives may need retouching to lighten or darken certain areas. This is performed by a lithographic artist.

Lithographic Artist

The necessary corrections are made by a *lithographic artist* who sharpens or reshapes images on the negatives. The work is done by hand, using chemicals, dyes, and special tools. Like the camera person, a lithographic artist is assigned to only one phase of the work and may have job titles such as *dot etcher, retoucher,* or *letterer,* the title reflecting the nature of the work being performed.

Stripper

After the line tone and continuous-tone negatives and positives have been made, they are stripped (pieced) together into a flat, with each page positioned into its proper place. *Strippers* arrange and paste negatives or positives of type and artwork on the layout sheets from which final photographic impressions are made for the press plates.

Platemaker

A *platemaker* covers the surface of the press plates with a coating of photosensitive chemicals. After exposing the sensitized plate to the negative, the platemaker chemically treats the plate to bring out the photographic images. The exposed image areas become ink receptive; the nonexposed areas, water receptive. The plates are now ready for the press operators.

Press Operator

The lithographic *press operators* install plates on the presses and adjust the pressure, water, and ink rollers for correct operation. In the pressing process the plate is first inked. The ink only adheres to the specially treated areas containing the images to be printed. The inked plate is then pressed against a rubber blanket. The rubber blanket picks up the ink from the metal plate. The inked rubber blanket is then pressed against the paper transferring the inked images to it.

By transferring the ink from the metal plate to the rubber blanket for application to the paper, instead of directly pressing the metal plate to the paper, a better image is formed because the soft rubber blanket is flexible, providing for better ink-to-paper contact and thus creating a clearer impression. This is the principle from which the term *offset printing* is derived. The press operators run the machines that perform this process.

Color Separator

The reproduction of color photographs cannot be done as simply as black-and-white photographs. It has already been shown that for black-and-white copy, intermediate tones of gray are reproduced by dot patterns with light and dark areas being determined by the size of the dots. The viewer sees the pattern as a tone. The same dot principle is used in color reproduction to vary the amounts of colored ink printed.

A printing press cannot selectively vary the amount of ink applied to the printing plate in different areas. It must deposit a uniform ink film over the entire surface of the plate. All colors are composed of varying degrees of four basic colors—yellow, red, blue, and black. Therefore, a color photograph can be broken down into its four primary colors. This process is known as color separation and is performed by an expert known as a *color separator*. After the colors have been separated, they can be applied to different plates for application to the same area of the paper to reproduce the original photograph.

The color separator takes four separate pictures of a color print, using a special color filter for each photograph to extract just one of the four primary colors out of the original picture. As in black-and-white lithography, the lithographic camera breaks up each color into tiny dots. After the colors have been separated into four negatives, each negative is used to make a separate plate in the same manner that plates are made from black-and-white negatives. Whereas the black-and-white plate is treated so that the exposed areas become receptive to black ink, each color plate is treated so that the exposed areas accept only one of the four primary ink colors. In reproducing the color print on paper, each one of the four plates (each possessing its own particular color of ink) is applied to the paper (via the rubber blanket) in the same spot. In this manner the colored dots from each plate are printed on the paper, thus reconstructing the colors from the original photograph.

TRAINING REQUIREMENTS

An apprenticeship program of four or five years is usually required in order to become a well-rounded lithographic craftsperson. A program may emphasize a specific craft, such as platemaking or press operating, although an attempt should be made to make the apprentice familiar with all lithographic operations. The apprenticeship training should be supplemented by classroom instruction or correspondence courses. The apprenticeship program may be substituted by the attendance of a two-year training program in a good vocational school that teaches all facets of the printing profession. Certain crafts, such as lithographic art, stripping and color separation, can be learned separately through a one-year training program in the craft plus some work experience.

For information on the varied training programs in the printing industry, write:

> *Printing Industries of America, Inc.*
> 1730 North Lynn Street
> Arlington, Virginia 22201

> *Graphic Arts Technical Foundation*
> 4615 Forbes Avenue
> Pittsburgh, Pennsylvania 15213

> *National Association*
> *of Photo-Lithographers*
> 230 West 41st Street
> New York, New York 10036

> *International Printing Pressmen*
> *and Assistants' Union*
> *of North America*
> 1730 Rhode Island Ave., N.W.
> Washington, D.C. 20036

> *The Graphic Arts International Union*
> 1900 L Street, N.W.
> Washington, D.C. 20036

SALARY AND EMPLOYMENT OPPORTUNITIES

The average salary of the various craftspeople employed in the lithographic profession generally ranges from $8 to $10 an hour. It has been reported that certain specialists, such as strippers and color separators, earn as much as $15 to $20 an hour.

Employment of lithographic workers is expected to increase in response to the continued growth of offset printing. More and more commercial printing firms and newspaper publishers are using offset presses in place of letter presses. Employment growth will also be stimulated by the greater use of photographs and drawings in printed matter and by the more widespread use of color in many printed products.

Lithography also presents many opportunities for the experienced crafts person to go into business as the owner of a printing shop. The cost of each shop will vary according to the amount of work the owner desires to turn out. A small shop will require approximately $20,000 to $40,000 worth of equipment. However, this cost can be reduced by purchasing used equipment at bankruptcy auctions or government surplus sales. The locations of government surplus sales offices can be obtained from a local office of the Small Business Administration. Also, in many instances it is possible to lease the necessary equipment to operate a printing shop.

A small shop owner can start business by soliciting orders for birth, wedding, and party announcements, and also the printing of brochures for various clubs and businesses. As one's business grows, additional equipment can be added and the type of work done expanded.

Most magazine and small newspaper publishers farm out their production operations to independent printing companies. If one can secure a printing contract to handle the printing needs of a good-sized publisher, it may be possible to borrow the capital needed for the necessary equipment from a local bank. Very often such loans are made on the strength of the contract alone, especially if the contract is with a publisher with a sound financial history.

Many a large printing organization started out as a small "mama-papa" type of organization and grew through aggressive business promotion on the part of the owner. In fact, some small printing shops have grown to dynamic proportions in just a few years. The owner of a small printing shop can make $25,000 a year. This figure can rise rapidly as business increases.

It may be impractical for small shops, and in some cases even large shops, to employ on a full-time basis some of the specialists needed in the printing operations. This presents the opportunity for certain specialists to develop businesses of their own performing free-lance work for printing shops. Examples of craftspeople in this category are lithographic artists, strippers, and color separators. In most cases these "independents" will charge $20 an hour and even more for their services. What is more, it has been reported that it is hard to hire these specialists; thus they can charge a higher rate. Moreover, because these people depend more on personal skill rather than expensive machines in the performance of their tasks, they can go into business for themselves with very little capital or overhead. Many specialists hold permanent jobs with a printing concern and do free-lance work during their off-duty hours. Therefore, their earning potential is enhanced.

The printing profession offers many opportunities for the skilled and ambitious craftsperson. The training is not expensive and the rewards can be great.

5

Paramedicine

The medical field presents unlimited opportunities to the man or woman interested in a career in one of the many specialties available. These opportunities will always exist. The reason is simple: no matter how many advances are made in medical treatment, there will always be more to be made—and they will be made! The human body can always be improved upon. This can readily be understood if you consider that at one time the life expectancy of the average individual was approximately age thirty. Through the years this gradually increased to the present time when the life expectancy is approximately age seventy-five. This increase has largely been due to the advances in medical treatment. After all, what finally kills someone is disease. The average life expectancy of an individual will not stop at seventy-five. It will continue to grow. It will be the continued medical research in diagnosis and treatment of disease that will allow it to increase. As the body increases in its life expectancy, new diseases will also appear. These new diseases will also eventually be conquered.

The advances in medicine will not happen automatically. A continuous supply of medical personnel will be required to work as technicians in medical research and diagnostic and treatment techniques. Moreover, the new advances will create new career opportunities that are unheard of today. These advances are constantly taking place and at a rapid pace. They can serve today's generation with many opportunities.

The health industry has become "big business." This claim is supported by the official forecast that estimates that the nation will be spending more than $110 billion on health care by 1980. Everyone in this country is being availed of modern health care. Many employers, whether large or small concerns, are offering medical insurance for their employees and their families.

In the past few years the federal government has sponsored many important health programs, such as Medicare (health insurance for the aged), Medicaid (expanded health services to the poor), and the Allied Health Professions Personnel Act.

Additional reasons for the expansion of the health field can be found in the growing national health consciousness and concern for the nation's population, which is increasing by 2 million a year. In direct relation, employment in the health industry is expected to increase to 6.3 million by 1980.

The practice of medicine and its administration are changing. One of the marked changes is a trend to free doctors from work that someone else can do in order to allow the physicians to concentrate on more of what only they can do. Thus, employment for various medical assistants is rising. In addition, the new medical equipment and techniques call for people with new skills.

Careers that involve assisting the physician in one way or another are known as *paramedical careers,* the prefix "para" meaning "helping in a secondary way" or "accessory." Technicians who practice these careers are known as *paramedical specialists.*

There are acute shortages in many of these positions. Prominent authorities in medical administration contend that many of our nation's health problems can be solved only if more people become paramedical specialists.

The variety of paramedical openings is enormous. They include medical secretaries and medical librarians as well as people who deal in diagnostic and treatment procedures. A number of these career fields are described in the following section.

TRAINING REQUIREMENTS

The length of training for the paramedical jobs that we will consider varies anywhere from six months to three years, with the average being two years. Many specialties can be learned in hospital-based programs where practical or clinical training is taught in addition to classroom work. The fees for many of these programs are very low. In many cases they are offered free of charge except for books. In fact, in some training programs the student is paid a small stipend while in training. The reason for this is that in many programs the student is also contributing to the functioning of the hospital as he or she is undergoing clinical experience. In areas where college courses are necessary to qualify for certification, many of the courses can be taken in a junior or community college where the fees generally tend to be low.

Whenever there may be a considerable financial expense attached to a career goal, there is always a chance for financial assistance from the federal government. Moreover, in some cases a certain percentage of a government loan may be exempt from repayment if the student agrees to practice the specialty in a designated shortage area for a specific period of time. This is one way in which areas deprived of health manpower can be serviced and the scarce supply of trained health personnel can be more equitably distributed.

For information on federal financial aid available to the paramedical professions, write:

Bureau of Health Manpower Education
National Institute of Health
Bethesda, Maryland 20014

In addition to the names and addresses of organizations that can offer information on the training programs available that are cited in the discussion of the different specialties, someone considering a paramedical career should consult the *Allied Medical Education Directory,* published by the American Medical Association. This volume lists, state by state and city by city, the paramedical training programs available in the United States. The following pertinent information is also included: entrance requirements, length of each program, student capacity, starting dates of each class, tuition (if any), stipends paid (if any), scholarships available, and the certification or degree granted.

This book should be available in your local public or high school library or may be purchased from:

American Medical Association
Order Department
535 North Dearborn Street
Chicago, Illinois 60610

As will be seen, there are many opportunities available in the medical field and many methods of attaining them.

MEDICAL RECORD TECHNICIAN

With the increased expansion of medical care in this country and the advanced methods of treating disease, the *medical record technician* has become more important. Today, whenever an observation, diagnostic procedure, or treatment is performed on a patient, the results are recorded on a personalized form known as a medical record, which is a permanent report on a patient's condition and course of treatment in a hospital, clinic, or other health care institution. This record includes such data as X-ray and laboratory reports, cardiogram tracings, diets, medications prescribed, and other pertinent information about the individual's medical history. Hospitals now employ experienced trained personnel to be responsible for the care and study of these records.

The medical record technician, under the direction of a medical record administrator, records all of the pertinent data on the record sheet or sheets and maintains and keeps track of all the medical records in the particular institution. A brief description of the *medical record administrator* follows this chapter, for it is a higher position to which a technician might like to advance.

Medical records are very important, for they assist the physician in diagnosing and studying the effects of treatment of the patient's diseases. The record can tell the doctor what has already been done, what did not work, and what did work.

The technician codes, according to a recognized classification system, the diseases, operations, diagnostic tests, and special therapies and their results and enters the data on the medical record. The coding system eliminates lengthy word descriptions in a person's record. It also makes it possible for the record to be processed in a computer system for future referral and medical research. Analyzing and cross-indexing these records also make up a large part of the technician's work.

Some medical record technicians are employed as consultants to several small health facilities. Some insurance companies employ experienced technicians to collect information from patient's records to determine liability for insurance payments. Public health departments hire technicians to supervise data collection from health care institutions and to assist in research to improve health care. Manufacturers of medical record systems, services, and equipment also employ medical record technicians to help develop and market their products.

It cannot be stressed too much how accurate medical records can assist in medical research and guide the destiny of our lives. Through periodic review of thousands of medical records (through computers or individual scanning) scientists may observe that many people with the same problems underwent similar medical or environmental experiences. Likewise, many people with very desirable health situations may be observed to have gone through similar medical treatments or environmental experiences. This data can show research scientists what conditions and situations should be excluded or added to a person's life-style to insure maximum health.

TRAINING REQUIREMENTS

There are many accredited one- and two-year programs that lead to certification by the American Medical Record Association as an Accredited Record Technician (ART). The association also offers a twenty-five-lesson home correspondence course for medical record personnel. This course and the other accredited programs include training in the biological sciences, medical terminology, medical record science, business management, and secretarial skills.

For information concerning the accredited medical record training programs and the correspondence course, write:

The American Medical
Record Association
875 North Michigan Avenue
Suite 1850
Chicago, Illinois 60611

SALARY AND EMPLOYMENT OPPORTUNITIES

According to the American Medical Record Association, the salary range for a properly certified medical record technician is approximately from $7,500 to $15,000 per year. As the health care systems in our country keep expanding and become more sophisticated, the demand for accredited medical technicians will continue to grow at a rapid rate.

MEDICAL RECORD ADMINISTRATOR

Whereas the medical record technician is responsible for the compiling and maintenance of accurate medical records, the *medical record administrator* is responsible for setting up and organizing efficient medical record systems, and for analyzing the data collected. An administrator may assist the medical staff in research by selecting and tabulating data from patients' records and may assist in the final preparation of research studies based on the medical reports. The medical record administrator supervises the work of the medical record department and is responsible for the selecting and training of the technicians and clerks in the department.

Besides hospitals and other health care institutions, the medical record administrator may become involved in important research programs in government, drug companies, and universities.

TRAINING REQUIREMENTS

There are several avenues open to becoming a medical record administrator. The candidate may enroll in a four-year program leading to a bachelor's degree in medical records. Or one may first take two years of undergraduate work at an accredited junior college and then transfer for the last two years to a college or university offering a baccalaureate program in medical records. As a third option, after completion of a baccalaureate degree in liberal arts, one may take the one-year certificate or diploma course in medical records. Therefore, if you are a college graduate who is "floating around" looking for a job, you might consider the possibility of one more year of training to insure a secure and rewarding career for yourself. Also, an accredited technician may advance to an administrator's position by taking the added curriculum. For a list of colleges and universities offering programs in medical record administration, write:

The American Medical
Record Association
875 North Michigan Avenue
Suite 850
Chicago, Illinois 60611

SALARY AND EMPLOYMENT OPPORTUNITIES

The salary range for an experienced and efficient medical record administrator is from $10,000 to $30,000 per year. And the field is wide open!

RESPIRATORY THERAPIST

Respiratory therapy is considered by many as the fastest growing allied health profession. Our whole life process depends upon the proper intake and utilization of life-sustaining oxygen. New advances in respiratory therapy have made the field a highly complex one requiring the total attention of specially trained practitioners—the *respiratory therapists.*

The respiratory therapist, in addition to aiding in many

respiratory procedures, is on the "front line" with the physician in many emergency life-saving procedures. This is readily realized when you consider that if someone stops breathing for just four minutes, there can be irreparable brain damage; and if oxygen is cut off for more than nine minutes, death can ensue.

The respiratory therapist is instrumental in the diagnosis, treatment, management, and preventive care of patients with cardiopulmonary problems. These patients may be found in the newborn nursery, the surgical and medical wards, the emergency room, the outpatient departments, and the intensive-care unit of a hospital. They may be suffering from a variety of acute and chronic conditions that are either life threatening or disabling.

The respiratory therapist must be competent in such areas as medical gas administration, intermittent positive pressure breathing (IPPB), bronchopulmonary drainage and exercises, cardiopulmonary resuscitation, mechanical ventilation, airway management, pulmonary function studies, blood gas analysis, and physiological monitoring.

Respiratory therapy personnel are involved in the treatment of such cardiac and pulmonary ailments as cardiac failure, asthma, pulmonary edema, emphysema, cerebral thrombosis, drowning, hemorrhage, and shock.

Various machines are used to administer medication to the lungs so that the medication can act locally on areas within the lung as well as become diffused into the body's circulatory system. It is the respiratory therapist who uses and supervises these machines.

Respiratory therapy employs a variety of testing techniques to assist both in the diagnosis of disorders and medical research and treatment. One example is the administration of radioactive gases or aerosols to the patient through the respiratory system. Various portions of the lung may then be screened and evaluated for abnormalities. The most common diagnostic examinations performed by the therapist are the measurement of lung volumes, flow patterns, and pressures.

New respiratory technology has been utilized to treat gangrene, carbon monoxide poisoning, tetanus, and many other disorders. The respiratory therapist is also being involved in dealing with problems of air pollution and in the advancement of aerospace medicine.

One of the prime goals of the respiratory therapist is to train asthmatics to breath properly

TRAINING REQUIREMENTS

The best way to obtain a top job in respiratory therapy is take a two-year inhalation therapy program in a college or hospital program approved by the American Medical Association, followed by one year of clinical experience. After completion of the clinical experience the therapist is then eligible for certification by the American Registry of Inhalation Therapists (ARIT). To be certified, one must pass written and oral examinations. After certification by the ARIT, the therapist is then awarded the title of Registered Inhalation Therapist.

For a list of schools offering training in respiratory therapy, write:

American Association
for Respiratory Therapy
7411 Hines Place
Dallas, Texas 75235

SALARY AND EMPLOYMENT OPPORTUNITIES

There is a tremendous demand for respiratory therapists in hospitals and medical clinics. Their skills can be utilized in emergency rooms, respiratory disease wards, and out-patient asthma clinics. They can even practice as independent practitioners who travel to the homes of people bedridden with respiratory ailments, supervising and instructing them in the proper use of their respiratory machines. This is naturally done under the auspices of the physician in charge of the patient.

At present, the salary for a well-trained and experienced respiratory therapist can go up to $1,724 per month. As an independent practitioner, it can even go higher. The therapist may even advance to a supervisory, management, or teaching position in a hospital or other medical institution.

For a satisfying and well-paying profession where one is really "wanted and needed," inhalation therapy is rated among the best.

PHYSICAL THERAPIST

The human body, when damaged, has the ability to heal itself. This ability can be enhanced by several methods. One, with which we are all familiar, is medication. Another is physical therapy. Physical therapy is just what the name implies: treatment through physical or mechanical means. Physicians and other medical authorities are realizing the vast potential of physical therapy in the treatment of many muscular, circulatory, and nerve disorders. Trained professionals, called *physical therapists,* stimulate and promote the refunctioning of these organ systems when damaged through disease or accident. Physical therapy has value in the treatment of a wide variety of diseases and injuries, such as multiple sclerosis, some nerve injuries, certain chest conditions, back problems, amputations, fractures, sprains, muscle spasms, arthritis, and cerebral palsy.

In treating a patient, the physical therapist will first evaluate the extent of damage by performing and interpreting tests for muscle strength, motor development, functional capacity, and respiratory and circulatory efficiency. The results of these tests will determine the treatment to be given.

The treatment may entail one or several physical therapy procedures, including exercise to strengthen damaged muscles, massage and heat to improve circulation and bring blood to the damaged area, electrical currents to stimulate paralyzed or damaged muscles, ultrasonic waves to penetrate deep into areas of the body to stimulate the functioning of damaged areas, and ultraviolet rays to provide heat to inflamed tissues. The physical therapist will then evaluate the effectiveness of the treatment and discuss the patient's progress with physicians, psychologists, occupational therapists, and other specialists. When advisable, the therapist will revise the therapeutic procedures and treatments.

Physical therapists also teach patients to help themselves at home through various exercise programs, and they work with amputees in teaching them to use their prosthetic devices.

A physical therapist must be somewhat of a psychologist. People who have suffered a serious accident or disease may become discouraged and mentally depressed. It is the responsibility of the therapist to build up the confidence of the patient and show him how the various treatments will allow him to function fully again.

TRAINING REQUIREMENTS

The practice of physical therapy on the professional level is regulated by state law. Each state requires licensure or "registration" through state examinations in order to practice. Exams are given at least once a year.

To qualify for the exam, an applicant must have been enrolled in a four-year program in physical therapy in an accredited college or university and been granted a bachelor's degree in the field. More than 52 colleges and universities offer a fully accredited physical therapy program. Essentially, the course is divided into several areas: a liberal arts program emphasizes the humanities and social studies. Study of the biological sciences includes anatomy, physiology, and pathology. Major emphasis in physical sciences is on chemistry and physics, including the fundamental principles of mechanics, thermodynamics, light, sound, and electricity. Specialization courses provide the fundamental knowledge and skill required to treat patients. Finally, supervised clinical practice completes the course.

If you already have a college degree and now desire to enter physical therapy, it is possible to do so providing that your major included numerous science courses. If you qualify in this area, you may attend a twelve-month certificate course that provides intensive and specialized training in physical therapy. Upon completion of the program a certificate is awarded. Graduates of certificate programs are considered equally as qualified as graduates of bachelor's degree programs. There are fifteen schools that offer twelve-month certificate programs.

If the cost of education is of concern to you, it may be possible to receive your preliminary liberal arts and science courses in a junior college in your community at a nominal fee, and then transfer to a university program for the completion of your bachelor's degree, after which you can still attend the certificate program if necessary. There are also scholarships available to persons pursuing professional education in physical therapy.

Several universities offer the master's degree in physical therapy. This is normally a two-year program. A graduate degree combined with clinical experience increases the opportunities for advancement, especially in research, teaching, supervisory, and administrative positions.

For a list of schools that offer the bachelor's degree in physical therapy, the certificate program, and the master's degree, write:

American Physical Therapy Association
1156 15th Street, N.W.
Washington, D.C. 20005

This organization will also inform you where to apply for scholarships and other financial assistance.

An experienced physical therapist will usually earn from $12,000 to $17,000 per year. Experienced high-level physical therapists in clinical, consultative, educational, or administrative positions can earn from $15,000 to $25,000 per year.

Physicians and other medical authorities are becoming increasingly aware of the benefits of physical therapy and its advantages over the use of drugs. The demand for physical therapists far exceeds the supply. Sources for employment include hospitals, schools for crippled children, nursing homes, rehabilitation centers, industrial firms, athletic teams, and government and armed forces facilities.

It is also possible for a licensed physical therapist to open a private office to treat patients referred by physicians. Some therapists lease space in small hospitals where they perform therapy for both inpatients and outpatients on a fee-for-service basis. Therapists in private practice can earn over $25,000 per year.

OCCUPATIONAL THERAPIST

The human body is a remarkable and resourceful machine. Most people function at only a partial of their full potential. When emotional or physical damage occurs in an individual, reaching down and tapping unused potential can allow the person to function again.

The *occupational therapist* is a very special individual trained to help handicapped people utilize their full potential. The therapist will instruct and aid an injured person to develop and maximize his/her inner talents and then to use these talents to compensate for that person's emotional or physical damage. If the person is physically healthy but in an "extreme" situation such as old age, poverty, or a hostile environment, occupational therapy may be used to aid the individual in coping with and overcoming this situation, thus enabling him to enjoy a higher quality of life.

If the person is an accident victim or victim of a disease, the occupational therapist will attempt to retrain him to perform in his same occupation. If this is not possible, the occupational therapist will retrain him to assume a new occupation.

Occupational therapists work with emotionally disturbed and retarded people to teach them to perform useful occupational tasks. This will accomplish several goals: first, it will give the patient a sense of worth and well-being. Second, it will prevent the patient from being a detriment to society by enabling him or her to contribute economically to himself and society. Third, the attainment of one level of increased ability can stimulate the patient to achieve higher levels of performance until his reserve is fully developed. When a person is suffering from both emotional and physical handicaps, the severest of the two is given initial preference. When one handicap is brought under control, further attention is given to the second handicap.

The profession of occupational therapy occupies an important place in the treatment programs of health facilities and institutions throughout the country.

When the patient is referred by the physician, the therapist makes an evaluation to determine the current level of functioning and to learn more about the patient as a person. After making the evaluation, the therapist can decide which activity would appeal to and provide the most benefit to the patient. The extent and speed of progress is very much dependent on the therapist's professional judgment. The following are some examples of the challenges presented to a therapist:

Would learning to type help develop hand coordination of an injured mechanic? Once the therapist has gained his interest, the mechanic responds eagerly, and the use of a practical skill aids him in reacquiring his former skill, thus allowing him to return to work.

Would weaving be the most beneficial activity for the woman with arthritic fingers? If this would help her to achieve a sense of progress in doing so and at the same time benefit her therapeutically, the answer would be "yes."

How will a little girl develop enough coordination in her movements to eat alone? First, she needs to learn to let her eyes and hands work together. The therapist may attempt to accomplish this by having the little girl toss a beanbag while sitting at a cut-out table. The accomplishment of this activity may eventually aid her in developing the coordination to feed herself.

Besides the ability to teach and to communicate with handicapped people and a general background of knowledge in the basic sciences and medicine, the occupational therapist needs specific knowledge in the various working skills used in therapy. Among these skills are potting, leatherwork, jewelry making, woodwork, metalwork, textile crafts, and printing. The therapist may also organize educational activities, such as creative writing, or may organize group activities, such as dramatic groups.

Many therapists administer occupational therapy programs, coordinate patient activities, or act as consultants to local and state health departments and mental health agencies. Some teach in colleges and universities.

TRAINING REQUIREMENTS

Occupational therapy requires four years of college training leading to the degree of bachelor of science. This is followed by a clinical training period lasting from six to nine months, after which the therapist is eligible to qualify for professional registration. For those who already have a college degree and now wish to enter occupational therapy, there is an advanced-standing course of eighteen to twenty-two months, divided between academic and clinical work. There is also a master's degree program offered in several universities. The master's degree would qualify someone to do administrative and consulting work. The college preparation for occupational therapy emphasizes physical and behavioral sciences, such as anatomy, physiology, neurology, psychology, and sociology. Other subjects would include manual and creative skills, education courses, and recreational activities.

If you have already started college and now wish to transfer to an occupational therapy program, it is possible to do so without losing credits as long as your training has included the biological and physical sciences, English, psychology, and sociology. If you are already in college and now feel you may be interested in this field, you may be able to participate in a summer experience program in occupational therapy. Students selected for this program work six weeks during the summer in the occupational therapy department of a hospital.

For information on schools offering programs in occupational therapy and on the six-week summer experience program, write:

American Occupational Therapy Association
6000 Executive Boulevard
Rockville, Maryland 20852

SALARY AND EMPLOYMENT OPPORTUNITIES

An experienced occupational therapist in senior and advisory positions can earn from $16,000 to $20,000 per year. Those with master's degrees can earn $120 a day performing consulting services.

Occupational therapists are usually employed in hospitals, rehabilitation centers, nursing homes, schools, outpatient clinics, community mental health centers, and government research centers.

It has been projected that by the year 1980 there will be a 151 percent increase in the demand for workers in occupational therapy. Research has shown that it is one of the most promising health fields.

PROSTHETIST AND ORTHOTIST

One of the most traumatic things a person can experience is the loss of a limb due to disease or accident. Fortunately, because of the fantastic work of a group of people known as *prosthetists*, many victims of this experience can get most of their normal function and appearance back through the use of artificial limbs.

The prosthetist is a highly trained individual who specializes in designing, fabricating, and fitting artificial body limbs (prostheses) to an amputee.

An allied field, known as orthotics, involves the designing, fabricating, and fitting of orthopedic braces (orthoses) for the support of a weakened body part, and/or for the correction of body defects of a handicapped or disabled person. The person who performs this work is called an *orthotist*.

A person may be both an orthotist and a prosthetist since similar training is involved in both professions. Modern technology is causing rapid advances in the creating and fabricating of many prosthetic and orthotic devices. In fact, not only are there lighter and better orthotic braces to support weakened muscles and bones, but today there are also devices that allow paralyzed persons to move and manipulate various appendages that are paralyzed.

The prosthetist in performing the work measures the arm or leg stump by length and circumference. He or she then makes a cast of the stump with plaster to get the exact shape of the remaining part in building the socket. The normal extremity has also been measured in order to attempt to duplicate it as accurately as possible. In building the prostheses, the prosthetist designs it in proportion to the size and weight of the person and colors it to simulate that of the normal skin tone of the wearer. After the device is finished, the prosthetist fits it to the wearer, making sure it is properly aligned and fits comfortably. In a small shop he or she may train the wearer in the proper use of the device. In a larger clinic-type operation there may be specialists whose job it is to work solely with patients in training them to use their device properly.

An orthotist accurately measures the portion of the patient's body that is being fitted for the brace. He or she designs the brace so that it corrects the patient's unique orthopedic or muscular problem. Due to the large number of people with back problems, an orthotist can do a lucrative business just in designing custom-made lumbosacral supports.

There are several important requirements in becoming proficient in this profession. You should have mechanical and artistic ability. You should have patience and be precise in your work habits. And very important, since you are dealing with people who are going through an emotional crisis due to their handicap, you must be a very understanding person who gains great satisfaction from helping other people. You must be able to reassure the patient of his or her returning to a normal and useful life. If you fit the description, you may have a rewarding and secure future ahead of you in these fields.

TRAINING REQUIREMENTS

You do not learn either type of work just anywhere. Most training institutions are located in big cities. You can learn this profession by on-the-job training in a prosthetic or orthotic shop. However, like so many other fields in medicine, formal professional training followed by certification by the professional group representing that profession can lead to higher paying jobs. There are schools that offer courses leading to an associate of arts degree in prosthetics or orthotics. The degree is followed by two years of practical training in a shop or clinic. After the practical training period (during which the trainee receives a salary) one is then eligible for professional certification by the American Board for Certification of the Prosthetic and Orthotic Appliance Industry.

For information on training programs, write:

*The American Orthotic
and Prosthetic Association*
Suite 130
919 18th Street, N.W.
Washington, D.C. 20006

*American Board for Certification
of the Prosthetic and
Orthotic Appliance Industry, Inc.*
411 Associations Building
1145 19th Street, N.W.
Washington, D.C. 20006

Rancho Los Amigos Hospital
Prosthetic Education
7601 East Imperial Highway
Downey, California 90242

University of California
Prosthetic-Orthotic Program
405 Hilgard Avenue
Los Angeles, California 90024

SALARY AND EMPLOYMENT OPPORTUNITIES

A well-trained and certified technician can earn up to $400 per week in either a small shop or large hospital or rehabilitation clinic. The technician can also open a shop (preferably in a large city) and earn well over $20,000 per year. Before doing this, it would be advisable to build a good reputation in a rehabilitation clinic and then solicit the recommendations of orthopedic surgeons in your area.

As far as employment goes, there are presently many employment opportunities for people in this profession. What is more, there are not enough qualified personnel to meet the present needs, and the demand is expected to increase until the late 1990s.

The modern operating room requires a highly trained team of individuals to facilitate its proper operation. Each member of the team is trained in one or several procedures to give maximum assistance to the surgeon in charge. An important member of this team is the *surgical* or *operating room technician.*

Operating room technicians assist surgeons and anesthesiologists before, during, and after surgery. They are supervised by registered nurses. They help set up the operating room with instruments, equipment, sterile linens, and fluids such as blood and glucose that may be needed during an operation. Operating room technicians also prepare patients for surgery by washing, shaving, and disinfecting the parts of the body where the surgeon will operate. They also help drape and position the patient on the operating table.

During surgery they pass instruments and other sterile supplies to members of the professional surgical team. They hold retractors, cut sutures, and help nurses count the sponges, needles, and instruments used during the operation. When the operation is over, a technician may help in applying the dressings to the incision. The experienced technician will also operate sterilizers, lights, suction machines, and diagnostic equipment.

TRAINING REQUIREMENTS

There are several avenues one can follow in becoming a surgical technician. Generally, this occupation can be learned in a one-year on-the-job training program in the surgical department of a hospital. These programs are divided into classroom training and clinical work. Some of the courses required are anatomy, physiology, and microbiology. Medic programs in the armed forces are also an excellent source of training. Some junior colleges do offer two-year programs leading to an associate's degree in surgical technology.

The Association of Operating Room Technicians awards a certificate to operating room technicians who pass their comprehensive examination. A Certified Operating Room Technician (CORT) is recognized as competent in the field and is generally paid a higher salary.

For information concerning training programs, write:

Association of Operating Technicians, Inc.
1101 West Littleton Boulevard
Suite 101
Littleton, Colorado 80120

SALARY AND EMPLOYMENT OPPORTUNITIES

Employment opportunities for operating room technicians are expected to be excellent through the 1980s. Graduates of a two-year junior college program should be especially in demand. The salary for an operating room technician generally ranges from $8,000 to $12,000 per year. Although this may not be a tremendous amount of money, this field can be used as a stepping stone to advanced medical specialities such as a surgeon's assistant, which will be discussed next.

SURGEON'S ASSISTANT

The *surgeon's assistant* is a skilled person qualified by academic and clinical training to provide patient services under the supervision and responsibility of a surgeon. The assistant may be involved with the patients of the surgeon in any medical setting which the surgeon is in, but most frequently a surgeon's assistant is found in a large medical center where there is an extensive division and specialization of tasks.

The assistant performs diagnostic and therapeutic functions in order to allow the surgeon to extend his or her services through the more effective use of his or her knowledge, skills, and abilities. The surgeon's assistant gathers the data necessary for the surgeon to reach a decision and then assists in implementing the therapeutic plan for the patient. Tasks performed by the assistant include transmission and execution of the surgeon's orders, patient care services, and also such diagnostic and therapeutic procedures as may be delegated by the surgeon. The assistant may be highly trained and specialize in areas in which his or her immediate supervisor has interest, or the assistant may remain in an area of surgery requiring a wide variety of procedures such as performed by general surgeons. The frequency of performance of certain duties will in part determine the degree of special expertise such an individual obtains in the care of patients. Since no one individual could participate in all the categories of work outlined, it is expected that a certain degree of limitation will occur. Intelligence, the ability to relate with people, a capacity for calm and reasoned judgment in meeting emergencies, and an orientation toward service are qualities essential for the assistant to the surgeon.

TRAINING REQUIREMENTS

Most training programs are conducted free of charge in large hospitals. To be allowed into a surgical assistant's program, a prerequisite of two years of college in a health-related field is necessary. We feel that an ideal preliminary training program would be that of an operating room technician, which has been previously discussed. The classroom and clinical work encountered in becoming an operating room technician provides an excellent background for the surgeon's assistant. In addition, working as an operating room technician provides not only an income, but also will give an individual the experience and time to decide on whether or not he or she wants to advance to the position of surgeon's assistant.

After satisfying the preliminary requirements, the surgeon's assistant trainee enrolls in a program that usually lasts for eighteen months, the length depending on the policies of the particular hospital. In the eighteen-month program the schedule is divided into nine months of classroom work and nine months of clinical experience. Previous education and experience of the student can shorten the time required to complete the program. Many hospitals supply the student with a small financial stipend while he or she is going through training.

The classroom work includes subjects such as anatomy, medical terminology, physiology, pharmacology, fundamentals of general surgery, surgical patient care, sterile techniques, medical history and physical examination, X-ray interpretation, electrocardiogram recording technique and interpretation, and pulmonary functions tests as well as inhalation therapy.

The clinical phase involves surgical services on a two-month rotation basis with responsibility for history and physical examinations, preoperative and postoperative care procedures, and assisting in surgery.

For information on this specialty, write:

American Medical Association
Department of Allied Medical
    Professions and Services
535 North Dearborn Street
Chicago, Illinois 60610

SALARY AND EMPLOYMENT OPPORTUNITIES

The salary for surgeon's assistants ranges from $10,000 to $20,000 per year, depending on experience and expertise. As the practice of medicine becomes more complex and more and more people are treated on a mass scale, the demand for the well-trained surgeon's assistant will increase tremendously.

ELECTROCARDIOGRAPH (EKG) TECHNICIAN

The heart gives off a series of electrical impulses as it beats. These impulses can be recorded on an electronic device known as an electrocardiograph (EKG) machine. It is the *electrocardiograph (EKG) technician* who operates and monitors these machines in the recording of this important data.

A normal heart will give off a characteristic series of waves. Likewise, an abnormal heart will give off its own series of recognizable waves. In fact, each abnormality will have its own specific wave characteristics. When properly interpreted by a cardiologist, these EKG recordings can aid in making a proper diagnosis for the patient. It can also aid in deciding the proper medication and other therapeutic measures to be taken, and then by later recordings, enable the physician to see how these therapeutic programs are working out.

It is very important for a well-trained EKG technician to do an accurate and thorough job in recording a patient's heartbeat; otherwise a wrong diagnosis by the cardiologist may result. All agree that the EKG technician is a critical link in the health care system.

In taking an electrocardiogram, the technician prepares the patient for the test, then places electrodes on his chest, arms, and legs before manipulating the controls on the machine. During the test the chest electrodes are moved to different positions to get several tracings. When the EKG machine picks up the impulses from the heart, the energy is transmitted to an armature equipped with a hot stylus that marks the impulses on a moving, calibrated strip of heat-sensitive paper. The lines recorded on the paper show the status of the heart: vertical lines show the intensity of the heart contractions, and horizontal lines show the frequency of these contractions.

During the test the technician must be able to recognize and correct any technical errors or interferences recorded on the electrocardiogram. She or he must also be able to recognize any deviations from the norm that call for a doctor's immediate attention.

EKG technicians occasionally conduct other tests such as basal metabolism tests, which measure energy usage, and phonocardiograms, which record the sounds of the heart valves and blood passing through them.

Since EKG technicians are trained to operate machines that record electrical impulses from the heart, it is easy for them to expand their training to operate machines that record electrical impulses from the brain and thus qualify to be electroencephalographic (EEG) technicians. (This field is discussed in the next chapter.) These two talents when combined can provide a physician or small clinic with a very valuable medical assistant. Thus, in accordance with the basic rules of economy, the more valuable you are, the more money you can command.

TRAINING REQUIREMENTS

Usually an intelligent man or woman with a high school diploma can be trained on the job in the EKG department of a good hospital to be an electrocardiograph technician. The training program is generally conducted by a senior EKG technician or a cardiologist and lasts for a period of approximately three months. Tuition is usually free. As new and advanced machines come into use in the field, the well-trained technician can learn to operate them by special instructions given by the companies that manufacture the machines.

Information on recognized training programs can be obtained from the following sources:

American Cardiology
Technologists' Association
Heart Station
University of Miami Medical School
Jackson Memorial Hospital
Miami, Florida 33136

American Hospital Association
840 North Lake Shore Drive
Chicago, Illinois 60611

American Medical Association
Department of Allied Medical Professions
535 North Dearborn Street
Chicago, Illinois 60610

SALARY AND EMPLOYMENT OPPORTUNITIES

A well-trained and experienced EKG technician can earn approximately $1,000 per month in a doctor's office, private clinic, large hospital, teaching facility, or government agency.

The demand for technicians is expected to rise very rapidly because of increasing reliance by physicians on EKGs in the diagnosis of heart diseases and the routine use of EKGs in the physical examinations of patients over a certain age.

The relatively short and inexpensive training period along with the reasonable pay scale makes the field especially suitable for a woman who is looking for a comfortable and interesting way to supplement the family's income.

ELECTROENCEPHALOGRAPHIC (EEG) TECHNICIAN

The brain emits a series of electrical impulses called brain waves. This phenomenon has opened up a whole new field in medicine—the study of the human brain and its functioning. Through an electronic machine, known as an electroencephalograph (EEG machine), these brain waves can be permanently recorded and studied to diagnose and pinpoint certain abnormalities in a person's neurological system. It is the skilled *electroencephalographic technician* (EEG technician) who operates this machine and is responsible for the proper recording of one's brain waves.

Through a series of electrodes attached to the scalp the EEG machine receives and amplifies these brain waves and converts this electrical energy into mechanical energy to move a row of pens on a sheet of paper. The pattern that results tells the story.

The waves that are emitted from a normal and healthy brain fall into a fixed pattern and are recognized as such. Various abnormalities in the brain will cause their own characteristic pattern on the EEG machine. It is the proper interpretation of these patterns taken by an EEG technician that aids the neurologist in making an accurate diagnosis. Therefore, the record of a patient's brain waves has become a valuable tool in diagnosing such brain conditions as injury from infection or accident, rupture of the blood vessels (a stroke), epilepsy, or tumors.

The EEG technician is responsible for carrying out the actual recording of a patient's EEG activity. The technician measures the patient's head and attaches the electrodes in the proper positions. These electrodes are connected to the recording instrument, and the technologist selects the proper combinations of electrodes and instrument controls that will provide the most meaningful record for interpretation by the neurologist.

162

Throughout the recording period the technologist observes the patient and keeps a careful record of his behavior. The technologist must have a fundamental understanding of the equipment being used and of the diseases that are encountered in day-to-day work. Recognition of normal and abnormal brain activity is necessary so that the collection of significant information can be made in an orderly manner.

The more adventuresome and talented technologist may become part of a highly specialized neurosurgical team. An experienced and ambitious EEG technician can become involved in teaching and research programs.

In addition to the duties just discussed, there is ample opportunity for the EEG technician to become involved in a new medical media known as biofeedback. This is a process in which a subject observes the electrical tracings of various parts of his or her body and then attempts to consciously and subconsciously control them. The brain is not the only organ that gives off electrical impulses. Many of the other organs of the body do so also. The same machines and techniques used to record the brain's electrical charges are used to record these impulses. When the patient is allowed to observe these recordings, he has the opportunity to learn to control them. One prime example of this is in the controlling of abnormal blood pressure and heartbeat.

Many behavioral patterns can be learned with EEG machines to enable psychologists to develop a deeper understanding of human emotions.

It seems it is very likely that the EEG technician's role will grow to encompass a great variety of medical responsibilities.

TRAINING REQUIREMENTS

An intelligent person can generally learn to be an EEG technician in a one-year program in a recognized hospital or clinic. The program is usually divided into two parts: six months of academic work and six months of on-the-job clinical experience. After completion of the training program, the technician is eligible to receive certification by the American Society of EEG Technologists as a Registered Electroencephalographic Technician and is entitled to use the letters R. EEG T. after his or her name.

For information on the recognized training programs in electroencephalography, write:

American Society of EEG Technologists
University of Iowa
Division of EEG and Neurophysiology
500 Newton Road
Iowa City, Iowa 52240

American Medical
Electroencephalographic Association
825 Nicollet on the Mall
Minneapolis, Minnesota 55402

American Board of Registration
of EEG Technologists
Secretary-Treasurer
Atlanta Neurological Clinic
3312 Piedmont Road, N.E.
Atlanta, Georgia 30305

SALARY AND EMPLOYMENT OPPORTUNITIES

The salary generally received by an experienced EEG technician is approximately $1,000 per month and can increase as one steps into higher supervisory and teaching positions.

The employment possibilities for a good technician are excellent as this field is still basically in its infancy. Electroencephalographic technicians are primarily employed in hospitals, medical clinics, and the private offices of neurologists. There is still a great deal of pioneering to be done. Why not join in exploring these "new frontiers?"

RADIOLOGIC (X-RAY) TECHNOLOGIST

Medical X-rays play a major role in the diagnostic and therapeutic procedures in medicine. *Radiologic technologists,* also called medical *X-ray technicians,* operate the intricate equipment used to perform these procedures.

The constant expansion in hospital and health services plus the increased application of X-ray in medicine is creating an ever expanding demand for the services of the qualified X-ray technologist. There is considerable evidence that those who are skilled and capable in this field will never lack opportunity for employment. Once an individual becomes a registered technologist, he or she can advance through the ranks to supervisory capacities. The rapidity with which an individual advances depends upon one's personality, character, ability to assume responsibility, and professional preparation. Professional preparation should be interpreted to include keeping abreast of the new and advanced radiological techniques long after completion of one's basic studies.

Most radiologic technologists use X-ray equipment to take pictures of internal parts of the patient's body. After determining the correct voltage, current, and desired exposure time, the technologist positions the patient and makes the required number of radiographs to be developed for interpretation by the physician. The technologist may use mobile X-ray equipment at a patient's bedside and in surgery.

Some radiologic technologists do radiation therapy work and are sometimes referred to as *radiation therapists.* They help physicians treat patients with diseases, such as certain types of cancer, by administering prescribed doses of X-ray or other forms of radiation to the affected areas of the body. They may also assist the radiologist in measuring and handling radium and other radioactive materials.

Other technologists work in the field of nuclear medicine and are referred to as *nuclear medical technologists.* In this field radioactive chemicals (known as isotopes) are used to diagnose and treat disease. It is possible for radiologists to inject these isotopes into the body and trace their path. By these methods the functioning of many organs can be observed. Also, since certain isotopes have an affinity for certain organs, radioactive isotopes can be sent directly to these affected organs to destroy certain types of tumors. The nuclear medical technologist helps the radiologist prepare and administer the prescribed radioisotopes and operates special equipment for monitoring the isotopes on their pathway through the body.

TRAINING REQUIREMENTS

Preparation for a career in X-ray technology is best done in one of the schools for X-ray technologists approved by the Council on Medical Education of the American Medical Association.

At present there are over 1,000 approved schools. A list of these may be obtained by writing:

American Medical Association
Council on Medical Education
535 North Dearborn Street
Chicago, Illinois 60610

The majority of the programs are of two years' duration and are tuition free. Some schools even pay a small salary during part of the educational program. One reason for this is that even while you are learning, you can provide a benefit to the hospital and its patients.

Candidates for admission to these schools should be high school graduates (or the equivalent) and have a background in mathematics and science, especially physics, chemistry, and biology.

After completion of training, the technologist is qualified to become certified by the American Registry of Radiologic Technologists as a Registered Radiologic Technologist.

SALARY AND EMPLOYMENT OPPORTUNITIES

As mentioned earlier, the demand for qualified X-ray technicians is growing at a rapid rate. The average salary for a technologist varies from $12,000 to $16,000 per year. Those employed as directors and administrators in large teaching institutions may earn $20,000 per year and more.

While most technologists are employed in large medical institutions, many are employed in small clinics and in doctors' offices. In fact, it is even possible for a technologist to be self-employed. Many patients, especially the aged, are confined to convalescent hospitals. Most of these institutions do not have X-ray equipment or technicians to operate such equipment. Therefore, when a physician finds it necessary to have a patient undergo diagnostic X-rays, an X-ray technician with a portable unit is usually called in. Many technicians make an excellent living offering such a service. It is so well recognized that practically all private and government-sponsored insurance programs pay for this service. It is possible for the self-employed technologist to make well over $20,000 per year in his or her mobile X-ray business.

As you can see, the X-ray field can provide an interesting and financially secure future.

DIAGNOSTIC
MEDICAL SONOGRAPHER

As new advances are made in diagnostic procedures, so are there new job opportunities for trained people to perform these procedures. The field of diagnostic medical sonography makes use of sonic energy to determine the contours and composition of body tissues. These procedures make it possible to visualize anatomical, pathological, and functional data to aid the physician in the diagnosis of disease and injury.

It is a fundamental principal of physics that when sound waves hit a solid object, they are bounced back in the form of "echoes." Different objects return different echoes. This simple principle is now being used in diagnostic medicine. Different tissues, whether normal or pathological, return different echoes depending on their composition and density. These echoes can be used to give visual impressions through the use of an oscilloscope of the object off which they are bounced.

By this method it is possible, for example, to measure an enlarged liver, to identify the presence and location of a tumor, or to find out whether the head of an unborn baby is too large to pass through its mother's pelvic arch. This is accomplished by means of a crystal ultrasound generating transducer connected by a flexible cable to an oscilloscope. The transducer transmits the ultrasound impulses and acts as a microphone to receive their echoes and pass them along to the oscilloscope. We have already mentioned that tissues of different density return correspondingly different echoes. Translating the returning signals into visual images, the oscilloscope displays them on a screen where their vertical deflections enable the *diagnostic medical sonographer* to identify and measure the object or organ with which he or she is concerned.

The sonographer should have knowledge of the patient's appropriate history and available clinical data. With this knowledge the patient is positioned in a manner that will faciliate optimum diagnostic results. The sonographer then surveys the area being studied to obtain preliminary sonographic information with respect to the acoustical properties of the patient as well as anatomical and pathological relationships. Based on this sonographic information, the sonographer adjusts the transducer to the settings that will best demonstrate the anatomy and/or pathology being studied. The sonographer then must perform a diagnostic scan and make a permanent record of the significant functional and/or anatomical and pathological data obtained for interpretation by a physician.

TRAINING REQUIREMENTS

The diagnostic medical sonographer must have an educational background in medical sciences and acoustical physics and technical and professional training related to diagnostic ultrasound. If the prospective sonographer has no background in medicine at all, it might be advisable to attend a junior college taking courses in science, physics, mathematics, anatomy, physiology, and medical terminology. After the completion of these basic courses, the student may enter a one-year hospital program, receiving training in acoustical physics and instrumentation and scanning techniques.

For information on available programs write:

American Medical Association
Department of Allied Medical
   Professions and Services
535 North Dearborn Street
Chicago, Illinois 60610

SALARY AND EMPLOYMENT OPPORTUNITIES

An experienced sonographer can earn anywhere from $10,000 to $20,000 per year, depending on qualifications and experience. As in many other medical specialties, the future holds great promise for technicians trained in this new diagnostic specialty.

In the treatment of disease an accurate diagnosis is half the battle. We have already discussed the diagnostic procedures and the technicians who perform them, such as X-rays, electroencephalography, electrocardiogram recordings, and sonography. Another major method of diagnosing disease is through the examination of body fluids and tissues.

There are many diseases that cause chemical changes in the blood, urine, and lymph fluid, such as increase or decrease in the amount of red and white blood cells, microscopic changes in the structure of the cells of diseased tissue and organs, and the presence of parasites, viruses, or bacteria in the blood or diseased tissue. The detection of the presence and degree of these conditions can be invaluable to the physician in making an accurate diagnosis of a patient's condition.

All laboratory testing of body fluids and tissues is done under the supervision of a physician known as a pathologist. The pathologist, like many other medical specialists, depends on a trained team of assistants in order to make an accurate diagnosis of pathological conditions.

The field concerned with assisting the pathologist is known as *medical technology* and embraces a number of occupational specialties. The specialists that we will discuss will be the medical technologist, medical laboratory technician, blood bank technologist, certified laboratory assistant, cytotechnologist, and the histological technician.

The following are a group of professional organizations that can offer a list of the names, locations, and scholarships available for the academic and clinical programs available for the training in the medical technology specialties to be discussed in the next five sections.

American Medical Association
Council on Medical Education
535 North Dearborn Street
Chicago, Illinois 60611

American Medical Technologists
710 Higgins Road
Park Ridge, Illinois 60068

American Society
of Clinical Pathologists
2100 West Harrison Street
Chicago, Illinois 60612

American Society
of Medical Technologists
Suite 1600
Hermann Professional Building
Houston, Texas 77025

Board of Registry of the
American Society of Clinical Pathologists
Box 4872
Chicago, Illinois 60680

National Committee for Careers
in the Medical Laboratory
9650 Rockville Pike
Rockville, Maryland 20014

International Society of
Clinical Laboratory Technologists
805 Ambassador Building
411 North Seventh Street
St. Louis, Missouri 63101

American Society
for Medical Technologists
5555 West Loop South
Bellaire, Texas 77401

Information concerning employment opportunities in government clinical and research hospitals is available from:

Department of Medicine and Surgery
Veterans Administration
Washington, D.C. 20421

Clinical Center
National Institutes of Health
Bethesda, Maryland 20014

Medical Technologist

In the medical laboratory the most highly trained of all of the technicians is the *medical technologist*. He or she works directly under the pathologist in coordinating and supervising the diagnostic procedures performed in the laboratory. All of the other lab technicians work under the technologist in carrying out the complex procedures performed. The medical technologist must not only know the proper performance of each laboratory test, but must also understand the scientific principles behind each test in order to recognize, correct, and prevent errors in test results.

Very often the technologist will use his or her knowledge in assisting in the proper interpretation of test results. The technologist must have the ability to establish and monitor quality control programs and is expected to be able to design or modify procedures.

The following are illustrations of the kinds of tests the medical technologist would be expected to perform and supervise:

1. Matching blood samples of donor and recipient in blood transfusions.

2. Growing "cultures" of bacteria found in a patient's blood,

sputum, feces, or discharge from a sore or wound and identifying the bacteria.

3. Searching for and identifying parasites (e.g., tapeworms, pinworms) living in the body.

4. Testing for the presence or absence of various chemicals in the blood and other body fluids.

5. Testing for antibodies and other disease-fighting elements in the blood.

6. Analyzing urine for evidence of illnesses such as diabetes, nephritis, infection of the bladder, cancer of the bladder, etc.

7. Performing blood tests to detect illnesses of the blood such as hemophilia, anemia, leukemia, and mononucleosis.

8. Examining tissue cultures for the presence of pathological conditions such as cancer.

Some medical technologists will participate in the performance or supervision of each of these tasks while others specialize in only one of these specific fields. In the performance of their duties technologists are trained to operate special apparatus and a wide array of precision instruments, such as electronic counters, automatic analyzers, centrifuges, microscopes, autoclaves, spectrophometers, polorimiters, microtomes, and computers.

TRAINING REQUIREMENTS

To become a medical technologist requires three years of college plus one year of clinical education in a school of medical technology approved by the Council on Medical Education and Hospitals of the American Medical Association. The three years in college should include sixteen semester hours of biological sciences, sixteen semester hours of chemistry, and at least one semester of college-level math.

Most schools of medical technology are located in hospitals. Many charge very little for the clinical phase of education. Some even pay a small stipend while the student is undergoing this phase. After completing the clinical phase, the graduate can receive certification from the Registry of Medical Technologists of the American Society of Clinical Pathologists by passing their exam. Individuals who pass are allowed to use the initial MT after their name.

SALARY AND EMPLOYMENT OPPORTUNITIES

The average salary range for a licensed medical technologist is from $12,000 to $25,000 per year, depending on experience and supervisory position reached. Most medical technologists work in hospitals, but they are in demand in independent laboratories that provide diagnostic services to private physicians; in public health laboratories, where the chief work is in communicable diseases; in medical research institutes; in companies that manufacture drugs, serums, vaccines, antibiotics, and diagnostic reagents; and in the armed services.

The education in medical technology also provides an excellent background for graduate work leading to advanced degrees in laboratory sciences, teaching, and administration. Medical Technology is the backbone in medical diagnosis, and the technologist is the mainstay of this field. New diagnostic procedures are constantly being developed. The technologist who keeps abreast of the new advances can be assured of a secure future in this important field.

Blood Bank Technologist

The *blood bank technologist* collects blood from donors and classifies, processes, and stores it so that it can be instantly available either as whole blood or as plasma. This work is done in hospitals, clinics, and special blood bank centers; thus, the blood bank technologist is not categorized as one of the medical lab technologists.

The blood bank technologist must demonstrate a superior level of technical proficiency and problem solving in areas such as:

1. Testing for blood group compatibility.

2. Investigating abnormalities such as hemolytic diseases of the newborn, hemolytic anemias, and adverse response to transfusion.

3. Supporting physicians in transfusion therapy, especially for people undergoing organ transplants.

Supervising, managing, and teaching comprise a considerable portion of this technologist's responsibilities.

TRAINING REQUIREMENTS

Blood bank technologists are certified medical technologists who have had an additional year of approved training in a blood bank school approved by the American Association of Blood Banks. Upon passing an examination, they may be certified by the Registry of Medical Technologists as blood bank specialists.

For information concerning training programs, write:

American Association of Blood Banks
30 North Michigan Avenue
Suite 1322
Chicago, Illinois 60602

The salary for a blood bank technologist ranges from $12,000 to $19,000 per year. There is a demand for this specialty, and as new advances are made in treating blood diseases and in transplanting organs, the demand will increase further.

Medical Laboratory Technician

Until recently most of the laboratory testing in medicine was done by medical technologists. However, the technologists have, for the most part, moved on to supervising and teaching. They still do some of the most difficult and complicated testing. Otherwise, all but the most routine testing is now done by the *medical laboratory technician* under the supervision of the medical technologist. (The routine testing is done by certified laboratory assistants, discussed next.)

TRAINING REQUIREMENTS

Preparation as a medical laboratory technician can be achieved in several ways. First, the student can attain an associate's degree in this field from an accredited junior or community college and then gain clinical experience in an approved laboratory. Students with this experience may receive certification as a medical laboratory technician (MLT) by the Registry of Medical Technologists.

The registry will also give MLT certification to high school graduates who have completed a combined two-year work-school experience program, that is, if the school program is approved by the Accrediting Bureau of Medical Laboratory Schools. The registry will also grant certification to students who have completed a fifty-week armed forces course in medical laboratory techniques. All applicants for medical laboratory technologists registry must pass a registry examination.

After the student has become certified as a MLT, he or she can go on to become a registered medical technologist by attending extra classes that supplement the academic education. What is required is sixteen semester hours each in the biological sciences and chemistry. As you can see in this field, like so many other fields mentioned in this book, many fine career positions can be attained by gradually using one position as a stepping stone to a higher career position. This can make your education more economical and in many cases more interesting.

SALARY AND EMPLOYMENT OPPORTUNITIES

A medical laboratory technician can earn from $8,000 to $10,000 per year. The job opportunities are great, for there are overwhelming laboratory requirements in hospitals and other medical facilities.

Certified Laboratory Assistant

The *certified laboratory assistant* works under the direct supervision of the medical technologist in performing routine laboratory procedures in bacteriology, blood banking, chemistry, hematology, parasitology, serology, and urinalysis.

TRAINING REQUIREMENTS

To qualify for certification, one must graduate from high school and complete a twelve-month training program in a certified laboratory assistant school approved by the American Medical Association.

Currently, hospital laboratory schools are being accredited to provide qualified high school graduates with one year of practical and technical training in routine laboratory work. We recommend that all laboratory training be taken in schools directly associated with a hospital. Graduates of these schools may become certified as a laboratory assistant by passing an examination given by the Registry of Medical Technologists.

The laboratory assistant may also receive limited certification as a laboratory technician from the registry by completing a twenty-four-month on-the-job training program in an approved laboratory. We would like to mention again that most on-the-job training programs in medical work do not require the student to pay any training fees. In fact, most training programs will pay the student a small stipend while he or she is working.

SALARY AND EMPLOYMENT OPPORTUNITIES

The average salary of a certified laboratory assistant is approximately $7,200 to $9,500 per year. The opportunities for employment are as good as in the other related laboratory fields.

Cytotechnologist

The technician responsible for detecting evidence of cell disease by microscopic study of cell samples is the *cytotechnologist*. Cellular samples are obtained from various parts of the body, such as the female reproductive tract, the oral cavity, and any body cavity shedding cells. After taking a sample from a patient, the cytotechnologist prepares the sample by special staining techniques. Using the microscope, the technologist is able to detect minute abnormalities of the cell that may be the warning signs of cancer. As soon as any abnormalities in the cell structure are observed, the technologist gives the material to the pathologist for further study.

It is through the findings of the cytotechnologist that the physician is frequently able to diagnose cancer long before it could be detected by other methods, as well as diseases involving hormonal abnormalities. This examination of tissue by the cytologist and pathologist is one of the most critical procedures in medicine, for it is here that the final patient diagnosis is made.

TRAINING REQUIREMENTS

Educational preparation for cytotechnologists requires two years of college work to include twelve semester hours in biology, followed by six months in one of over 100 American Medical Association's approved schools of cytotechnology and six months' experience under supervision in an acceptable cytology laboratory. The student is then eligible to take the certifying examination given by the Registry of Medical Technologists and upon passing may place CT after his or her name. The cytotechnology curriculum will include a historical background of cytology, cytology as applied in clinical medicine, cytology in the screening of exfoliative tumor cells, as well as areas of anatomy, histology, embryology, cytochemistry, cytophysiology, endocrinology, and inflammatory diseases. Many of the biological sciences can be taken in a two-year junior college program at very little expense, and the clinical program in most cases is free.

SALARY AND EMPLOYMENT OPPORTUNITIES

The salary range for a cytotechnologist is from $10,000 to $15,000 per year. Due to the increased concern for early cancer detection and cure, there is a massive routine examining program in this country of all tissue that is susceptible to cancer. The "pap" smear that many women have done is a typical example. Cytotechnologists are directly involved in these programs, and will be able to count on a secure and financially rewarding future in their important function.

There are occasions where a cytotechnologist has opened up his or her own diagnostic laboratory, subcontracting the services of a licensed pathologist to act as director during his or her spare time. Stocking the laboratory with the basic equipment—a tissue slicing machine (microtome), staining solutions, and a high-power microscope—the enterprising cytotechnologist solicits the patronage of medical offices, either prepares the slides or has this done by a histologic technician, examines the slides, and turns any suspicious ones over to the pathologist, who gets paid on a fee-for-service basis. In this situation, incomes well over $50,000 a year have been reported.

Histologic Technician

Cuts and stains of tissues that have been removed from the body are made by the *histologic technician* so that the cytologist and the pathologist can examine the tissues microscopically for any signs of malignant or questionable cells. The slide must be prepared properly by the technician to insure proper interpretation.

When the tissue is cut from the body, the histologic technician slices it to the correct thickness for examination under the microscope, usually by imbedding it in melted paraffin wax, allowing the wax to harden, and then slicing the wax containing the tissue on a microtome machine. After this is done, the tissue is placed on the slide and properly stained by the technician to accentuate each component and make it readily visible to the pathologist. The technician must know which stain to use on each type of tissue and must carry out each step precisely. Since histologic laboratory work may deal with life-and-death matters, this work requires precision, dependability, manual dexterity, and a strong sense of responsibility.

TRAINING REQUIREMENTS

A high school graduate who has had an adequate background in the biological sciences can qualify as a histologic technician by taking a twelve-month clinical program in histologic technique given in a medical laboratory approved by the American Medical Association.

SALARY AND EMPLOYMENT OPPORTUNITIES

The average salary for a histologic technician is from $7,000 to $10,000. The employment opportunities are very good in this field.

REGISTERED NURSE

The professional *registered nurse* is by far the most important of all the paramedical specialists assisting the physician. As the practice of medicine becomes more widespread and the techniques of diagnosis and treatment become more complex, physicians and hospital staffs alike will become increasingly dependent on the well-trained nurse to carry out many medical procedures. Besides general nurses, there are nurses who specialize in various fields of medicine. In fact, as many medical specialties as there are in practice, there are almost as many corresponding nursing specialties.

Nurses supervise and administer medications; observe, evaluate, and record symptoms, reactions, and progress of patients; assist in rehabilitation of patients; and help maintain a physical and emotional environment that promotes patient recovery. They may carry out these functions on a general basis or in the specialty in which they decide to practice.

Registered Nursing Specialties

In a hospital setting there are many opportunities for specialist nurses.

The *psychiatric nurse* assists in observing and treating patients hospitalized for emotional problems. Nurses in this field are trained to recognize symptoms and changes in a patient and to report findings to the psychiatric staff to aid in diagnosing. The psychiatric nurse will see to it that the proper medications are given to the patient and will observe the results obtained. Many times the psychiatric nurse will act as an intermediary consultant to the patient and offer advice (under the supervision of the psychiatrist) to the patient that will hasten his or her recovery. The increased recognition of the presence of emotional problems afflicting people from all walks of life, and the desire to remedy this situation, has brought about an increased awareness of the important role that the psychiatric nurse can play not only in the hospital, but also in outpatient clinics, mental health facilities, school campuses, and even industry.

In the *cardiac care* unit, *respiratory care* unit, and the *intensive care* unit the *nurses* are trained to care for and observe the condition of the seriously ill patients in these respective units. These nurses monitor the complex machines that are connected to the patient and record all of the patient's vital signs. The nurse in this position must be quick to recognize any change in a patient's condition and report it to the physician in charge. In many cases one nurse will monitor the readings of six or more patients at the same time. Whenever there is a negative change in a patient's condition, the nurse must be knowledgeable and prompt in administering emergency procedures.

The *maternity nurse* works in the delivery room where she prepares the expectant mother for delivery and then assists the physician in the delivery. After delivery, she will cleanse the baby and aid the physician in checking for any abnormal conditions in the newborn. The maternity nurse will also instruct the mother in the proper care of her new child.

The *child care nurse* works in the children's ward in administering medication and treatment to children. Besides the usual nursing skills, the child care nurse must have a fondness for children and be able to make them feel comfortable in their distressed state and strange surroundings.

The *orthopedic nurse* will assist the orthopedic surgeon in the very intricate procedures of orthopedic surgery.

The *neurosurgery nurse* will likewise assist the neurosurgeon in the extremely delicate procedures involved in neurosurgery.

The general *operating room and surgical nurse* is responsible for everything that goes on in the operating room, including the proper preparation by operating room technicians for a scheduled operation. The surgical nurse must know what instruments are needed for the different types of surgery, have them ready for the surgeon, and then assist in handing them to the doctor during the operation.

The *gynecology nurse* assists the gynecologist in the examination and treatment of females. She will also instruct women on the practice of proper personal hygiene.

There are also areas other than hospitals that nurses may practice their profession.

Office nurses assist physicians in private practice or clinics. Sometimes they perform routine laboratory and office work in addition to their nursing duties.

Public health nurses care for patients in clinics, homes, schools, and other community settings. They instruct patients and families in proper health care and give periodic examinations and care as prescribed by a physician. They may also instruct groups of patients in proper diet and arrange for immunizations. These nurses work with community leaders, teachers, parents, and physicians in community health education. Some public health nurses work in schools.

Nurse educators teach students the principles and skills of nursing, both in the classroom and in direct patient care. They also conduct continuing education courses for registered nurses, practical nurses, and nursing assistants.

Industrial nurses provide nursing care to employees in industry and government. They treat minor injuries and illnesses occurring at the place of employment, provide for the needed nursing care, and arrange for further medical care if necessary. They offer health counseling and may also assist with health examinations and inoculations.

A growing movement in nursing, generally being referred to as the *nurse practitioner program,* is opening new career possibilities. Nurses who wish to take the extra training are preparing for highly independent roles in the clinical care and teaching of patients, such as nurse-midwifery, clinical research, physician assisting, and teaching.

TRAINING REQUIREMENTS

To become a registered nurse requires three years of training. Many university-connected hospitals provide the complete three-year program at very little cost to the student. The registered nurse can then supplement his or her education with an extra year of college training to earn a bachelor of science degree. Nurses desiring to enter the upper levels of nursing education and/or clinical research may extend their studies and fulfill the requirements of a master's degree. Very often the advanced degrees can be obtained while employed in general nursing. This can lighten the financial hardships of higher education.

For information on approved schools of nursing, nursing careers, loans, and scholarships, contact:

ANA Committee on Nursing Careers
American Nurses' Association
2420 Pershing Road
Kansas City, Missouri 64108

SALARY AND EMPLOYMENT OPPORTUNITIES

The average nursing salary is from $12,000 to $18,000 per year. Higher salaries are paid to nurses with graduate degrees who become involved in teaching, research, and primary care specialties, such as midwifery (which will be discussed later in this book). Nursing can be a very exciting career, offering a great deal of variety to match the interests of the individual nurse practitioner. Today many convalescent hospitals employ registered nurses with administrative ability to function as chief administrators of these facilities. These positions can be very financially rewarding, depending on the size of the facility.

A rapid increase in the employment of registered nurses is expected because of rising population, improved economic status of the population, extension of prepayment programs for hospitalization, expansion of medical services as a result of new medical techniques, and, more important, the ever increasing realization that physicians alone cannot provide all of the medical care necessary to the patient and society.

LICENSED PRACTICAL NURSE

Because of the expanding professional responsibilities of the registered nurse, the *licensed practical nurse* (LPN), also known as a *licensed vocational nurse* (LVN), is trained to work under the supervision of the registered nurse in administering health care.

LPNs are employed in hospitals, public health agencies, rehabilitation agencies, private homes, physician's offices, clinics, nursing homes, and such special institutions as psychiatric hospitals and children's hospitals.

The licensed practical nurse is starting to provide a large share of the bedside nursing care in hospitals and nursing homes. A LPN is trained to administer medication, including injections and intravenous solutions, under the supervision of a registered nurse. There is an increasing demand for men as licensed practical nurses, especially in the area of psychiatric and rehabilitation nursing.

TRAINING REQUIREMENTS

State-approved practical nursing schools are operated by hospitals, community agencies, junior colleges, and public vocational schools. Most approved schools offer a twelve-month course. After completion of the program the student is eligible to take a state examination to become licensed as a practical or vocational nurse, with the initials LPN or LVN after his or her name. The twelve-month program provides classroom and clinical experience. It includes instruction on the care of medical, surgical, and obstetric patients and instruction on special care for infants, children, the elderly, and the chronically ill. Selected background information in the behavioral and biological sciences is also provided.

For information regarding training programs, write:

National Association for
Practical Nurse Education and Service
1465 Broadway
New York, New York 10036

National Federation
for Licensed Practical Nurses
250 West 57th Street
New York, New York 10017

SALARY AND EMPLOYMENT OPPORTUNITIES

The average salary for an LPN is from $7,000 to $10,000 per year. A licensed practical nurse can look forward to a secure employment future since the supply falls far short of the demand. It is possible to supplement one's education with additional courses in order to receive certification as a registered nurse.

Years ago, before medicine became as sophisticated as it is today, many babies were delivered by midwives instead of doctors. These women were specifically trained for this function. Many times their experience was gained by "on-the-job" training under the guidance of other midwives. They were independently hired to be on hand at the expected time of delivery and to handle the complete delivery themselves. In most cases, where there were no complications, they did an excellent job.

As the practice of medicine advanced, the job of child delivery was performed by a physician specialist—the obstetrician. However, as medicine advanced even farther and the population increased even more, it became evident that there were not enough obstetricians to perform this task without putting a great deal of physical strain on them. After all, obstetricians have a full day at the office and having to be available at all hours for child delivery puts an undue strain on them, which subsequently could be detrimental to their patients.

As medical officials became more aware of these facts, they recalled the effectiveness of the original midwives and decided that people performing the same function—but with better training—could effectively substitute for the obstetrician at a normal delivery.

Today the *nurse-midwife* is a registered professional nurse who after successfully completing a recognized program of study and clinical experience in obstetrics has been certified in nurse-midwifery. The midwife provides prenatal care, performs the actual delivery, and then provides postpartum care. Guidance, emotional support, and reassurance are offered to each mother in this important life-giving function.

During the prenatal care the nurse-midwife performs the total physical examination of the mother, including breast examination, abdominal palpation, complete pelvic examination and evaluation, and taking the papanicolaou smear. As long as the course of labor is normal, the nurse-midwife will manage the labor and perform the delivery. The obstetrician to whom the midwife is responsible is consulted whenever there is any deviation from the normal. Any treatments, infusions, and medications, such as sedatives and analgesics, are prescribed by the nurse-midwife in accordance with the hospital's approved rules for nurse-midwifery service. After delivery the nurse-midwife provides immediate care of the newborn and, if necessary, performs simple resuscitation. The midwife also signs the birth certificate and performs the postpartum examinations of the mother. Women who have given birth via a nurse-midwife instead of a physician have reported complete satisfaction with this system. So, the prognosis is that this practice will continue to grow.

TRAINING REQUIREMENTS

A person must first become a registered nurse in order to become eligible for the nurse-midwife program. This program takes approximately eight months and provides an intensive course of theory and clinical experience leading to a certificate in nurse-midwifery. Schools of nurse-midwifery must be approved by the American College of Nurse-Midwives. At present about ten institutions in the United States and Puerto Rico offer basic education for nurse-midwifery and related internship programs and refresher courses. Scholarships are available to eligible applicants in almost all programs.

Information on scholarships and location of programs may be obtained by writing:

American College of Nurse-Midwives
50 East 92nd Street
New York, New York 10028

The salary range for a nurse-midwife is in the $20,000 a year category. The demand for nurse-midwives is expected to increase in order to free obstetricians to see more patients in their offices and clinics.

PHYSICIAN'S ASSOCIATE

As you read through this book, you will notice that there are many technical specialties that aid the physician in his or her role of diagnosing and treating patient illnesses. However, until now the physician has lacked someone with a broad paramedical background to assist in all phases of the doctor's responsibilities in patient care. The American Medical Association has recognized the need for such a person and has started programs to train and certify individuals to assume the role and title of *physician's associate* (PA), also known as *physician's assistant* in some medical circles. The American Medical Association has defined the physician's associate as a "skilled person qualified by academic and practical on-the-job training to provide services under the supervision and direction of a licensed physician who is responsible for the performance of that assistant. The functions of the physician's associate are interdisciplinary involving medicine, surgery, pediatrics , psychiatry, and obstetrics." Thus, the person being defined can also be categorized as an assistant to the primary care physician.

Some of the services that a physician's associate provides follow:

1. Receiving patients, obtaining case histories, performing an appropriate physical examination, and presenting meaningful data to the physician.

189

2. Performing or assisting in laboratory procedures and related studies in the practice setting.

3. Giving injections and immunizations.

4. Suturing and caring for wounds.

5. Providing patient counseling services.

6. Referring patients to other services.

7. Responding to emergency situations that arise in the physician's absence (within the associate's range of skills and experience).

The last function makes the PA especially useful in rural areas where a doctor is not always available.

TRAINING REQUIREMENTS

The physician's associate program, which is taught at several universities throughout the country, has an average course time of twenty-seven months, that is, nine academic quarters. Acceptance into the program requires a high school diploma with an extensive background in chemistry and the biological sciences. People who have undergone medical corps training in the military service in addition to their high school diploma make excellent candidates for this program. Likewise, people from other paramedical backgrounds, such as registered nurses or the many medical specialties discussed, also are excellent candidates.

The program, which consists of classroom and clinical work, is constructed in three phases so that students with different degrees of experience and proficiency may enter at different levels based on previous educational experience.

This training can be expensive—in some universities as much as $1,000 per quarter, making a total of approximately $9,000 for the entire nine quarters. However, various types of financial aid are available. The Bureau of Health Manpower Education will grant stipends of up to $3,000 per year to needy students. Information on scholarships and loans can be obtained by writing:

Bureau of Health Manpower Education
National Institute of Health
Bethesda, Maryland 20014

After completion of the requirements the student is awarded the title of physician's associate and is allowed to use the initials PA after his or her name. The physician's associate must then be licensed by the state in which he or she works. Most state boards license the associate to work under only one designated physician. When the associate changes physician employers, it must be done with the approval of the medical board. However, this is usually no problem providing that the new physician employer is competent.

Information on programs leading to certification as a physician's associate can be obtained by writing:

American Medical Association
Council on Medical Education
535 North Dearborn Street
Chicago, Illinois 60610

Physician Association Program
Division of Allied Health Professions
Emory University School of Medicine
Atlanta, Georgia 30322

Association of
Physician Assistant Programs
2120 L Street, N.W.
Washington, D.C. 20027

SALARY AND EMPLOYMENT OPPORTUNITIES

An experienced physician's associate can earn over $20,000 per year. The position has been created because of the shortage of physicians and the need to have personnel available to allow doctors to extend their knowledge and expertise to everyone in the community. This fact alone will insure a secure future to the well-trained physician's associate.

ORTHOPTIST AND
OPHTHALMIC TECHNICIAN

The work of the *orthoptist* and *ophthalmic technician* will be discussed under the same heading as the work of these practitioners overlap each other.

The orthoptist is mainly concerned with administering eye exercises to people with cross-eyes in the attempt to straighten them. The ophthalmic technician does everything the orthopist does but is authorized in addition to carry out other ophthalmic procedures in the assisting of ophthalmologists in their treatment of patients. Obviously, the ophthalmic technician requires further training than an orthoptist (about six months more), but then again, an expanded job market with higher salaries is open to the ophthalmic technician.

Orthoptics is an organized auxiliary to ophthalmology and is a science dealing with cross-eyes related to eye coordination. The ophthalmic technician is essentially an orthopist with advanced training to perform all diagnostic tests that are essential for diagnosing such anomalies as glaucoma and field defects and to assist in such other areas as surgical procedures and retinoscopy. Both the orthopist and the ophthalmic technician work under the supervision of an ophthalmologist. Upon graduating from a certified school, these technicians will be qualified to work in a university or hospital system where they will teach or see private patients or they will work in an office of an ophthalmologist in private practice.

The orthoptist determines, by special tests, how patients

use their two eyes together. He or she teaches them to develop and use binocular vision (focusing both eyes) and uses instruments, such as amblyoscopes and prisms, designed to train patients in the correct use of their eyes. The orthoptist works largely, though not exclusively, with children since juveniles respond more readily to treatment.

The ophthalmic technician, in addition to doing orthoptic work, is authorized to carry out other ophthalmic procedures, such as administering glaucoma tests, testing visual perception, testing visual acuity, measuring the eyeball for the acceptance of contact lenses, and training the patient to wear contact lenses. Since the ophthalmic technician is trained in the anatomy and physiology of the eye, in addition to a variety of ophthalmic procedures, he or she is the likely candidate to assist the ophthalmologist in the operating room. This is another extension of the training received.

TRAINING REQUIREMENTS

To be accepted into an orthoptic or ophthalmic technician program, one must have an associate of arts degree from a junior college. This can be readily obtained at one of the many junior colleges in the country at very little expense. It is recommended that a student wishing to enter this field take courses in mathematics, physics, science, chemistry, biology, and anatomy.

While in junior college one might apply for a job in an ophthalmologist's office doing routine work. This could give the student a greater understanding of the field and a deeper appreciation of the upcoming studies.

The student orthoptist may take training either in a training center or a preceptorship (instructorship). A preceptorship is usually a thirteen-month training program in an accredited office or clinic. Before, after, or during this course the student will take an eight-week basic course in orthoptics and ocular examination techniques sponsored each year by the American

Orthoptic Council. Students trained in preceptorships are required to take the basic course. Most preceptorships do not charge a tuition fee, but there is a fee for the basic course. The basic course is given every summer at the University of Iowa in Iowa City, Iowa. After completion of the preceptorship and the basic course the student is eligible to take the examination for certification by the American Orthoptic Council. The cost of the basic course is $300.

Instead of taking a preceptorship and the basic course, the orthoptic student can combine everything in one program at a training center accredited by the American Orthoptic Council. Training centers provide both practical and theoretical training concurrently. The usual period of training is fifteen to eighteen months. Some schools have extended this program to twenty-four months. Students in training centers are not required to enroll in the basic course since training centers provide both practical and theoretical training.

Our investigations have shown that the average tuition at a training center runs about $200 to $800 for the complete program.

It is the purpose of this book to inform people of the occupational options open to them. At the same time our research will show us what avenues provide the greatest financial remuneration and job security. It is because of this that we highly recommend that a prospective student take the combined orthoptic and ophthalmic technician program at an accredited training center. This is usually a two-year course. The tuition for this program varies from university to university, but we have found the average to be about $1,000 for the complete course; living fees are extra of course.

If the student successfully completes the combined program, he or she is then eligible to take the national written examinations. One is given by the American Orthoptic Council and the other is given by the Joint Commission of Allied Health. Upon completion of these exams, he or she is then eligible to take the oral and practical examinations and will receive certification from both the American Orthoptic Council as an orthoptist and from the Joint Commission of Allied Health Personnel in Ophthalmology as an ophthalmic technician. Double certification in these areas expands job opportunities and salaries for the student.

We suggest you write to the official training centers to find out which ones offer the combined program.

For further information on training programs, write:

The American Orthoptic Council
555 University Avenue
Toronto, Canada M5G 1X8

For further information concerning the basic course, write:

William E. Scott, M.D.
Department of Ophthalmology
University Hospital
Iowa City, Iowa 52240

SALARY AND EMPLOYMENT OPPORTUNITIES

There are almost unlimited career opportunities in this field, since the demand for orthoptists and ophthalmic technicians far exceeds the small number being trained each year.

The salary range of an orthoptist is approximately $9,000 to $12,000 per year. The salary range for an ophthalmic technician is from $12,000 to $20,000 per year, which is why we recommend the latter.

Because a well-trained ophthalmic technician can help an ophthalmologist to increase his or her work load and see more patients, thus increasing income, the technician may be able to get even higher salaries.

DENTAL HYGIENIST

The only people besides dentists who are licensed to work in a person's mouth are *dental hygienists*. Although the work is varied, the principal function of the hygienist is the cleaning of teeth. Research conducted in dentistry has revealed that more people are losing their teeth due to gum disease rather than to the actual decay of teeth. Also, it is being noted that the tartar and other debris that is deposited under the gums is one of the prime causes of gum disease.

The hygienist is trained to reach into the areas between the gums and the teeth and remove this tartar and debris. The process is generally known as "scaling." In doing this, the hygienist uses a variety of dental instruments and must be highly trained in their use. It is recommended that a person return to the hygienist every six months to have this process repeated as the tartar buildup is a continual process. The hygienist will also instruct the patient on the proper home care of the teeth and gums. In addition to the cleaning of teeth, a hygienist may also perform oral inspections and chart oral conditions, apply topical medicaments to reduce dental decay, and take and develop dental X-rays.

The work of a hygienist is not to be confused with that of the *dental assistant* whose primary function is to assist by passing instruments to the dentist, mixing filling materials, and attempting to make patients comfortable.

The majority of dental hygienists work in private dental laboratories. However, some are employed in government medical agencies and other large medical institutions that offer dental services. Also, many are employed in the dental hygiene programs of city school systems. In this capacity they become involved in the mass inspection of children's teeth, observing for oral conditions that should be referred to a dentist, and in instructing children in the proper care of teeth and gums.

The hygienists who work in private dental offices may do so

under a variety of employment situations. Some may work for a dentist on a permanent basis, receiving a fixed salary. In this capacity they will usually carry out other patient procedures in addition to cleaning teeth. Others may work for a dentist just doing scaling (cleaning) work. In this capacity they will book their own appointment schedules and receive a fee of approximately 60 percent of the dentist's fee. A complete scaling takes about forty-five minutes. A good hygienist can earn an average of about $95 a day. Some hygienists may perform their services for several dentists. This is done by spending certain days in different offices and booking appointments for that dentist's patients on the days they will be in that particular office. In this manner they make maximum use of their time. Also, in this capacity they are actually functioning as their own boss.

TRAINING REQUIREMENTS

To become a fully accredited dental hygienist, one must take an accredited two-year dental hygiene program followed by a licensing examination given by the National Dental Hygiene Board. Many community and junior colleges offer this program. Moreover, the tuition is very low and in many cases completely free except for instruments. A list of accredited dental hygiene programs can be obtained by writing:

The American Dental Hygienists' Association
211 East Chicago Avenue
Chicago, Illinois 60611

SALARY AND EMPLOYMENT OPPORTUNITIES

A dental hygienist can easily earn a salary of approximately $19,000 per year.

Due to an expanding population and the growing awareness of the importance of regular dental care, the employment of dental hygienists is expected to rise sharply. Also, now that many medical insurance programs are paying for dental care, many people who at one time could not have afforded complete dental care can now receive it. In many areas of the country the demand for dental hygienists far exeeds the supply.

PHARMACY TECHNICIAN

The pharmacy profession is striving to relieve its many practitioners from many of their routine tasks, such as typing prescription labels and counting pills, so that pharmacists can utilize their knowledge toward a more professional nature, such as providing professional information on drug usage and pointing out potential dangers of certain drug combinations.

This goal has given rise to a new technical specialty—the *pharmacy technician*. It is the proposed purpose of the pharmacy technician to work under the supervision of the pharmacist to type prescription labels, assist in counting pills, answer the phone, maintain patient drug files, and act as liaison between the pharmacist and the public.

TRAINING REQUIREMENTS

As yet, there are no definite training requirements for this field. Much of the knowledge needed can be acquired in approximately six months of on-the-job training in a retail pharmacy or hospital pharmacy working under the direction and supervision of a registered pharmacist. The American Association of Hospital Pharmacists can provide information on approximately forty-two hospital programs throughout the country designed to train pharmacy technicians. For information on these programs, write:

American Society of Hospital Pharmacists
Director of Professional and
  Scientific Services
4630 Montgomery Avenue
Washington, D.C. 20014

SALARY AND EMPLOYMENT OPPORTUNITIES

The typical salary of a pharmacy technician is approximately $5 to $6 an hour plus benefits. The work is clean and can be very interesting.

6

Creative Fields

HORTICULTURIST

During the past decade people in our country have become acutely aware of the need for increased food production and the beautification of our environment. One professional, in particular, is directly involved in this two-fold task—the *horticulturist*. We might define a horticulturist as a scientific gardener who provides us with both food-bearing plants and trees and ornamental plants and flowers for home and landscape use. The food-bearing plants include orchard products that supply us with fruits and nuts and garden plants that furnish us with vegetables. The ornamental plants are all of the plants and flowers used to decorate our environment.

Today, even in the United States, we are in a food crisis. Horticulturists can play a role in alleviating this crisis, for they are directly involved in developing newer and improved varieties of food-bearing plants. They may work in a laboratory developing new growing techniques for others to apply, or they may apply their knowledge and experimentation as a "commercial grower."

For instance, they may strive to produce tomatoes that are acid free, various fruits and nuts without pits, and larger and firmer cucumbers, corn, and tomatoes. In other words, for whatever food product in existence, they try to improve the size and taste while diminishing any undesirable qualities. For reasons of economy they will try to develop fruits and vegetables that will ripen at the same time on the tree or vine and have a firmness or hardness that renders them easily harvested by today's automatic and mechanical harvesting machines.

To be successful in the endeavors, horticulturists must be familiar with the functions of the parts of the plants and the factors controlling the plants' growth. It is necessary to have a thorough knowledge of botany and to know how to cross-pollinate plants to develop the desired products.

Horticulturists study plants, pests, and diseases and their control. They attempt to breed plants that will grow abundantly in areas where the climate is adverse and where they are commercially important, and to breed strains resistant to certain diseases.

The conservation of natural resources is another avenue of work for horticulturists. They are concerned with the planting of trees, grasses, and other plants that will help conserve natural resources and stabilize the land. In this area a horticulturist would most likely be employed by the government or privately owned landscaping and commerical development companies.

Many horticulturists are lawn specialists concerned with turf production and maintenance. They deal with homeowners and industry to assist them in developing more beautiful lawns. In this area a horticulturist might act as a consultant to a company that builds golf courses.

Because they are familiar with the chemicals, fertilizers, and insecticides necessary for good crop production, some horticulturists may become involved as field representatives for commercial chemical or equipment manufacturers. They visit farms to determine the effect of new chemicals on the crops. If they desire, they can combine their scientific knowledge along with their sales ability to promote the sale and distribution of a company's products. Canners and freezers will use horticulturists to contract farmers to grow crops for them and provide them with advice on the proper growing methods of these crops.

One of the biggest areas that horticulturists can practice their profession and grow financially is in horticultural sales. This is a field within itself. In this area the horticulturist is concerned with the commercial growing and selling of vegetable and ornamental plants. Because of increased food prices, many people are buying partially grown food plants and replanting them in their own gardens. Also, people have a new awareness and interest in the use of plants in decorating the inside and outside of their homes and apartments. Plants provide an economical, interesting, and creative way to decorate homes, apartments, and offices. People develop a sense of accomplishment in caring for their plants and watching them grow. Today ornamental horticulture has become a multibillion dollar industry in this nation.

There are several avenues to be taken in horticultural sales. A horticulturist can own and operate a greenhouse where plants are grown and resold on a wholesale basis to retail plant stores, landscape companies, or to private individuals. A horticulturist can open a retail plant store selling plants purchased from the greenhouses to the public. The horticulturist's knowledge on the care of these plants can be used to advise the plant customer. In this way the shop owner can establish a reputation as a good source from whom to buy plants.

Another retail avenue for the horticulturist is opening a garden shop specializing in the sale of seeds, fertilizers, insecticides, and gardening machinery for the people who want to start and develop their own plants and gardens. Here again, one's scientific knowledge can act as a supplement in developing a large clientele. Also, a horticulturist may become involved in working in or owning his or her own floral shop, growing and designing floral arrangements. The ability to telegraph floral orders from one part of the world to another has greatly increased the demand for qualified florists and designers.

An individual can work in, or open just one type of shop, or combine several operations under one roof. For instance, one may have a plant shop and house and garden center all on the same premises. The possibilities are many. There are over 81 million amateur gardeners spending several billion dollars annually on lawns, plants, and gardening.

TRAINING REQUIREMENTS

A lot of greenhouse and house and garden work can be learned by on-the-job training. However, to maximize one's career potential, it is advisable to receive some formal education in horticulture. There are many technical institutes and junior colleges offering two-year programs covering the various phases of horticulture and landscape design. This training will provide a greater opportunity for rapid advancement in all phases of the industry. If one has one's own business, knowing the fundamentals of plant characteristics and cross-pollination can provide the imaginative person with the resources to be unique in the development of many of one's own special breeds of plants.

An individual may even go beyond a two-year technical program to receive a bachelor's, master's, and even a doctor of philosophy degree in horticulture. These advanced degrees would prepare one for research and teaching positions in universities and government agencies.

For information regarding training programs in horticulture, write:

American Association of Nurserymen
230 Southern Building N.W.
Washington, D.C. 20005

American Horticultural Society, Inc.
901 North Washington Street
Alexandria, Virginia 22314

Information Services
California State Polytechnic College
San Luis Obispo, California 93401

National Landscape Association
230 Southern Building
Washington, D.C. 20005

SALARY AND EMPLOYMENT OPPORTUNITIES

It is hard to give a salary range for this type of work. An experienced greenhouse worker will probably receive from $10,000 to $12,000 per year. A teaching, research, or consultant salary can go to over $25,000 per year. As mentioned earlier, the increased interest in ornamental horticulture and gardening has opened up new opportunities for horticulturists to go into business for themselves as greenhouse operators, house and garden shop proprietors, etc. In this capacity the sky is the limit.

The growing emphasis on environmental improvement plus the need to improve food production in a world where hunger is becoming more prevalent has opened up vast horizons for the intelligent horticulturist. What is more, the modern technological developments in this field provide the ambitious individual with the resources to exploit these horizons.

ARBORIST

For years people have recklessly cut down trees because they were plentiful. They were cut down to clear land for farming and to build homes and other products requiring wood. Little attention was paid to replacing them for the use of future generations. Large wooded areas were literally depleted. The folly of such a policy is now being realized the world over. The supply of trees is becoming scarce, and there is not enough to satisfy the demands of an expanding world population. Trees are important to us not only in providing beauty and wood products, but also in nourishing soil to allow other vegetation to grow.

The recent realization of the crisis that could occur if our trees were not cared for properly has brought the occupation of the *arborist* into sharp focus. The arborist, also known as a *tree surgeon,* is a professional trained in all phases of caring for trees. The term "tree surgeon" is very appropriate for this occupation because a tree is a living thing and needs proper care and treatment by a trained professional, just as the human being needs the care of a good doctor. Trees need proper nutrition just as human beings do; they also get diseases just as humans do. The arborist takes care of the needs of trees by performing such tasks as transplanting, fertilizing, spraying, pruning, and removing trees.

Fertilizing trees is an essential part of a good tree maintenance program and is especially recommended for trees that show sparse foliage due to undernourishment. The arborist will drill holes around the tree with an electrically powered soil auger and then fill these holes with a tree food mixture.

Spraying trees is an important phase of the arborist's work, both as a preventative and as a corrective measure to control insects and plant disease. Power sprayers are used to apply the proper chemicals. Also, the arborist must be able to diagnose the diseases encountered by trees and know what chemicals and procedures should be used in their treatment.

Pruning trees is another important task. It is done to improve the shape of trees and also to remove dead or diseased limbs. Pruning may also be necessary to remove branches that are interfering with power lines or dwellings.

Quite often the arborist will be called upon to transplant a tree from one area to another for beautification purposes. This must be handled with great care in order to preserve the continued life of the tree. If a tree does die, an arborist must be skilled in removing it without damage to the surrounding structures.

TRAINING REQUIREMENTS

Much of the training can be learned on the job by working for a tree service company, landscape contractor, or tree maintenance department of the department of parks and recreation of a large city. On-the-job training can also be supplemented by taking special outside courses in a junior college in the community. These courses should include basic botany, soil chemistry, entomology (study of insects), plant physiology, and plant pathology. Also, a lot of general and specific information can be obtained by reading books and periodicals on tree maintenance. These books can usually be found in the public library. It should be noted also that since the work of an arborist requires a lot of climbing and other strenuous maneuvers, the aspiring worker should be physically strong and healthy.

Information on college or university training programs in tree care may be obtained by writing:

National Arborist Association, Inc.
3537 Stratford Road
Wantagh, New York 11793

Information Office
Forest Service
Department of Agriculture
Washington, D.C. 20250

SALARY AND EMPLOYMENT OPPORTUNITIES

A good arborist can expect to earn approximately $10,000 to $12,000 per year working for someone else. It is feasible for a good arborist to go into business for himself. From $10,000 to

$15,000 will buy the necessary equipment (power saws, a truck with a winch and boom, spraying equipment, rope, and small tools) to start a business. Some of the equipment can be leased or financed.

The self-employed arborist should solicit home building and developing companies to maintain the trees on their developments, city governments to maintain trees in parks and along city streets, and county and state governments to maintain trees in the countryside. Also, many private organizations such as colleges, hospitals, universities, manufacturing plants, golf courses, and other establishments with trees on their premises are good candidates for customers. Of course, homeowners will need the service. A successful business can net an arborist well over $20,000 per year.

The employment and business opportunities are excellent due to the increased interest in beautification everywhere—highways, streets, downtowns, parks, and home grounds. Real estate developers and homeowners are realizing how beautiful and well-maintained trees can greatly improve the appearance of a neighborhood and thus increase the value of each individual home.

LANDSCAPE GARDENER

Today people are becoming increasingly concerned with the environment in which they live. They want to be in an atmosphere conducive to good living. This includes not only "internal environment," but also "external environment." It is common to hear people speak of "beautifying America" and "Let's Keep America Beautiful." The *landscape gardener* plays an important part in creating and maintaining a pleasant outdoor atmosphere in which to play, work, shop, or just relax.

Landscape gardening tends to blend the best of nature with the type of architecture it is intended to enhance. A landscape gardener might be called an "exterior designer," for the gardener does with the outside area of a building what the "interior designer" does with the inside. Landscape gardeners can create "programs" for parcels of land, from small gardens to large commercial properties. In addition, they maintain the soil, grass, trees, and plants utilized in a landscape scheme.

The landscape gardener plans and executes a variety of landscaping operations that includes the cultivation and maintenance of grounds of private residences, business establishments, schools, government buildings, hospitals, and other institutions. After a basic design has been laid out, he or she participates with landscape laborers in preparing and grading the terrain; applying fertilizers and insecticides; seeding, sodding, and repairing lawns; and planting and transplanting shrubs, trees, and plants. One must always keep in mind the uses to which the land will be put. For insance, will the area have heavy traffic or light traffic, or will it be used for an ornamental or play area? Care must also be taken to use seed mixtures and fertilizers that are recommended for a particular type of soil or geographic location. A landscape gardener also designs and installs sprinkler systems to make sure a project is properly irrigated.

Landscape gardeners may be in their own business executing their own or their client's designs, or they may be in the employ of a landscape architect or large landscape contracting firms. They may also own and operate, or work in, nurseries, greenhouses, or home and garden shops. A landscaper who is in business as an independent contractor or in a supervisory position with a large landscaping firm will be called upon to make a large number of field decisions and be the sole individual commissioned to execute and oversee the complete design as well as its future maintenance.

An important phase of landscape gardening involves the use and maintenance of equipment ranging from basic tools, such as rakes, hoes, clippers, trowels, and spades, to power equipment, such as mowers, tractors, edgers, sprayers, and spreaders.

TRAINING REQUIREMENTS

The most important requirement for success as a landscape gardener is to have an interest for growing things, an affinity for the out-of-doors, and an eagerness to learn new developments and methods of doing things. Although you may not be able to change Mother Nature, there is always the opportunity to improve upon her and enhance her beauty.

One of the best ways to prepare for a career in landscape gardening is to work several years for a large landscaping firm where you can gain experience in all phases of the business. It is a good idea to supplement work experience with some formal academic training in landscaping. This training can be acquired during day or night classes at various junior colleges. A good academic program should include basic principles of landscape design where the ornamental and functional aspects of design are combined. You should also take the fundamentals of watering, irrigation, and fertilization. The use of chemicals and sprays and the recognition and control of diseases and pests should also be covered. Pruning, trimming, and turf management will also add to a trainee's proficiency. In addition, the principles of design, function, operation, cost and care of hand tools, power tools, and other equipment will prove valuable to a landscape gardener, especially if you plan to go into business for yourself.

SALARY AND EMPLOYMENT OPPORTUNITIES

The employment opportunities in this field are vast. Some of the projects calling for a landscaper's talents include the planning, design, and landscape gardening of zoological and botanical gardens, of historical sites and monuments, of river and lakefront developments, of playgrounds, of municipal, state, and national parks, of individual residences, of housing projects and urban renewal projects and of colleges, hospitals, and other institutions. These are just a few of the areas where landscape gardeners may apply their talents. In addition, more and more department stores are adding retail plant sales and accompanying services to their merchandise inventories—offering promising employment to landscape gardeners.

A gardener employed by a private landscape contractor or a local or state government agency will usually earn approximately $5 an hour. In a supervisory position, this wage may go up to $7 an hour. As is true for so many other fields, the best situation is to be in business for yourself. An independent landscape contractor usually charges between $11 and $13 an hour for services plus a charge for the trees, plants, grass, sprinkler systems, and other items necessary to complete a landscape design. The charge for the materials usually represents a 50 percent profit for the landscaper. Therefore, a work order consisting of a sprinkler system, a small decorative fountain or statue, plus grass, plants, and other vegetation might easily amount to $1,000, allowing the landscaper a profit of $500 plus the labor fees.

Landscaping is a highly competitive field. However, there are many ways of succeeding in this potentially lucrative area.

The most important thing is to make yourself and the quality of your work known to every potential customer of landscaping services. There are many ways of accomplishing this. First, you should contact every building developer in your area. Whenever a housing project is built, the homes are usually erected with very little landscaping around them, except for the model homes. Many real estate developers elaborately furnish and landscape several model homes in a development to use them as sales aids in promoting the sale of the rest of the homes in the development. An industrious landscape gardener can approach the owner or manager of a development and offer to do the landscaping for the model homes at a very low price. In return for the price concession, the developer will usually allow the landscaper to erect small signs on the landscaped area taking credit for the work and informing onlookers where to reach the landscaper. The buyers of the other homes frequently will hire the landscaper to do the landscaping on their newly purchased homes.

It is always a good idea to obtain lists of the names and addresses of everyone who has just purchased a home in a particular area, whether it be new or used. When people purchase a home, they are usually very excited about it and enthusiastic about fixing it up to their own likes—including the landscape. Therefore, recent home purchasers may be very receptive to the services of a good landscaper if they can see how the landscape artist can add to the appearance of their new possession. After all, buying a home is one of the major financial investments in a person's life, and each buyer wants to keep it as attractive as possible.

The names of new purchasers can be found in the legal section of local newspapers, in the county recorder's office, and from local real estate brokers.

Another excellent method of making one's landscaping talents known to the public is through the erecting of various types of gardens at county fairs or garden shows. Most officials of county fairs search for people who can help beautify the fair grounds and add to the total environment of the fair. To accomplish this, they will usually allow landscapers free display space to erect attractive gardens. In fact, they will even give prizes to the landscapers with the best gardens. This offers ample opportunity for the industrious landscaper to erect an original and creative garden at every county and state fair. The landscaper will be allowed to erect signs informing onlookers who created the beautiful garden that they are looking at. Many homeowners and large real estate developers go to these fairs expressly for the purpose of finding new and creative landscape artists.

Garden shows sponsored by local garden clubs and other organizations also furnish excellent exposure for the landscape gardener. In most cases you must be invited to be an exhibitor, and generally you are charged a fee for erecting a display. But the prospective opportunities for attracting new clientele warrant the expenditure.

Very often landscaping contracts totaling thousands of dollars can result from the gardens displayed at these fairs and shows. Many city, county, and state government agencies award large landscaping contracts for parks and recreational areas to qualified landscape gardeners.

There is a lot of money to be made in this field. And it does not take a large financial investment to get started! The most expensive item needed is a large flatbed truck which can usually be bought used or leased. The tools necessary to operate a full-scale landscaping service can be purchased for approximately $1,000. After the initial investment all you have to supply is your head and your hands.

INTERIOR DESIGNER OR DECORATOR

Have you ever walked into an apartment house, home, restaurant, office, hotel, or other type of building and become immediately aware of the elegance and style of the surroundings? Some interiors seem to put you into another world of warmth, beauty, and good taste. Many rooms seem to possess a theme all of their own, one that pleasantly engulfs the inhabitants. This is accomplished through the artistic science known as interior design, also known as interior decorating.

The American Institute of Interior Designers defines an *interior designer,* the practitioner of this science, as follows:

The interior designer and decorator is a person qualified by training and experience, to plan and supervise the design and execution of interiors and their furnishings, and to organize the various arts and crafts essential to their completion.

The designer is concerned with a human's spaces. He or she must recognize his or her surroundings, the materials he or she is working with, and the activities to be provided for. The relation of spaces to these elements and to the relation of spaces to each other constitutes design. The interior designer uses his or her knowledge of styles and periods of furniture, of fabrics for draperies, slipcovers, bedspreads, and the like, of wall and floor coverings, and of lighting fixtures and various art objects and puts them together in just the right blend so that all elements merge pleasantly and functionally with each other.

Interior designers—or interior decorators, as they are commonly called—plan and supervise the design and arrangement of building interiors and furnishings. They help clients select furniture, draperies, fabrics, floor coverings, and accessories. They also estimate what the furnishings or labor will cost. They may prepare sketches or other drawings so clients can visualize their plans. After a client approves both the plans and the cost, a designer may make arrangements for buying the furnishings, supervise the work of painters, floor finishers, cabinetmakers, upholsterers, carpet layers, and other craftspeople, as well as supervise installing and arranging the furnishings.

Interior design was once a luxury profession and the services of an interior decorator were used almost exclusively by the wealthy in furnishing their homes. People have since learned, however, that even modest homes can have charm and individuality and that people with modest means can afford to use the services of a professional designer to design their homes. In fact, many people are realizing that it is economical to hire the services of a professional decorator. A good decorator can select inexpensive items for a client and arrange them in such a manner as to give charm and elegance to a room. Small businesses, as well as large, have found that it is simply good business to have well-designed offices and public areas. Hotels, theaters, clubs, department stores, hospitals, schools, banks, and other establishments find it of great value to provide well-planned, tasteful interiors.

The designer must know materials—textiles, woods, metals, plastics, paints, papers, ceramics, fibers, and plasters—used in the creation of an interior. It is necessary to be able to advise a client on the quality and suitability of materials and furnishings. Every designer must have a knowledge of line, proportion, color harmony, and an understanding of space.

The interior designer must combine artistic talents with business ability. He or she must know about wholesale sources for the design profession. A thorough knowledge of buying procedures is essential, as quite often the designer contracts to buy all materials and furnish the labor for the job.

TRAINING REQUIREMENTS

The first requirement for entering the interior design profession is to have imagination and possess artistic and creative ability. There are aptitude tests that can help determine whether or not a person possesses the artistic ability necessary for this field. Once it has been established that an individual possesses the necessary talents, there are many avenues he or she can pursue in becoming qualified to practice as a professional interior designer.

Many junior colleges and vocational schools offer two-year programs leading to an associate's degree in interior design. Courses can be taken in high school and college night school programs. There are several correspondence courses approved by the National Home Study Council that offer training in interior design. Very often it is possible to gain excellent experience and background combining saleswork in a furniture or home furnishings store with full- or part-time academic training.

Membership in either the American Institute of Interior Designers (AID) or the National Society of Interior Designers (NSID), both professional societies, is a recognized mark of achievement in this profession. Membership usually requires the completion of three or four years of college training in interior design, followed by several years of practical experience in the field.

It should be pointed out, however, that going four years to college and becoming a member of either of the professional societies are not necessarily criteria for success. As in many career fields that we have discussed, if you possess the native ability plus the desire for success, conscientious study in a two-year college, night school, or correspondence program, plus practical experience, can provide an individual with the ingredients for success.

For information concerning training programs in interior design, contact:

American Institute
of Interior Designers
730 Fifth Avenue
New York, New York 10022

National Association
of Interior Designers, Inc.
312 East 62nd Street
New York, New York 10021

Foundation of Interior Design
Education Research
1750 Old Meadow Road
McLean, Virginia 22101

Also, the publication entitled *American Art Directory,* which may be found in most public libraries, contains a list of schools offering programs in interior design.

A good designer who can sell a client on using his or her ideas can earn anywhere from $10,000 to $50,000 a year, and even more. There are many ways to do it.

First, an individual can obtain a job in a furniture or home furnishings store selling items for a basic salary plus commission on the items sold. The commission is usually 10 percent of the sale. Therefore, if an individual sells a couch for $800, the commission would be $80. Once an individual gains experience not only in design, but also in selling, it is possible to gain the confidence of potential customers and sell them the furnishings necessary to furnish completely a room or home. Sales such as this can range from $3,000 to $10,000 and provide the decorator-salesperson with commissions of from $300 to $1,000.

Besides providing a salesperson with decorating experience plus income, working in a furniture or home furnishings store provides an individual with many types of contacts. These contacts include not only customer associations, but also associations with manufacturers. It is possible for a decorator salesperson to open his or her own design shop selling furniture and home furnishings from manufacturers' catalogues. The experience as a salesperson will give the decorator information on what manufacturers make the best products and also how to contact them and develop business relationships. A decorator who gives good service to customers during job-holding days can retain the patronage of many clients when opening up his or her own establishment.

In setting up a design shop, it is not necessary to tie up money in large inventories. Generally, all that is needed to open a design shop is to find a retail location with reasonable "foot traffic" and then tastefully decorate it with an eye-catching furniture and accessory display. The next step is to contact reputable manufacturers of all types of furniture and home furnishings for the purpose of selling their products through attractive display catalogues, which they can furnish to you. A good manufacturer is not going to sell to just anyone. However, once serious intent has been shown in becoming a professional decorator, it is fairly easy to obtain good manufacturing accounts. The fact that an individual has opened one's own shop and has had successful experience as a salesperson in a large retail establishment will usually qualify the individual in the eyes of the manufacturer. Moreover, the contacts made with manufacturers' representatives during job-holding days generally pave the way for sales agreements.

Once a design shop is set up with decorative display and manufacturers' catalogues on hand, the decorator can sell clients the products on individual orders from the catalogues. A manufacturer will usually allow a decorator-proprietor a profit margin of approximately 60 percent. To induce clients to buy from the shop rather than from the large retail stores, the decorator may have to offer a discount in addition to providing quality decorating services. Even with a discount, this will usually leave the decorator with a profit of approximately 40 percent. Therefore, if a designer furnishes a client with $3,000 worth of decorator furniture, it leaves a profit of $1,200. The furniture is usually "drop shipped" to the decorator's shop or warehouse and is later delivered to the client by the decorator via a delivery service. Practically anyone offering decorating items for sale will give an established decorator a "trade discount." Therefore, if a shop does not normally handle a certain item, the supplier of that item will usually give a discount to the decorator, allowing the decorator to derive a profit from it. Even upholsterers will give special price considerations to decorators.

There are many ways for a decorator to build up a clientele. First, there is the tried and true method of newspaper advertising. In addition, it is a good idea to establish contact with real estate offices. Very often a person who is hesitant to purchase a house can be persuaded to do so if the sales agent can convince the individual that the house will look marvelous with the proper decorating scheme. To do so, the agent calls in the decorator. One can establish these "leads" by personally contacting real estate people and also by going to various meetings and conventions of the real estate industry.

Another way to solicit patronage is to give speeches to various clubs and civic organizations on proper decorating techniques for home and offices. If an individual in the audience is in the need of decorating services at the present or a future date, he or she may contact the decorator for his or her services. Furthermore, once a decorator develops a reputation for doing quality work at reasonable prices, this reputation spreads fast, and before long people are seeking out the decorator. Excellent results can also be obtained by advertising in the yellow pages of the phone directory.

Sometimes a restaurant or hotel chain will hire a decorator to work for the organization and redesign new and established outlets on a full-time basis. Sometimes large architectural firms will hire full-time decorators.

There are also opportunities for good decorators to work from their homes advising people on decorating schemes on a consultant basis. In this capacity the decorator does not stock or order any merchandise for the client. Instead, he or she selects an attractive and functional decorating scheme for the client and then helps to select the necessary items in retail furniture and decorating stores or special companies that sell only through decorators. This practice is usually done with clients who are willing to pay top prices for extremely fine furnishings. For the service the decorator will usually charge a flat fee or a percentage of the cost of the goods purchased by the client.

The utilization of the services of interior designers is expected to increase with the availability of well-designed furnishings at moderate prices and the growing recognition among middle-income families of the value of professional design services. Also, the increasing use of design services by commercial establishments should contribute to the demand for decorators.

The interior design field offers a variety of fascinating opportunities for individuals to express themselves in exciting and creative ways and to profit handsomely from doing so.

FASHION DESIGNER

The time has long since passed in most parts of the world that clothes are bought (or made) primarily to protect the wearers from the elements. This is no longer primarily true. We have become a style- and fashion-conscious society. Well-styled clothes allow us to express our individuality. People want to look attractive, and clothes do a great deal to enhance a person's looks and even personality.

As a result of this, clothing styles are constantly changing. The people responsible for this constant change are the *fashion designers*. There are four seasons in a year—winter, spring, summer, and fall. There is a clothing style for each season, and each year the styles for each season change. There is really no practical reason for this except for the old adage "variety is the spice of life." People from every economic level want fashion changes, and the fashion designers provide them with it.

Fashion designing is very competitive, and we cannot recommend it as offering the same job security as many of the other occupations discussed in this book. However, we chose to include this profession because it can offer the person with artistic and creative style ability a great deal of excitement, challenge, personal satisfaction, and large financial returns. Although we will not guarantee job security, the opportunities for success do exist for a person who is flexible, hard working, and innovative to rise to the upper echelons of this field. A good candidate for a career in fashion design should possess artistic and mechanical aptitude.

A fashion designer usually starts a new fashion with a pencil sketch. This sketch may be inspired by a variety of experiences: traveling, observing different life-styles, and seeing the work of other designers. Many designers travel to Paris, Rome, and other fashion capitals of the world to attend fashion shows. If a designer sees a fashion or trend that seems interesting, original, and suitable for sale, she or he may copy the original and adapt it to her or his own tastes. The outright copying of an original takes a great deal of judgment and style sense. When a designer for the ready made market designs a garment or copies one, the designer must be able to adapt it to make it feasible for mass production at competitive prices.

After the original sketch is complete, the designer and an assistant make an experimental garment. They cut materials and pin, sew, and adjust the garment on a form or live model until it matches the sketch. The experimental garment is then used as a guide in cutting and sewing fabrics to make a finished "sample" of the dress. After the sample is completed and approved (by the manufacturer who will market the garment), it is used as a guide to make a master pattern of each segment of the garment. Each master pattern is then measured and modified to allow the garment to be produced in various sizes. Each master pattern serves as a guide to cut and mass-produce hundreds or thousands of garment segments, which are later assembled and sewn together.

Most designers do not start their careers by producing the original design. Most likely, they will be employed assisting in one or several of the steps just mentioned. After proving themselves in the secondary positions, they may move up to senior designers.

A designer's work habits are varied. There are four showings a year, and it is not unusual for a designer to be required to turn out from 30 to 100 creations for each showing. This usually means putting in long hours getting each garment ready for final showing. However, after the garments are ready, the designer can usually take some time off for vacationing and relaxing before getting ready for the next season. This is a good field for the person who likes to work hard and then play hard.

Many designers specialize in just certain types of outfits, be they designers for ladies', men's, or children's clothes. Some will specialize in the designing of sports clothes, others in formal wear, some in coats and suits, others in blouses, or still others in men's shirts. Certain designers like to specialize in clothes for certain age groups. For every type of outfit there is, usually there is a corresponding design specialty.

TRAINING REQUIREMENTS

There are no set training rules for becoming a designer. The most important qualification is to have a flair for style. This flair can be developed by attending a good design school and then getting on-the-job training. This combination will enable a person to prepare for positions as senior designers.

A list of schools offering training programs in fashion design may be obtained by writing:

The Alumnae Advisory Center, Inc.
Box AC 541 Madison Avenue
New York, New York 10022

The International Association
of Clothing Designers
12 South 12th Street
Philadelphia, Pennsylvania 19107

Many junior colleges in your community offer this training at very low fees. Information on these colleges can be obtained by contacting high school guidance departments. There are schools that offer a four year program leading to a bachelor of arts degree in fashion design. Two such schools are:

The Fashion Institute of Technology
227 W. 27th Street
New York, New York 10001

Pratt Institute
215 Ryerson Street
Brooklyn, New York 11025

SALARY AND EMPLOYMENT OPPORTUNITIES

There is a great variance in the wages and employment opportunities for a fashion designer. A designer may start out with a large manufacturing company in one of the assisting categories for under $200 a week. Once a person has become established as a good designer, he or she can advance to senior design positions earning up to $50,000 a year and more. As long as a designer's creations keep selling, a large income is virtually assured.

Designers who want to be on their own and not have to depend on the decisions of their superiors for advancement have other avenues to pursue.

One may operate his or her own retail shop featuring garments designed by and manufactured for the designer. Independent manufacturers who specialize in just assembly production will sew the garments. Some designers own and operate their own high-fashion design salons where they custom design and manufacture individual garments for a more select clientele who are willing to pay high prices for personalized fashions.

A designer with a good reputation may become an independent contractor, designing clothes for several small manufacturing companies who do not wish to maintain a full-time design staff.

Designers can even start their own companies by designing a line of clothing and then subcontracting a manufacturing company to produce a number of samples of each creation. These creations are then put in the hands of commission salespeople who show it to, and take orders from, retail store buyers. As the orders for each style are received, they are turned over to the manufacturing company for production and shipment. In this manner, by subcontracting the actual production work to a production company, a designer can literally have his or her own clothing line without tying up enormous sums of money in machine and assembly-line personnel. Designers who operate their own businesses are limited in income only by talent, energy, skill, and resourcefulness in promoting their ideas.

JEWELRY AND FLATWARE DESIGNERS

The wearing of jewelry has always been one of the most popular ways of enhancing one's appearance, second only to clothing. As with clothes, styles in jewelry design constantly change, providing continuous sales opportunities for new creations. Not only is the wearing of fine expensive jewelry always popular, but now, with the improved materials used in custom jewelry, there is a tremendous market for well-designed, less expensive, costume jewelry. Moreover, it has been observed that as the country experiences economic hardships, the sale of well-designed costume jewelry increases. People crave personal identity, and when they face hard times and can no longer afford expensive cars or clothes, they turn to jewelry to glamorize their appearance and call attention to themselves.

Also, a popular activity in our society is the giving of fashionable dinner parties. This has created a demand for well-designed tableware to complement the dining atmosphere.

These trends have led to the development of new and vast opportunities for the imaginative and skilled jewelry designer and flatware designer.

Since jewelry and flatware designers are people with similar educations and backgrounds, they are considered together in this discussion. However, they work in completely different areas. The *jewelry designer* creates original designs or modifies existing ones for use in making jewelry. The *flatware designer* performs the same functions to produce flatware, which consists of spoons, forks, knives, and other tableware. Usually each designer makes sketches of a new or revised design or pattern and then finalizes the drawing so that it can be used directly, by transfer to the material or to form a mold, to manufacture the final article.

Jewelry and flatware designers are both specialized artists. They work at the drawing board or make models in metal, plaster, or wax to produce the required designs. In order to produce unique designs, they use their imagination or draw upon their observations of existing art forms around them, those in nature and those created by man. They may have recorded this information in a sketch book where they have drawn various art forms such as flowers, plants, shells, animals, birds, and fishes, and even such forms as raindrops, snowflakes, and ice crystals. They may use these as a basis for their designs, extending the forms into various designs.

Both jewelry and flatware designers must be constantly aware of the demands of the marketplace and what is considered "in" in order to gain an advantage over their competition. For this reason they may attend various art, fashion, and other exhibitions throughout the world to keep abreast of the latest fashion and household developments, thus enabling them to design jewelry and flatware that harmonizes with forthcoming fashions and styles.

Once designs are finalized and approved, the designers must transfer them to the material, as we already noted. For individual pieces of jewelry this can be done by tracing the design from the paper onto the material and then, using instruments, decorating the metal to conform to the design. For manufactured articles a model is made in wax by the craftsperson.

When the wax model is completed, it is cast into a plaster of paris mold into which melted bronze is poured. The bronze model is placed in a die-cutting machine to make a steel die. The die is then used in the mass production of the article.

Jewelry and flatware designers must possess a combination of artistry and practicality. It is essential that they be able to draw and sketch. The person who likes to sketch can learn to be a designer, but in addition to drawing, one must have imagination and possess the ability to be creative and original. The designer must be able to take an example, an idea, even a hint, visualize its development, and project it into a finished product.

TRAINING REQUIREMENTS

Since jewelry and flatware designers are artists, their training should emphasize art, design, and a knowledge of materials used to produce suitable designs for their craft. Many design schools offer majors in silversmithing. Such schools are the logical place to look for initial training. Some junior colleges grant an associate's degree in jewelry design. Another path to a design position is through apprenticeship and work in some phase of jewelry or flatware manufacture. There are also trade and industry schools that have courses in jewelry making and jewelry design, thus providing practice in both the craft and the associated design.

For information concerning training programs and career opportunities in jewelry and flatware design, write:

Manufacturing Jewelers
and Silversmiths of America
Suite 75, Biltmore Hotel
Providence, Rhode Island 02902

Retail Jewelers of America
10 Rooney Circle
West Orange, New Jersey 07052

Industrial Designers Society of America
60 West 55th Street
New York, New York 10019

American Jewelry Manufacturer
[Magazine]
Chilton Company
56th Street and Chestnut Street
Philadelphia, Pennsylvania 19319

SALARY AND EMPLOYMENT OPPORTUNITIES

The wages of experienced jewelry or flatware designers will vary from $300 to $500 a week. Usually these designers work for large jewelry or flatware manufacturing firms.

However, numerous jewelry designers own their own shops, designing and creating their own articles. They may create the pieces for mass production or custom make individual pieces for individual customers. Some designers custom design their creations, farm out the production requirements to a manufacturing firm, and then hire salespeople on a commission basis to present the creations to department, jewelry, and gift stores around the country. By supplying salespeople with samples to solicit orders from, the designer can then have the items mass-produced by a manufacturing production company, once the sales contracts have been secured. In this manner overhead and cost of going into business can be greatly reduced, as the sale is made before the samples are mass-produced. Prominent designers with distinguished reputations can do free-lance work providing design services to large jewelry manufacturing firms. The wearing of jewelry has become more popular and has increased the scope of opportunities for designers.

The improvements in the process for the production of stainless steel flatware now provide tableware that looks like sterling and that matches sterling flatware patterns. This has brought styled flatware within the cost range of the average household.

The number of large-volume stores selling jewelry and flatware continues to rise along with many small shops. This has contributed to increased sales of jewelry and flatware and the corresponding increase in the demand for skilled jewelry and flatware designers.

COMMERCIAL ARTIST

"A picture is worth a thousand words"—no truer statement can be made. Essentially, this is what commercial art is all about. A picture can be drawn to make a certain impression on the observer. Most *commercial artists* work in various areas of the advertising media to convey the message of the advertiser to the reader.

Although photographs are used in advertisements, very often a drawing can be structured to make an impact that a photograph cannot. The commercial artists use color and black-and-white drawings to emphasize or dramatize the theme of the ad. The field of commercial art can offer the artistically inclined individual the opportunity to turn an interest in art into a full-scale career.

Commercial artists create the concept and artwork for a wide variety of items. These include direct-mail advertising, catalogues, counter displays, slides, and film strips. They also design or lay out the editorial pages and feature articles of publications and produce the necessary illustrations to accompany them. Many commercial artists specialize. For example, some do only fashion illustrations; others, book illustrations; still others, technical drawings for industry.

Artists may also retouch photographic prints, prepare charts and maps, draw movie cartoons, and do freehand and mechanical lettering. Well-trained commercial artists are capable of designing containers and the labels that are attached to them. They also sketch and color designs for greeting cards, and design and illustrate television commercials.

Most commercial artists work as staff artists for advertising agencies, commercial art studios, advertising departments of large companies, printing and publishing firms, newspapers, textile companies, television and motion picture studios, department stores, and a variety of other business organizations.

Many are self-employed as free-lance artists. Some salaried commercial artists also do free-lance work in their spare time, adding to their income.

As you can see, the areas where commercial art is applicable are extensive. In any case, the commercial artist does work to fit the requirements of a specific client or employer.

In an advertising agency's art department, for example, the artist first confers with the copywriters and account executives to determine the message or theme that is to be delivered in the drawing for the "product." After ascertaining the general theme of what is being attempted, the illustrator begins rough sketches. This is difficult because the artist must decide how to establish the mood of the picture and what color combinations, background, and composition to use. For the first rough sketches felt-tip pens, chalks, crayons, or pencil are generally the art tools used. After these preliminary sketches, the artist may do many sketches in color before beginning the final illustration. Most artists are skilled in the use of several types of media, such as black-and-white pencil drawings, water color, pastels, acrylics, tempera, or oil. However, usually they find one particular media that is most suitable for their individual style of illustration. In some cases several types of media are used in the same picture.

Free lancing is the eventual aim of most illustrating commercial artists. It affords them the opportunity to specialize in the type of illustration in which they excel and allows them to develop original styles. Moreover, it affords them the greatest opportunity for large financial gain. The free-lance artist must have a good grasp of advertising design and possess originality of thought in order to suggest original plans and advise clients.

TRAINING REQUIREMENTS

The most widely accepted training for commercial art is the instruction given in art schools or institutes that specialize in commercial and applied art. Many universities and junior colleges offer two- to four-year programs in commercial arts.

Numerous colleges also offer night programs. Several correspondence schools listed in the *Home Study Blue Book* (available from the National Home Study Council, 1601 18th Street, N.W., Washington, D.C. 20009) offer courses in illustration.

The most important factor for success in this field is creative and artistic ability, that is, the power to conceive ideas and project them in graphic form. Whether or not an individual possesses this ability can be determined by taking aptitude tests administered by high school or college guidance departments, the state department of vocational guidance, or any other impartial testing agency. Be wary of tests administered by small private art schools. Once a student is assured of his or her artistic ability, he or she can then pursue a training program.

If a private school is decided upon, make sure all the rules discussed in the section "How to Pick a Good School," in the beginning of this book, are followed.

A good curriculum should include drawing logic, advertising procedures, illustration theory, advertising design, theory of color and values, airbrush photo retouching, production procedures, and commercial design.

For more information on opportunities and training programs in commercial art, write:

National Art Education Association
1916 Association Drive
Reston, Virginia 22091

SALARY AND EMPLOYMENT OPPORTUNITIES

Employment of commercial artists is expected to increase. One reason is an anticipated rise in business expenditures for visual advertising such as television graphics, packaging design, and poster and window displays. The expanding field of industrial design also is expected to require more qualified artists to do three-dimensional work with engineering concepts.

Commercial artists in top positions usually earn from $350 to $450 a week or more. Earnings of free lancers vary widely. In general, a free lancer may receive from $40 for a single black-and-white fashion sketch to $850 for a figure in full color, from $1,000 to $2,000 for a color cover for a national magazine, or from $75 to $300 for a book jacket or record album cover.

There are many ways you as a free-lance artist can promote yourself. First, you should have a portfolio of all of the quality work that you have completed. You should then present this portfolio to advertising agencies and newspaper, magazine, and book publishers. Department stores or any other type of retail establishment that might use illustrations in their advertisements should also be contacted. Very often real estate agencies and developers will show black-and-white illustrations of homes for sale in the real estate section of local newspapers. This is a good place for a beginner to get a foothold in free lancing, since new drawings have to be continually made as old houses are sold and new ones listed. Check hotels for the various types of conventions to be held. Many organizations in a particular industry are in constant need of good artwork for company brochures and advertisements. It is very often possible for an illustrator to secure a small booth at these conventions to show his or her portfolio. The beginning can be very rough for a free-lance artist, but once a good reputation is established, many potential clients will then seek out the artist.

TECHNICAL ILLUSTRATOR

Just about every product sold today, from a simple toy to the most complex piece of machinery, is accompanied by descriptive literature and graphic illustrations concerning its assembly, operation, maintenance, and other facts about it. These detailed illustrations are the work of a *technical illustrator.*

Very often it is easier for an engineer, production superintendent, or consumer to understand the assembly and proper functioning of a product through an accurate, clear, and concise drawing. The illustrator not only draws a picture of an item to show every detail, but also constructs the drawing in such a manner to accentuate the important aspects of the product, bringing it to the attention of the observer. Whereas the commercial artist draws for beauty, the technical illustrator draws for accuracy and detail. The latter's drawing must be primarily informative, realistic, and technically correct.

The technical illustrator's work appears in booklets or manuals that tell the purchaser or user of equipment how to operate the new product. In many cases the illustrator draws several pictures of the product in different stages of disassembly to enable the observer to gain a greater understanding of the product.

In order to do the work properly, the illustrator must learn a great deal about the product being drawn. The drawings must illustrate function, relationship, and assembly of parts in their exact perspective. To acquire knowledge of the product, the technical illustrator studies blueprints, samples, models, and photographs. He or she also visits the working areas to observe processes and materials and often meets with engineers and others to discuss preliminary sketches for correction or approval. The technical illustrator must be able to convey engineers' ideas and sketches into visual form easily understood by technicians and laypeople.

The illustrator may prepare simple diagrams on instructions for assembling a toy or may draw illustrative proposals of machinery, weapons, or other equipment being submitted by a manufacturer to the government for the purpose of obtaining a contract. A million-dollar contract and employment for many engineers and production workers may depend on the accuracy and style of an illustrator's drawings.

In addition to drawing equipment, technical illustrators are called upon to supply the artwork for charts, graphs, and the diagrams required for booklets and manuals. They also prepare training manuals used to give visual descriptions of operational steps or processes. Their drawings may illustrate the step-by-step process of constructing a building, manufacturing a product, or various do-it-yourself projects.

Some illustrators specialize in preparing illustrations of products being submitted to the United States Patent Office for patenting. Very often a real estate developer will hire a technical illustrator to prepare an "artist's concept" of a development not yet built in order to secure funds for the project or presell the entire project or units of the project.

TRAINING REQUIREMENTS

The technical illustrator must like mathematics and have good spatial perception to enable him or her to visualize parts and equipment from blueprints or models. A thorough knowledge of blueprint reading and mechanical drawing is necessary. In addition to having great patience and the ability to give attention to detail, the illustrator should be artistic and imaginative and mechanically inclined as well.

Technical illustrating is taught in many vocational schools, junior colleges, and technical institutes. It is generally a one- to two-year program. Among the subjects that should be included in a good program are blueprint systems, technical construction, layout and composition, rendering techniques, art production techniques, perspective drawing, schematics, theory of color, isometric freehand sketching, and graphic design.

For more information concerning career opportunities and training programs, write:

Society for Technical Communication
1010 Vermont Avenue, N.W.
Washington, D.C. 20005

There are many areas in which a technical illustrator may be employed. It is possible to work for any company that manufactures products, or for a firm that specializes in preparing descriptive and technical literature, or for a company specializing in technical manuals, or be self-employed as a free-lance illustrator working for firms in any of these categories.

An experienced technical illustrator employed in industry or for a technical publishing firm can earn from $1,200 to $1,500 a month. A free-lance illustrator in great demand can earn as much as $20,000 per year, and sometimes even more.

The increased realization by manufacturers of the valuable aid technical illustrations provide places new importance on the work of the technical illustrator. Today's mass production of complex machines and equipment increases the need for visual instruction to provide knowledge regarding production, assembly, operation, and maintenance. Illustrations are becoming increasingly favored in personnel training programs. As our society becomes more mechanized, it is logical to assume that this occupation will grow—not only in size, but also in importance.

DRAFTSPERSON

Every object built today, whether it be a room addition, electric motor, television set, office building, or space capsule, must be built from a series of drawings. These drawings will reflect the external and internal functioning of the object. The engineer, scientist, or architect makes the rough sketches of the proposed object plus a list of specifications desired and gives these to a *draftsperson,* who, in turn, prepares detailed drawings based on the information provided. The draftsperson also calculates the strength, quality, quantity, and cost of materials required. The final drawings by the drafting staff contain a detailed view of the object as well as specifications for materials to be used, procedures to be followed, and other information needed to carry out the job. It is from these drawings and specifications that workers can proceed to build the object.

Draftspeople may specialize in a particular field of work, such as mechanical, electrical, electronic, aeronautical, structural, or architectural drafting.

In preparing drawings draftspeople use compasses, dividers, protractors, triangles, and machines that combine the functions of several devices. They also use engineering handbooks, tables, computers, and slide rules to help solve technical problems.

In mechanical drafting craftspeople must learn the latest shop procedures in allied industries. This means a great variety of interesting investigations, which keeps the draftsperson on the alert to stay abreast of manufacturing problems. Versatility and creative expression, as evidenced in the designs and drawings done, will be the measure of the draftsperson's advancement and salary.

Draftspeople are classified according to the work they do or their level of responsibility. Senior draftspeople translate engineers' or architects' preliminary plans into design layouts (scale drawings of the object to be built). Next down the line, draftspeople known as detailers draw each part shown on the layout and give dimensions, materials, and other information to make the detailed drawing clear and complete.

In architectural drafting the draftsperson is trained to make complete working drawings of one- and two-story frame residences and apartments, small commercial and industrial buildings, shopping centers, medical centers, and manufacturing establishments. These are achieved by combining the knowledge of drafting with an understanding of construction materials and methods. The study of perspective, layout, and design offers a continuing challenge to the draftsperson's creative ability, with unlimited opportunity for self-expression. For the architectural draftsperson opportunities for employment are unlimited. New building materials are constantly being developed, and methods of using them are continually changing. This can provide continuous challenge to the draftsperson. In addition to architectural firms, architectural draftspeople may work with builders and contractors, structural engineers, oil companies, cabinet makers, tile manufacturers, and steel companies and with city, state, and federal agencies.

TRAINING REQUIREMENTS

Persons interested in becoming a draftsman or draftswoman can learn this profession in a two-year educational program given in many technical institutes and junior colleges throughout the country. Others may qualify through company-sponsored on-the-job training programs.

Technical schools and junior colleges offer two types of drafting programs. The first is architectural drafting, which is a specialized two-year program leading to an associate's degree in this field. This degree prepares the student for architectural work already discussed in this chapter. The second type of program is a two-year program leading to an associate's degree in mechanical drafting. The scope of mechanical drafting is large and includes the fields of aircraft, tool design, mechanical design, machine and electrical drafting, as well as many other technical fields. After completion of an associate's degree extra courses in engineering, design, and mathematics sometimes enable draftspeople to transfer to engineering and design positions. A good drafting program will not only teach a student to make completed drawings, but will also familiarize the student with the various types of materials used in building the object being drawn.

For schools offering programs in drafting, write:

American Institute for
Design and Drafting
3119 Price Road
Bartlesville, Oklahoma 74003

American Federation
of Technical Engineers
1126 16th Street, N.W.
Washington, D.C. 20036

SALARY AND EMPLOYMENT OPPORTUNITIES

Employment opportunities for draftsmen and drafts-women are very good, especially when you consider that practically everything built today requires the services of a skilled draftsperson to initiate production. As designs and production procedures become more complex, more skilled draftspeople will be needed to facilitate production.

A well-trained individual who is willing to apply himself or herself and keep up with new design and production methods can advance to senior draftsperson, to technical illustrator, to designer, to drafting supervisor, to chief draftsperson, and to manager of a drafting department.

According to the American Institute for Design and Drafting, the top salaries for the various levels of draftspeople are $1,418 per month for a draftsperson, $1,679 per month for a senior draftsperson, and $2,557 per month for a designer. A designer is a draftsperson whose experience and extra training allow him or her to participate in the original formulation of many designs.

It should be noted further that as a result of the energy crisis, practically every utensil supplying or requiring energy will have to be redesigned for greater efficiency, thus providing even greater opportunities for draftspeople.

SIGN MAKER

The need for signs grows with the economic development of our country. Signs are used to advertise and identify everything from the sale of underwear in a department store to the advertising of a product on a large billboard. They are painted on trucks to advertise the businesses represented by them. Factories, schools, hospitals, and office buildings utilize signs to identify different offices and departments and to give directions to visitors. Every commercial business enterprise has a sign over its entrance to identify itself and project a desired image.

Few signs are alike in quality, color, and design simply because each sign is created to meet an individual need. This individualism of design gives the *sign maker* the opportunity for creative self-expression and the chance to make a good living as an independent businessperson. The individual who can interpret what a client wants and then can produce a graphic illustration of these ideas can build up an excellent clientele and prosper.

TRAINING REQUIREMENTS

There are many ways to learn sign making. Very often it can be self-taught through books and correspondence programs, supplemented by some night school courses. Commercial artists and technical illustrators can adapt their talents to the needs of the sign-making profession.

Many junior colleges and vocational schools offer two-year programs leading to an associate's degree in sign graphics. Among the courses taught in such a curriculum are the following: brush and pen lettering; show card production; sign construction; exterior sign production; window lettering; gold leaf lettering; masking methods; screen printing; layout and design; paint composition; color mixing and pattern making; and enlarging methods. These courses can aid in developing an individual's talents to handle many types of sign projects for the commercial market.

SALARY AND EMPLOYMENT OPPORTUNITIES

The average fee charged by the self-employed sign maker is approximately $15 an hour plus materials. Many even charge a $10 to $20 consultation fee. An individual can get started in a sign-making business with approximately $250 worth of equipment. One can operate the business from one's home or apartment, an office or a small studio. The following are some cost studies of various types of signs:

Panel Truck Sign

Consultation fee		$17.00
Materials		5.00
Hourly rate	$15.00	
Time required	8 hours	
Labor fee		120.00
TOTAL PRICE		$142.00

Gold Leaf Lettering on Window
(70 letters plus insignia)

Consultation fee		$18.00
Materials		25.00
Hourly rate	$15.00	
Time required	12 hours	
Labor fee		180.00
TOTAL PRICE		$223.00

Showcard Sign in Department Store
(50 letters on 14″ × 39″ piece
of white cardboard)

Consultation fee		$2.00
Materials		1.00
Hourly rate	$15.00	
Time required	1½ hours	
Labor fee		22.50
TOTAL PRICE		$25.50

Real Estate Sign
(18″ × 48″ piece of plywood
covered with black aluminum;
50 letters plus insignia)

Consultation fee		$25.00
Materials		55.00
Hourly rate	$15.00	
Time required	12 hours	
Labor fee		180.00
TOTAL PRICE		$260.00

*Painting Advertisement on Side
of Large Trailer Truck*

Consultation fee		$20.00
Materials		10.00
Hourly rate	$15.00	
Time required	14 hours	
Labor fee		210.00
TOTAL PRICE		$240.00

Hanging Wood Sign over Floral Shop
(24″ × 36″; 42 letters plus insignia,
plus frame and scroll work)

Consultation fee		$10.00
Materials		15.00
Hourly rate	$15.00	
Time required	8 hours	
Labor fee		120.00
TOTAL PRICE		$145.00

We have given only a few examples of the various types of
signs a sign maker constructs and the time and pay involved.

Many signs, such as "point-of-sale" signs in retail stores,
have to be changed constantly with the addition of new merchandise and price changes. This offers a great source of repeat
business to the sign maker. The artistic quality and craft that go
into a sign also serve as an indicator as to the quality of the
product, business, or service that the sign attracts attention to.
Therefore, many businesspeople will not quibble over the price
of a well-made and functional sign.

Eventually a sign maker may become involved in the designing and developing of large illuminated outdoor signs. After
soliciting a contract for an outdoor sign, he or she can design it
and then have a large sign manufacturing company fabricate it.
When it is completed, the sign maker can then solicit the services
of an installation service to hoist and place the sign in place and
hook up the electrical connections. This eliminates having to tie
up large sums of money in plastic cutting and molding equipment. When business warrants, the sign maker can purchase all
the necessary equipment for manufacturing large, illuminated
outdoor signs.

Practically anything that involves lettering or graphic designs can be handled by the sign maker. An individual can even
set up a small concession in a department store printing

custom-made message on tee shirts, for example. This is done by purchasing the letters beforehand and when an order is received, arranging them on the shirt to state the desired message, after which the letters are ironed right onto the shirt. This takes but a few minutes. The total cost of the letter is approximately 35¢ and the tee shirt, if purchased in bulk quantities, costs the concessionaire approximately $1 each. The total job (shirt plus lettering) can be sold for as much as $5. Many people are prospering from this business alone. The training necessary for this type of operation can be accomplished in just a few weeks. The letters can be purchased from a wholesale sign distributor. Another project that can be accomplished with shirts is the transferring of pictures (say that of the wearer) to the shirt via a silk screen process. This procedure takes several months to master. However, it can bring the operator a great deal of money for his or her services.

A sign maker can promote business in many ways. There is advertising in the phone directory's yellow pages of services. A personal call on every type of retail business (clothing stores, grocery stores, department stores, etc.) to solicit their sign-making business is very worthwhile and can even result in a great deal of repeat business. Real estate development companies should be contacted to find out about new buildings about to be constructed or already under construction. When completed, many facilities such as office buildings, hospitals, schools, and factories require a great deal of sign work on office doors and walls. A sign maker should leave a business card with building managers and leasing agencies of already established buildings, for whenever new tenants move in, they will require their names to be put on their office doors.

Sign making not only allows an individudal to develop and use artistic talents, but it also allows a variety of interesting ways to prosper from these talents.

An interesting source of information and opportunities in the sign business can be found in the magazine entitled *Signs of the Times,* published monthly by the Signs of the Times Publishing Company (407 Gilbert Avenue, Cincinnati, Ohio 45202). It may be found in your local library, or you can send away for a copy.

BEAUTY CULTURE

The desire to be beautiful is universal. The modern beauty culture business is an extensive and important industry. It is rated by some experts as the fourth largest industry group in this country. Beauty culture is a field that knows no seasonal recessions. Over $1 billion is spent annually in beauty shops.

Beautician

Changing hair styles and the development of new beauty processes and methods are stimulating the demand for skilled *beauticians*. Beauty culture offers tremendous opportunities for men and women who want a large income along with independence. Moreover, the training period is relatively short, especially when considering the potential for sizable financial return in addition to being your own boss. There is just one "catch"—you must be *good* at it. The fact cannot be stressed too much. The good beauticians make the top money, while the mediocre ones make just an average worker's salary.

One of the first signs of suitability for this career field is a real interest in beauty culture. Finger dexterity is important and can be easily determined through an aptitude test. An "artistic sense" helps to determine line, color, and proportion in hair arrangements. Information concerning aptitude tests can be obtained by contacting a local office of the U.S. Employment Service, which is listed in your telephone book.

Once it has been reasonably established that an individual

has the ability to succeed as a beautician, he or she can then pursue a training program in this high-paying field.

The work of a beautician includes manicuring, shampooing, hair styling, permanent waving, hair coloring, facial treatments, and make-up for stage, screen, or television. A beautician may perform all of these functions or just specialize in one or several. For instance, manicuring is usually a job in itself and is performed by someone performing just this one operation. The most popular and lucrative area of specialization is in hair styling, permanent waving, and hair coloring, combined.

Hair Stylist

Hair styling involves the creation of hair styles that are becoming and distinctive. It calls for a great deal of artistic ability. Some hair stylists become eminent artists in the field of beauty culture and command high returns for their services. The stylist studies the features, neckline, and head contour of the patron and observes the texture, color, and quantity of the hair. He or she then selects the most becoming arrangement and does the cutting and shaping necessary for the styles being created. Hair stylists may do the shampooing and setting, or this may be done by other people under their direction. A hair stylist may specialize in either women's or men's hair. Today many stylists do both.

Permanent-wave Specialist

Permanent waving is another high-income specialty in beauty culture. It may be done by the hair stylist or an individual specializing in just this one operation. Permanent waving involves changing the texture of the hair to make it wavy or curly or to just give it enough extra body to make it lay differently. The principles used in permanent waving are also used to straighten curly hair.

Hair Colorist

Hair coloring, including tinting and bleaching, is another phase of beauty culture that requires a high degree of skill. This procedure may be performed by the stylist or, again, a technician specializing in this one operation. The hair-coloring technician depends on the manufacturer's directions in the coloring process, but for a successful and natural-looking result a knowledge of the composition and use of chemicals is desirable.

Facial Treatment Operator

Facial treatment operators specialize in improving the condition and appearance of a patron's complexion. They examine the skin and determine its type and condition as to whether it is dry or oily. They give facial treatments with creams, lotions, and astringents, apply cosmetics, and advise on the most effective use of cosmetics. They may also sell cosmetics to their clients.

Manicurist

Manicuring involves the treatment of the fingernails. An operator usually specializes in just this one operation. A manicurist grooms the patron's nails by removing cuticles and trimming, filing, and polishing the nail. Many people go to a manicurist on a weekly basis to have this done. Some manicurists also give *pedicures*, which is the grooming of the toenails similar to a manicure. In some beauty salons one person does only pedicures.

TRAINING REQUIREMENTS

Hair-styling training is offered in many public and private schools and a few vocational schools. Courses usually last from six to eleven months. For specialties such as manicuring the time required is usually less. After completion of a formal styling training program it is advisable to undergo a one-year apprenticeship program in a good styling salon in order to become a top-notch stylist. All states require a beautician or barber to be licensed. To obtain a license a person must have graduated from a state-approved beautician school and passed a state-administered exam.

For more information concerning training programs in this field, write:

National Association of
Barber Schools, Inc.
338 Washington Avenue
Huntington, West Virginia 25701

National Association
of Cosmetology Schools, Inc.
3839 White Plains Road
Bronx, New York 10467

SALARY AND EMPLOYMENT OPPORTUNITIES

A top hair stylist working for someone else can earn $400 a week or more. A stylist who works for someone else usually is paid on a commission basis, receiving 60 percent of the fee for the work performed. A stylist who owns a shop receives 40 percent of the fee for the work performed by the employees and, naturally, 100 percent of the work done by himself or herself.

Generally, beauty salons are divided into three main categories: budget, regular, and "high-class" shops—the difference being the type of fixtures used and very often the experience of the beauticians employed. The following are the typical average fees charged by the different classes of shops. A cutting is approximately $3 in a budget shop, $7 in a regular shop, and

$20 in a high-class shop. The approximate time required for a hair-cut is thirty minutes. A permanent is $16 in a budget shop, $23 in a regular shop, and $40 in a high-class salon. It requires approximately ninety minutes to perform this operation. A hair coloring is approximately $5 in a budget shop, $13 in a regular shop, and $22 in a high-class shop. It takes approximately thirty minutes to perform. A manicure costs between $3.50 and $4 in all shops and requires approximately twenty-five minutes of work.

From the preceding statistics, you can compute what types of income can be derived as an employee or an owner of the different types of shops.

An added inducement to opening one's own beauty parlor is that it is not terribly expensive to equip a shop. Since the amount of equipment necessary is proportional to the number of chairs to be put into operation, the cost can be calculated on a per chair basis. The cost to equip each of the three main categories of shops follows: $1,500 per chair for a budget shop, $3,000 per chair for a regular shop, and $5,000 to $7,000 per chair for a high-class shop. Remember, however, the quality of a hair style is dependent on the skill of the stylist—and not on the furnishings of the shop. Therefore, if you build up a reputation as a top-flight stylist when employed by someone else, it may be easy to open your own shop with very modest fixtures and still charge high-class prices.

Some stylists like to open a hair-styling salon for men only. This can be especially lucrative when you consider you can charge $20 for a simple cutting and shaping that takes only twenty minutes to perform.

Today, regardless if times are good or bad, people are increasingly conscious of their appearance, especially of their hair grooming. This stress on personal appearance offers a future of independence and excellent earnings to the qualified beautician.

ELECTROLOGIST

Practically the entire human body is covered with an extremely fine growth of hair. Normally, this growth is so fine that it is hardly noticeable. However, as nature will have it, many things do not occur as they are supposed to.

Quite often, due to heredity or glandular irregularities, some women develop coarse and unsightly hair on their face and other areas of their body. The appearance of a beautiful woman may be marred by this undesirable hair. We have all seen women who have sprouted moustaches and chin whiskers. The use of tweezers and chemical hair removers only alleviates the condition temporarily, and in many cases may stimulate the regrowth of much darker, coarser, and more deeply rooted hair.

The most acceptable way to deal with this problem is to remove the hair permanently. Fortunately this can be done by a process known as electrolysis. It is the well-trained technician known as an *electrologist* who performs this work.

In order to understand and fully appreciate the work of the electrologist, let us first review the basic anatomy of a strand of hair. The human skin contains thousands of hair follicles. These are shafts or folds in the skin that contain the root and shaft of the hair strand. Beneath the hair root (at the bottom of the follicle) is the papilla. The papilla is the nutritive tissue responsible for producing and sustaining each strand of hair.

If the papilla is destroyed, the strand of hair that normally grew from it is destroyed forever. The electrologist is involved in destroying the papilla by sending an electronic current through it. The current is generated by a special machine—the electrolysis shortwave machine. This is basically what electrolysis is all about—each strand of unwanted hair being destroyed selectively, one by one. Some hairs, however, may require several treatments before they are finally destroyed.

The electrologist inserts a needle leading from the electrolysis machine into the hair follicle and into the papilla. Then a current of electricity is sent through it by pressing a foot switch, which releases the electricity from the machine. The needle is then removed, and the hair lifted out with a tweezer. Since the papilla is destroyed, the hair slides out easily. The current needed to accomplish this is so weak that the patient hardly feels anything, and the surrounding tissue is unaffected. However, exact and precise insertion of the needle is required for each strand of hair.

By this selective destruction of individual hair strands, the electrologist can not only remove every bit of hair from a certain area such as the face, but also, if a client so desires, thin and permanently shape eyebrows. Because each hair is destroyed one by one, it will take several visits by the patient to do a complete job.

TRAINING REQUIREMENTS

Most states require an electrologist to pass an examination and become licensed. A good electrolysis school can usually train and prepare a person for work and for the exam in about 150 hours of instruction. This short training program makes this profession ideal for a person who is limited on funds and time available for training.

For information concerning good schools, it is advisable to consult with practicing electrologists in your area or to write:

The Electrolysis Society of America
701 Seventh Avenue
New York, New York 10036

SALARY AND EMPLOYMENT OPPORTUNITIES

Approximate rates for electrolysis work are $6.50 for a quarter-hour, $10.00 for a half-hour, and $20.00 for a full hour. When you work for someone else, you usually receive 60 percent of the fee. When you are in business for yourself, you naturally keep the full payment.

Electrolysis can be an extremely lucrative field and one that does not require a large investment. A modern office can be set up and equipped for under $2,000. The future for this profession looks extremely bright as more and more women are turning to electrolysis treatments as a normal beauty procedure.

PROFESSIONAL PHOTOGRAPHY

Photography can allow an individual to turn a hobby into a profitable profession. The field offers one literally scores of varied and interesting opportunities. A career in photography takes an individual into the thick of things. It allows one to meet interesting people and take part in events as they happen. Along with the fun, excitement, and activity, there is money to be made as a *photographer.*

A good photo transmits a message. A good photographer is one who can make a picture talk, one who can capture a feeling, a mood, a moment. A professional photographer accomplishes this through technological skills coupled with an artistic awareness enabling him or her to identify, create, and record a good shot.

There is almost no field of human endeavor that does not require the services of a trained photographer. Business and industry alone consume millions of dollars worth of photographs to advertise their goods and services.

Everything that can be seen, and much that cannot, is photographed today. The professional photographer has a completely unlimited choice of career goals. The areas of specialization include portrait photography, social events (such as weddings), advertising, fashion photography, child photography, photo journalism, illustrative photography (such as creating book jackets and record album covers), and scientific photography (which includes biomedical and scientific research). The vast new areas of underwater exploration and the boundless exploration of outer space open up new horizons in photography. In an age where international communication is so vital, photography is truly the universal language. To the educated and imaginative individual it can offer an exciting and profitable career.

Portrait Photographer

Portraiture is a very popular type of photography. Families like to have portraits taken of their kin. This is especially true when children grow up and travel away from home. Business executives and political figures enjoy having fine portraits of themselves in their offices and board rooms. A good portrait photographer can capture a person's true personality with a camera. Many top portrait photographers enjoy widespread reputations in the upper echelons of society.

Fashion Photographer

Fashions change rapidly. Each season brings with it a completely new line of clothing apparel. The manufacturers of apparel require their creations to be modeled by professional models and then photographed by professional photographers to bring out their elegance. These photos are used by manufacturers for catalogues and local and nationwide advertising campaigns. In this field the photographer must know how to direct the models to make them look glamorous and natural at the same time in order to enhance the appearance of the clothing being modeled. This is true in the men's clothing field as well as the ladies. Fashion photographers who can effectively capture the elegance of today's fashions are among the highest paid in the industry.

Wedding Photographer

A wedding is one of the most significant events in a couple's life. Likewise, it is an event of joy and remembrance for the parents of the bride and bridegroom. No matter if a wedding is large or small, it is almost always accompanied by an album of professionally taken photographs of the wedding ceremony and the celebration that follows. A wedding assignment usually means the producing of three sets of albums—one for the wedding couple, one for the bride's parents, and one for the bridegroom's parents. A good photographer does not just take pictures and place them in the album at random. He or she chooses and arranges the photos so that the wedding album tells a story. A typical wedding can put about $300 profit in the photographer's pocket for just one day's work.

Child Photographer

Have you ever known parents who could resist photographs of their child, especially those taken of situations that are spontaneous and depict various characters of the child? A child photographer does not necessarily have to solicit work assignments first. He or she can take free-lance shots at amusement parks, playgrounds, ice skating rinks, or any place where children are most apt to be themselves and project the most self-expression. After the shots have been taken, the photographer can give his or her card to the parents of the child, inviting them to see the proof pictures. These proofs are very inexpensive to make and can serve to induce the parent to have a full size print made. An 8″ × 10″ black-and-white print costs the photographer about $1 to make and can sell for as much as $10 to $25.

Of course, many parents will bring their children to a child photographer to have special portraits taken of them or will hire the services of one to take impromptu shots at a birthday party or similar event. There are child photographers who make $50,000 a year and more in this speciality.

Photo Journalist

The field of photo journalism involves pictures illustrating newsworthy events. Magazines and newspapers could not exist without crisp, on-the-spot camera work. The demand for fresh material is never ending, whether a photographer is a regular staff photographer for a newspaper or magazine or a free-lance photographer working on his or her own. Very often a free-lance photographer is the only one present at the site of an unexpected happening. The free lancer then can find a ready market for the pictures taken.

Newspapers, magazines, and trade papers use more photographs today than ever before, and the demand for fresh material is constant. Pictures taken of public figures in spontaneous and unrehearsed moods are always in demand and very often command high prices.

Theater and Motion Picture Photographer

Servicing the tremendous photographic needs of the entertainment industry can be a profitable, full-time career by itself. Photographers work among famous actors and actresses of the stage, television, and motion pictures to make pictures for publicity, advertising, lobby displays, and the personal scrapbooks of the stars themselves.

Industrial Photographer

Many industries use photographers to take pictures of their research, development, and production techniques. These photos are used for advertising and public relations purposes in addition to providing informative and instructional material for communication among management, researchers, and production personnel.

Commercial and Advertising Photographer

No matter what product is put on the market today, photography plays a big part in promoting it. Photographs by the thousands flow from cameras and studios to magazines, newspapers, direct-mail advertising, brochure producers, designers, packagers, and just about every business and service you can name. Photographers who can take distinctive pictures of commercial products are in demand by advertising agencies and manufacturers.

Scientific Photographer

In recent years there has been a growing demand for scientific photography. This area covers methods, techniques, and procedures of biological photography including applications in medical science as well as naturalist and field photography. Biomedical photography is a specialty in the scientific field that shows promise for a great deal of future growth. It involves taking pictures of various specimens under the microscope, normal and abnormal tissue cultures, diseased organs before and after treatment, areas inside the body via special instruments, surgical procedures, and many other types of medical phenomena and techniques. Professional biomedical photographers may have permanent staff positions with large research hospitals, medical and dental schools, pharmaceutical companies, and government agencies. A senior staff photographer of a large medical facility can earn $20,000 a year and more.

There are many opportunities for biomedical photographers to do free-lance work. Many physicians, such as dermatologists and plastic surgeons, publish research papers in order to become known among other physicians for the purpose of obtaining referrals. Very often they will use the services of a free-lance biomedical photographer to illustrate their work.

Research institutions document preliminary research with scientific photographs in order to obtain government and philanthropic grants. Pharmaceutical companies use scientific photographs in many of their advertisements to the medical world. Publishers of scientific books use the services of biological photographers to illustrate their text.

A new and potential future for biomedical photographers is in the medical malpractice area. Many doctors are becoming involved in expensive malpractice suits. One simple way of defending against and discouraging such suits is to photograph, either by still photography or motion picture photography, the steps taken in performing many medical procedures. This would serve to illustrate the skill used in the performance of many procedures performed by doctors.

The future in biological photography is just beginning; as science advances, so should this specialized profession.

TRAINING REQUIREMENTS

There are special courses in commercial photography. However, the techniques needed to take professional quality photographs may be learned by working and experimenting with the various techniques in photography. Many people who start in photography as a hobby wind up practicing it as a full-time and profitable profession. Practical experience can be supplemented with correspondence and night school courses. There are many technical and vocational schools offering two- and four-year programs in commercial photography leading to associate's and bachelor's degrees. The Professional Photographers of America, Inc., publishes a booklet giving the names and locations of colleges and universities throughout the country offering instruction in photography. To obtain this booklet, write:

> *Professional Photographers of America, Inc.*
> Education Committee
> 1090 Executive Way
> Des Plains, Illinois 60018

It is hard to pinpoint an average salary for a professional photographer. The ultimate goal of many photographers is to set up their own studio or laboratory and work on a free-lance basis. A great deal of money can be made doing free-lance work. Rates will vary according to subject material, the artistry and originality intrinsic in it, and the area of its distribution (local vs. national). A photographer for billboard illustrations might work at the rate of $50 an hour for a billboard illustration to be displayed locally and $100 an hour if the illustration is for national distribution. A book jacket or record album cover might bring from $75 to $200 for a black-and-white illustration and $200 to $1,000 for a color illustration. Television stations will often pay from $50 to $200 for still shots for advertising purposes. A high-class fashion shot for national distribution might bring as much as $1,000 to $2,000. Likewise, a distinctive shot of a commercial product for national distribution might bring the same amount. A fine portrait might bring anywhere from $50 to $500. Everything depends on the uniqueness of the photo and the sales ability of the photographer.

There are many ways a free-lance photographer can promote himself or herself to a variety of customers. Instead of going from one potential customer to another passing out business cards or showing a portfolio, the industrious photographer should create a series of shots applicable to the prospect's needs and then call on that customer to show what can be done for him. It is not expensive to do this. It just takes some imagination and time. The rewards can be great. For instance, a photographer might take some unique architectural shots of a factory or office headquarters of a particular business organization. If he or she shows these photos to the president or other executives of the firm, it is quite possible that the firm might purchase the photos for one of its sales or stockholders brochures. The photographer might even receive assignments for more work.

A free-lance photographer might take a series of pictures telling the story of a community, a photo story that puts the community in its "best light." These pictures might be purchased by the chamber of commerce for some of its brochures. This is especially possible in communities that are trying to attract resort business or new industry. Pictures taken of people enjoying themselves in a commercial facility, such as an amusement park, ice-cream parlor, or skating rink, might be purchased by the proprietor of that establishment for advertising purposes.

A series of shots illustrating the facets of a particular industry might be purchased by one of the official organizations representing that industry for public relations use. The *Encyclopedia of Associations,* found in most libraries, lists the names and addresses of all of the official organizations representing practically every industry in the United States. This can serve as a source of ideas and potential clients for a photographer's work. By attending major conventions of various industries, a photographer might easily be able to sell industrial photos to members of a particular industry in addition to receiving future assignments.

A series of shots concerning a central theme such as wildlife animals, rare birds, children at play, people at work, people at play, or people in a particular social or economic predicament can be brought to a book or magazine publisher for the purpose of producing a special book on that particular theme, using the photographs along with captions as the main contents of the book or magazine article.

On various occasions imaginative photographers have thought of original shots of a commercial product to improve the advertising and sales potential of that product. Upon presenting the shots to the manufacturer of the product, the photographer not only found a ready purchaser, but also made a contact that led to future photo assignments.

These are but a few of the ways a free-lance photographer can promote himself or herself. Once a reputation for quality work is established, the free-lance photographer may be sought by many people, companies, and industries to handle their photo needs.

One important thing should be pointed out to the beginning photographer—do not be afraid to charge a substantial fee for your work. It will make you more appreciated, for the quotation of a significant fee adds credibility to you as a photographer and to your work. In photography, the opportunities for growth are limited only by one's initiative, imagination, and determination.

7

Special Fields

DEEP-SEA DIVER

Approximately two-thirds of the earth's surface is covered by water. As many of our natural resources on land are beginning to disappear, we are turning to the ocean floor in search of new products.

A new frontier lies under the sea—a frontier as challenging as the unexplored reaches of this country in the days of the pioneers, a frontier as demanding as outer space.

As science and industry inquire into the great potentials of the ocean, new jobs are created in many fields. No matter what is done under the ocean, it must be done by a *deep-sea diver*.

Being a commercial deep-sea diver means being a skilled technician who is vital to an important undersea activity. Commercial divers are involved in the installation of complex equipment for research in oceanography. Many times they will be called upon to salvage a sunken ship or repair ocean survey equipment. Many divers even become involved in the taking of still and motion pictures under the sea. These visual presentations of undersea conditions enable petroleum engineers who do not dive to make problem-solving decisions. The construction and repair of bridges and dams also require the services of the commercial diver.

A new area that is creating a great demand for the services of the commercial deep-sea diver is that of offshore oil drilling. Our world is in a serious energy crisis due to the depletion of land-based oil products. Recent exploration and research indicates that there are vast oil deposits under the ocean floor. This offshore oil can be pumped out of the ocean floor through the use of offshore drilling platforms. The construction of these gigantic platforms requires the work of the commercial deep-sea diver with construction skills. Offshore oilfield diving is in its infancy and will be around for a long time.

As new advances are made in diving technology, the equipment used by the diver will vary. However, we will briefly describe the current equipment used and the procedures taken by the deep-sea diver.

The commercial diver wears a waterproof suit and a metal helmet with a glass face plate to see through. Special shoes and a weighted belt enabling the diver to walk underwater complete the "uniform." While working undersea, the diver is connected with the surface vessel by an air line, a telephone line, and a life line. The surface vessel is usually a diving barge or boat containing air-gas machines, compressors, hoisting apparatus, and all of the tools necessary for completion of the underwater work. A *tender* assists the diver in preparing for the dive and looks after the compressors, life line, telephone, and hoisting equipment on the surface boat. The tender is also an accredited diver. Many new divers start out as tenders.

Once underwater, the diver generally performs the work of a construction worker. In salvaging operations the diver will use underwater burning equipment to cut through metal parts; in construction and repair work, underwater welding equipment to weld metal parts together.

Although a good diving school will teach the fundamentals of underwater construction, it is a good idea for the diving candidate to have a general knowledge and working experience in construction work. This can include mechanics, carpentry, electrical work, pipe fitting, rigging, and welding. It is not necessary to be an expert in all of these fields, but a diver should become proficient in just one of them. This will insure steady employment. Also, one can practice these fields on land to supplement earnings between diving assignments.

Most divers perform their work at a depth of about 150 feet below the surface. However, a new technique—bell diving—is enabling divers to reach depths of 200 feet and more. In bell diving a special bell or container is suspended between the surface boat and the underwater work area. The bell can be thought of as a special satellite from which the divers work. In the bell system the workers get into the bell on the surface; the bell is lowered to the desired depth; then the workers leave the bell to perform their work. When the underwater work is completed, the divers return to the bell, which is then hoisted to the surface.

The advantages of using a diving bell are numerous. It is a safer method for getting divers to the underwater work site, even through rough surface weather. The "umbilical" (air-hoses and safety lines) from the bell to the diver is much shorter than all the way from the surface. The bell serves as a source of power for lights and diver tools, a source of stable supplies of breathing gas, a source of hot water for heated suits, and a center for communication lines. It is a resting and safety refuge. The bell has many other strong points that provide the diver with better support to do a more efficient job.

Bell diving is being used in areas requiring heavy construction, such as the building of offshore oil wells. To become a bell diver requires extra training and certification.

Deep-sea diving candidates should be from 20 to 30 years of age, be in excellent health, and enjoy working with their hands. In fact, as mentioned earlier, divers should have a surface construction skill. They should possess a "feel" for the water. In fact, most diving schools require candidates for admission to be already certified *scuba* divers. These are divers trained to use self-contained underwater breathing apparatus for shallow diving. Let's face it, if you do not like this activity, you would not enjoy deeper diving.

Diving candidates must realize that they will have to travel all over the world on their job assignments. This can be a form of adventure for many people. Others may find this unsuitable for their desired life-style and should, therefore, not enter the field. Diving takes a great deal of intelligence; thus, the prospective student should also possess reasonable scholastic skills. If you can say "yes" to these prerequisites and desire the adventure and good pay of a diver, then deep-sea diving may be for you.

The average diving school offers a fifteen-week course and the fees total approximately $1,800. After completion of the course, the top students are usually invited to attend a special ten-week course in bell diving.

In the diving school curriculum, in addition to the actual acts of diving, the student will learn how to mix gas and air, handle compressors, and handle hoisting equipment. The trainee will learn underwater cutting and welding, offshore oil work procedures, rigging procedures, decompression procedures, blueprint reading, diesel and compressor maintenance, diving physiology and medicine, emergency first-aid procedures, oceanography equipment repair and maintenance, demolition theory, salvage and construction diving, and underwater photography and television.

There are training facilities for divers at the following institutions:

Highline Community College
240th and Pacific Highway South
Midway, Washington 98031

Santa Barbara City College
Marine Technology Department
721 Cliff Drive
Santa Barbara, California 93109

Divers Institute of Technology
P.O. Box 70312
Seattle, Washington 98107

Coastal School of Deep Sea Diving
320 29th Avenue
Oakland, California 94601

Commercial Diving Center
272 South Fries Avenue
Wilmington, California 90744

Ocean Corporation
5709 Glenmont
Houston, Texas 77081

Coastal Diving Academy
106 C West Main Street
Bayshore, New York 11706

SALARY AND EMPLOYMENT OPPORTUNITIES

A diver can earn anywhere from $65 to $195 per day depending upon experience and job assignment. Overseas workers receive higher wages. This can add up to an income of $30,000 per year. Quite often 60 to 70 percent of the student body of a training school will receive job offers before graduation. To the well-trained student who applies him- or herself, the future is almost unlimited. At present there is a big shortage of trained personnel to meet the new demands for offshore oil well construction.

To summarize, with the new demands that society has of the ocean, the field of commercial deep-sea diving offers endless opportunities to the qualified individual.

HUNTING AND FISHING GUIDE

Occupations and careers are not limited just to those vocations learned in a school or an apprenticeship program. Very often a hobby or side interest can be turned into an enjoyable and successful way of making a living. If there is a need for a service, there is a profit to be made in supplying that service. If you have an interest in hunting and fishing and enjoy the freedom of the outdoors, you may find your niche as a *hunting and fishing guide.*

Many people in sedentary occupations want new outlets and adventures during their vacation time. They are not content to just relax by the pool of some large resort. They want to feel that they are a "part of the action" in the great world of the outdoors. The problem is that no one person has the time to become proficient in everything. This is especially true in hunting and fishing and exploring the great outdoors. This is where competent hunting and fishing guides come in. These men and women are responsible for leading the inexperienced adventurer toward vacation accomplishments.

The guide is an expert sportsman or sportswoman who plans, organizes, and leads hunting and fishing expeditions and is responsible for making all the plans for clients whether they are moderately experienced outdoors men and women or inexperienced tenderfoots.

A good guide plans the trip long before its onset and will advise in advance what provisions should be brought along. The guide will, if necessary, provide the provisions (being reimbursed, of course) and will transport the sportspeople to hunting and fishing areas, select good camping sites, make camp and prepare meals for the group. Knowledge of the area, the sport, and the habits of the wildlife being dealt with can often spell success or failure for the expedition and can help or hinder the reputation and future income of a guide. Many times the guide will give instructions to the inexperienced hunter or fisherman.

The guide works independently since the occupation calls for little or no formal training. Your interest and pursuance of your career is your training. There are no regular hours, no minimum wage, no fringe benefits. Your earnings depend entirely upon your own initiative, skills, and reputation.

Geography plays an important part on where you will work. States with vast amounts of wilderness and wildlife are where most guides work. Some guides, depending on their preference, will specialize in certain types of hunting and fishing. A guide may lead a party of bass or trout fishermen, organize a quail hunt, or supervise a lengthy big game expedition. Work may occupy half a day, several days, or even two weeks or longer. The guide may operate a powerboat or paddle a canoe to a fishing area, may drive a jeep or truck, or ride the lead pony when guiding parties on horseback to remote hunting or fishing areas.

TRAINING REQUIREMENTS

There are no formal training programs for this type of work. A thorough familiarity with the area you plan to work in is a necessity. The type of person to go into this type of work should have a background in hunting, fishing, and boating. A course in basic navigation is essential. Most important, you should enjoy working with people and have a great deal of patience.

If you would like to become a guide and have little experience, do not despair. It is possible to obtain practical experience by working part time for a competent local guide. You may also contact your state department of conservation or department of wildlife on courses given on hunter safety and hunting and fishing skills. The address of your department of conservation or department of wildlife can be found in the phone book or by contacting your local chamber of commerce. The Outward Bound Schools, Inc. provide excellent orientation and training programs in living and surviving in the wilderness. They have six schools located in Colorado, Maine, Minnesota, North Carolina, Oregon, and New Mexico. For further information concerning their programs and school locations write:

Outward Bound, Inc.
165 West Putnam Avenue
Greenwich, Connecticut 06830

SALARY AND EMPLOYMENT OPPORTUNITIES

There is no set wage for guides. However, there are general fees for various types of expeditions. A fishing guide may charge anywhere from $10 to $35 a day per person. The variance usually depends on how far into the wilderness the guide takes a group. A guide may charge $15 per day per person to hunt small game, such as duck, geese, or deer. In hunting big game, such as cougar, a guide may charge a group a flat fee of $500. With the large fees, success in locating the game must be guaranteed. Some guides charge a standard fee plus a bonus if the hunter catches something. For example, in hunting wild boar, a guide may charge $50 per day per person plus $35 on each animal caught. Some states have formed guide's associations. These organizations suggest fees as a guideline to both the guides and the sportspeople.

At present there is a shortage of skilled guides. The demand should increase as many Americans keep turning to the great outdoors to relieve the pressures of urban living.

As you can see, being a guide is not for everyone. However,

if you possess a love for the outdoors and have a genuine interest in the habits of wildlife, this occupation may be for you. It is a truly independent profession. You can work as hard as you want and as long as you want. If you do your work well, you will eventually build up a reputation that will insure you constant patronage.

TUNA FISHERMAN

In today's modern society there are still some occupations that retain the romance and adventure of days gone by and still offer the potential of an attractive financial return. Fishing on the high seas is still the source of income for many people. Ocean fishing is an occupation that goes back in ancient times and will always be a necessity in feeding the world's population. In this segment we will discuss the work of only one type of fisherman—the *tuna fisherman*.

Tuna fishing has become a highly mechanized occupation. Large tuna clippers, varying in length from 70 to 100 feet, travel the world over in search of schools of tuna. From the United States they will sail as far as Africa and stay for several months, if necessary, to get a profitable catch. Average trips last between 45 and 80 days. The ships' crews, of approximately 14 to 16 people, usually take turns in performing most of the necessary fishing tasks.

On an average fishing trip the captain will head the vessel to an area that is known to have large schools of fish swimming in it. A mastman will spend a great deal of time in the crow's nest scanning the ocean for the fish. As the boat nears the fishing grounds, the mastman may also be aided by an operator who starts to scan the fish with a fish scope. The fish scope gives a televisionlike picture of the waters beneath the boat.

When the school of fish is located, the captain maneuvers the ship so that a large net (called a *purse seine*) can be set in front of the school and then dropped into the sea. The net, which is made of nylon and is about one-half mile in width and about 300 feet deep, can be thrown around the vast schools of fish and drawn in without breaking.

Dropping the net takes a great deal of skill. It is lowered to the water and placed in position by the use of a motorized skiff. After the fish swim into the purse created by the fold in the net, the net is hoisted and the fish are dumped on deck. A power scoop then shovels the catch into refrigerated fish wells where they are frozen. The net is again set via the motorized skiff.

The crew is divided into engine and deck gangs. The engine room gang stands watches in the engine room and helps the engineer and his assistants in operating or repairing the engines. The deck gang stands watches and performs all duties above the engine room. It is responsible for the skiffs, the net, the fish well, relieving the mastman, and other duties.

TRAINING REQUIREMENTS

Much of the training for tuna fishing can be acquired by actually working on a fishing boat and participating in the operations. The person going into this field should be healthy, have great physical strength and endurance, and be able to get along with others. One should have a cool head and be able to react quickly to emergency conditions encountered on the high seas. These requirements apply in all commercial fishing.

Training for a career in fishing can be supplemented by taking a variety of short courses taught in high schools, junior colleges, and vocational schools in various seaport areas. These courses can include handling (seamanship), meteorology, navigation, communication, marketing, and biology. Service at sea with the navy or coast guard could be helpful to someone planning to enter commercial fishing.

For information concerning training and jobs in commercial tuna fishing, contact:

National Marine Fisheries
300 S. Ferry St., Room 2016
Terminal Island, California 90731

American Tuna Boat Association
1 Tuna Lane
San Diego, California 92101

Also visit various tuna boat owners in San Diego and San Pedro, California.

SALARY AND EMPLOYMENT OPPORTUNITIES

Tuna fishermen do not get a straight salary. They share in the sale of the ship's take. After the ship returns to shore, the owner of the vessel receives approximately 40 percent of the money made on the take; the captain receives about 10 percent. The remaining 50 percent is shared by the crew. This can amount to an average salary of from $12,000 to $30,000 a year for a crew member, depending on the size of the boats worked on and how often one decides to ship out to sea.

The future of the seagoing fisherman is good. The importance of fish as a nutrition source is becoming more and more vital today. Seafood contains vitamins, minerals, and proteins and lacks the cholesterol content possessed by meat products. Also, fish is cheaper than meat. As more and more people are becoming aware of the advantages of eating fish, the need for people to provide the fish will increase.

TRUCK DRIVER

Practically all manufactured items, including the components used to make them, depend partially or entirely on trucks and *truck drivers* for delivery to their final destinations. Trucking plays a vital link between manufacturer and consumer. As our economy and technology increase, so will the opportunities in the trucking industry. It is estimated that by 1980 over 400,000 more truck drivers will be needed.

Truck driving is an excellent field for the young person who desires the adventure of the open road and freedom from close supervision by employers. Trucking can offer an individual a good paying job with a large trucking firm or the chance to be in business for oneself as an independent "owner-operator" of one's own diesel tractor, doing contract work for commercial trucking companies.

TRAINING REQUIREMENTS

The trucking industry offers great opportunities to those possessing the proper qualifications and the right training to become truly professional truck drivers. The line-haul driver has about $40,000 worth of truck and trailer in his or her care plus a freight load that can be valued as high as $100,000 or more. Therefore, the driver must be alert, well coordinated, healthy, skilled in all types of driving conditions, and have a cool head to handle all types of emergency situations that may occur on the highway. The role of the driver of a large tractor trailer is similar to that of the captain of a large commercial jet airliner.

With good instruction the conscientious individual can learn to master a large tractor trailer in approximately four weeks. Some carriers have their own driver training programs.

Special private schools make a business of training line-haul drivers and the better ones do a thoroughly professional job. Among the recommended public and private truck driving schools are the following:

> *North Carolina Truck Driver Training School*
> (North Carolina State University)
> Raleigh, North Carolina
>
> *P.M.T.A. Truck Driver School*
> Harrisburg, Pennsylvania
>
> *Northeastern Training Institute*
> Scranton, Pennsylvania
>
> *Ryder Truck Driving School*
> Chicago, Illinois
>
> *C.T.A. Truck Driver School*
> Los Angeles, california
>
> *Truck Drivers' Training Program*
> Manpower Training Center
> Ohio Department of Labor
> Cleveland, Ohio

A pamphlet entitled, "What to Look for in a Truck Driver Training School," is offered without charge by the Education Section, Public Relations Department, American Trucking Association, 1616 P Street, N.W., Washington, D.C. 20036. Once you decide on a school, ask truckers in the area of their opinion of that particular school.

It is also a good idea for a driver to learn some fundamentals of diesel repair. This is especially helpful to an individual planning to go into business privately as an independent owner-operator of a diesel tractor. The money he or she can save by doing many of the repairs can contribute greatly to the total profit picture.

A truck driver can work as a company driver for one of the many carriers in this country. The average salary is approximately $9 an hour plus benefits, such as vacation pay, medical insurance, and retirement programs. These extra benefits bring the hourly pay in many companies up to approximately $11 an hour.

A driver can also be independently employed as an owner-operator of his or her own tractor and work as a "lease-contract" driver for many of the nation's trucking companies. This type of arrangement is becoming increasingly popular in the industry. There are two parts to a truck: the tractor (also known as the cab) and the trailer, which is pulled by the tractor. The tractors are very expensive (about $35,000 new). Many freight companies and manufacturing firms requiring cross-country transportation services find it more practical to concentrate their money and efforts on the actual running of their freight enterprises rather than in expensive trucks and the labor force needed to operate them. These companies will usually own the trailers (which cost about $10,000 each) and depot and office facilities and then hire owner-operators of tractors to attach their tractors to the company trailers and transport them to their destinations.

The contract drivers are paid approximately 40¢ a mile. The overhead can be cut down by the driver who is capable of doing much of the required repair work. This leaves approximately 25¢ a mile profit. If an owner-operator drives 400 miles a day and works only 25 days a month, it amounts to 10,000 working miles a month. This adds up to $3,500 net profit a month. If the owner-operator wants to take a vacation, he or she can lease the tractor to a freight firm or individual driver and still derive an income from it while relaxing.

Owner-operators can also use their tractors to contract for transportation assignments from household moving companies. The pay scale here is different. Instead of being paid by the mile, the driver is paid approximately 40 to 60 percent of the total revenue derived from the transportation fee. A medium-sized load going from Los Angeles to New York brings about $2,800 in revenue; 60 percent of this is $1,680. The driver can also arrange with the same company or a different company to bring another load back on the return trip. If desired, and if time allows, the owner-operator of a tractor can use the tractor for both freight and moving assignments.

A good diesel tractor costs about $35,000 new. However, a good used one can be purchased for about $12,000 to $20,000. This is the most advisable arrangement for the beginner. These tractors can go approximately 400,000 miles before requiring a major overhaul. Very often an independent contract driver can obtain year-long driving contracts with well-established trucking companies. On the strength of these contracts alone, it is often possible for a driver to obtain a business loan from a bank to buy a truck.

Truck driving can offer an individual the opportunity to be "one's own person" and profit from it also.

Administrative and Clerical Fields

The practice of law has become very involved and complex. Not only are there new specialities in law, but each specialty has become overrun with new details that have been added to it. Lawyers have joined the growing list of professionals who are hiring paraprofessional assistants to help them handle large volumes of important but time-consuming details. *Legal assistants* perform complex research and interpretation of matters of law in order to free lawyers to make complicated decisions and plan legal strategy based on the assistant's research.

A Special Committee on Legal Assistants of the American Bar Association (ABA) has defined the function of the Legal Assistant as follows:

Under the supervision and direction of the lawyer, the legal assistant is trained to provide the following services:

1. Apply knowledge of law and legal procedures in rendering direct assistance to lawyers engaged in legal research.

2. Design, develop, or plan modifications of new procedures, techniques, services, processes, or applications.

3. Prepare or interpret legal documents, or write detailed procedures for engaging in the practice of certain fields of law.

4. Select, compile, and use technical information from such references as digests, encyclopedias, or practice manuals.

5. Analyze and follow procedural problems that involve independent decisions.

A survey of a number of law offices shows the following to be the tasks more frequently performed by legal assistants:

1. Searching and checking public records.

2. Preparing probate inventories.

3. Assisting with inheritance and federal and estate tax returns.

4. Contacting clients for information.

5. Indexing documents and preparing digests.

Attorneys generally set high standards of character and education for legal assistants. Intelligence, analytical ability, and discretion are essential qualifications. Legal assistants must be responsible and mature individuals thoroughly conversant in legal terminology and procedures.

TRAINING REQUIREMENTS

Formal training programs for legal assistants are offered by private vocational schools, junior and community colleges, and even some law schools in special legal-assistant programs. The average length of such a program is from one to two years. The Committee on Legal Assistants of the American Bar Association recommends provisional certification for the legal assistant upon the completion of the committee's recommended two-year course, with full certification after one year of employment as a legal assistant.

For information concerning training programs, write:

American Bar Association
Special Committee on Legal Assistants
1155 East 60th Street
Chicago, Illinois 60637

SALARY AND EMPLOYMENT OPPORTUNITIES

An experienced legal assistant can earn from $12,000 to $20,000 a year. Besides working in law offices, legal assistants are employed by banks, corporations, professional trade associations, and government agencies.

There are many indications that this field has great promise for well-trained individuals. The widespread establishment of prepaid group plans for legal services may stimulate a tremendous increase in the number of people availing themselves of legal services. To provide personalized quality legal services to a vastly increased population of consumers could trigger a substantial need for attorney support personnel.

It is highly probable that as the practice of law becomes more involved and more people are able to avail themselves of legal services, the required efficiency, economy, and humanization of such services will tend to assure employment opportunities for legal assistants.

COURT REPORTER

In every courtroom throughout the country every bit of testimony and dialogue that takes place among the participants must be recorded and transcribed. This will then allow for a permanent record of the proceedings that can later be referred to in making further judicial decisions.

This work is done by a *court reporter,* who listens to and puts down everything he or she hears in the courtroom proceedings. Naturally, no one can take down everything in longhand. Therefore, the court reporter is trained in using a special device known as a shorthand machine. This machine is portable, silent, lightweight, and is capable of taking dictation faster than anyone can speak. The court reporter uses the touch system of writing. The machine prints "sounds" of syllables and words, when various combinations of keys are pressed. After the day of recording is over, the reporter reads and interprets the symbols recorded and then, with the use of a typewriter, transcribes them on paper to give a word-for-word description of the proceedings.

There are many other areas that a reporter may work in. He or she may do deposition reporting. This involves the questioning of a witness prior to the actual trial, and it usually takes place in a lawyer's office. If a witness during an actual trial testifies differently from the way he or she did during the deposition, the court reporter's records will immediately show that the witness is possibly lying. The record can thus influence the outcome of the trial.

Court reporters also sit in on various government hearings recording the testimony of witnesses that may uncover wrongdoings in various government agencies. State legislatures and the Congress of the United States also employ court reporters to record and transcribe exact records of their proceedings.

A reporter can also work outside the legal system. Very often a group of business or professional people want an official transcript of everything said and agreed upon at a meeting. To be sure that nothing is missed, they will hire a court reporter to record the session rather than an office secretary. Many types of conventions employ the services of a court reporter for the same reason.

To become a qualified court reporter, one must attend an accredited court-reporting school. To become competent takes approximately two years as a full-time student or three years as an evening student. The training is very rigorous. Court reporting requires a high degree of concentration, alertness, and accuracy. Much of the training is concentrated on the use of the shorthand machine. A court reporter must be able to record 200 to 250 words per minute.

The student will learn a great deal of legal and medical terminology. The latter is stressed due to the fact that many trials involve personal-injury cases.

After completion of the course the student is eligible to take a special exam to become a Certified Court Reporter. After certification, the reporter is ready for employment.

To obtain a list of approved schools offering court reporting, write:

The Executive Secretary
National Shorthand Reporters Association
Suite 608
2361 South Jefferson Davis Highway
Arlington, Virginia 22202

The salary of a competent court reporter can vary anywhere from $13,000 to $30,000 per year. The broad salary range is due to the fact that some reporters may do more free lancing in deposition work and business meetings than others. (The usual rate for this is approximately $100 per day.) Also, in addition to the recording done in the courtroom and other areas, the reporter receives transcription fees for transferring the shorthand symbols to typewritten sheets of paper. Interested parties in the proceedings may purchase copies. This fee is usually $1 per page.

Municipal, superior, and federal courts will generally pay a court reporter from $13,000 to $18,000 per year plus transcript fees. A court position usually provides complete civil service benefits plus a retirement pension. A good court reporter is always in demand. In fact, the demand far outweighs the supply. As our judicial and business system becomes more complex, the demand for good reporters will continue to increase.

MARKETING RESEARCH WORKER

It takes a lot of money to develop, produce and market (sell) new products and services. Manufacturers and developers of these products and services cannot afford to make mistakes. They have to know exactly what the public wants. Discovering what the public mood is toward new products and ideas is performed through marketing research. Such research furnishes vital information to all types of businesses.

Today the manufacturer is many times removed from the consumer. Meaningful communication between the producer and the user is difficult. *Marketing research workers* help fill the communications gap between producer and consumer by furnishing manufacturers with information about the market.

Businesspeople require a great deal of information to make sound decisions on how to sell their products. Marketing research workers provide much of this information by making surveys and conducting interviews. By collecting and analyzing the results of the interviews, they are able to make recommendations on what types of products should succeed in the marketplace, what the product should look like, the type of container it should come in, and what type of advertising should be used.

Marketing research work can be divided into four main categories:

1. Planning research projects

2. Field work, such as consumer interviews

3. Tabulation of data collected

4. Analysis and reporting of research results

In any marketing research project it is necessary to decide which questions will obtain the needed information and which groups of people will be the most qualified to furnish the answers. These questions are usually composed by a *questionnaire writer*.

The next step is to have the questions answered, which is usually done through consumer interviews. It is common practice for even large business firms to hire an independent research firm as a *field supervisor* to conduct the actual marketing survey. The agency hires personnel to complete the survey in an allotted period of time and assumes responsibility for the accuracy of the work performed. *Interviewers* go out into the field to ask the questions on the questionnaire prepared by the client concerning preferences for a particular product or opinions of a service performed. They approach only those groups that the client has designated and carefully record the answers. They are generally part-time or temporary workers. Because the work is part time, many housewives, students, and retired people can work as interviewers.

When all of the questionnaires are collected and verified, the field supervisor sends them to the client for coding and tabulation.

Increasingly, tabulating machines are used to tally the data and print them on tape. However, it is the responsibility of a person called a *tabulator* to build statistical tables using data collected in the survey.

A *statistician* collects, analyzes, and interprets the numerical data to determine its significance.

An *analyst,* along with the statistician, uses the interpreted data to make sound policy decision on the exact products and services to be provided by the manufacturing or service firm.

Many small industries and institutions throughout the country are now using the services of marketing research firms to make important policy and marketing decisions. Institutions and groups as diverse as public libraries, hospitals, and symphony orchestras use marketing research techniques to determine public interest, how they may better serve the public, and how they might attract financial contributors. Politicians use marketing research services to measure voters' feelings on public issues. Radio and television stations use marketing research to determine listeners' and viewers' program preferences. Colleges and universities often use attitude and opinion polls to determine the willingness of alumni to support activities. All are potential employers of marketing research workers.

TRAINING REQUIREMENTS

Marketing research is primarily a problem-solving activity, and the ability to define and solve a problem creatively is an asset. An inquisitive interest in people, mathematical aptitude, and the ability to express oneself clearly are all necessary for a successful career in marketing research.

It is not necessary to have a college diploma to conduct interviews. However, if one desires to reach executive levels in marketing research, a college education is an asset. People in the executive levels of marketing research are the ones who determine what questions should be asked and then interpret and analyze the data collected.

College courses considered to be valuable preparation for work in marketing research are statistics, English composition, speech, psychology, and economics.

For more information on educational programs and career opportunities in marketing research, write:

American Marketing Association
230 North Michigan Avenue
Chicago, Illinois 60601

SALARY AND EMPLOYMENT OPPORTUNITIES

The majority of marketing research workers are employed by large manufacturing and service companies, advertising agencies, and independent research firms. Independent research organizations range in size from one-person enterprises to organizations having a hundred employees or more.

The salaries in this field vary widely. An interviewer in the field will earn from $3 to $5 an hour for interviews arranged in advance by the employer. Very often an interviewer must find and arrange his or her own interview sources. In this case the interviewer is paid a predetermined amount of money per interview. This fee can sometimes reach as high as $20 an interview. If the interviewer arranges the questions and answers concisely, one interview can sometimes be completed in a half hour. As you can calculate, this could lead to a sizable salary for a good interviewer. Also, as mentioned, an interviewer does not necessarily have to be a college graduate. Salaries for executive positions in marketing research vary from $13,000 to $35,000 a year depending on the level of responsibilities assumed and the efficiency with which they are carried out.

It is possible for an industrious worker to start his or her own marketing research firm. This can offer almost unlimited opportunities to the imaginative and industrious worker. The owner of a marketing research firm may contract large organizations and businesses to conduct the surveys created by that particular organization or business. Moreover, the owner of a small marketing research firm may contract organizations to conduct their "entire" marketing research needs—from developing the questions to be asked, conducting the survey, to collecting, interpreting, and analyzing the results of the project. One way that the owner of a marketing research firm can stimulate business is to approach various business organizations and inform each one how the firm can formulate research campaigns to pave the way for increased sales growth for that organization. If the presentation is made properly, business organizations who were not intending to avail themselves of marketing research services might just be inclined to do so in the hopes of improving business.

Opportunities for starting and developing an independent marketing research organization are almost limitless for the well-qualified person with imagination and talent for creative problem solving. A plus for someone seriously considering to do so is that it costs very little money to start an organization. About all you have to pay for is office space and some furniture—you are selling your brains, not a product. The results can be both financially and emotionally rewarding.

The demand for marketing research services is expected to grow very rapidly through the next decade. Existing marketing research organizations will expand, and new marketing research departments and independent firms will be set up. Business managers will find it increasingly important to obtain the best information possible for appraising marketing situations and planning marketing policies.

LIBRARY
TECHNICAL ASSISTANT

We are in the midst of an information explosion. Areas that just a matter of a few years ago were beyond imagination are being explored, and information is growing at a rapid pace. Each day

1,000 books are printed. Librarians and library technical assistants make information available to people. They select and organize collections of books, pamphlets, manuscripts, periodicals, clippings, and reports, and they assist readers in their use. In many libraries they also provide phonograph records, maps, slides, pictures, tapes, films, paintings, braille and talking books, microfilms, and computer tapes and programs.

In this chapter we will focus on the *library technical assistants*. These aides support and assist professional librarians in providing information. They are supervised by a librarian and have duties in either technical services or reader services.

In technical services library technical assistants prepare the library's materials and equipment for reader use. For example, they may keep current files of special materials such as newspaper clippings and pictures. Library technicians also assist in purchasing and cataloguing library materials.

In reader's services library technical assistants furnish information on library services and facilities and assist people in finding the information that they need.

A technical assistant may work in a particular subject field, such as law, medicine, economics, or music. By specializing and becoming familiar with all of the informational sources of a particular field, an assistant is more apt to render quicker and superior services to members of that field.

TRAINING REQUIREMENTS

Library technical assistants may receive training for their work either from on-the-job experience or in a formal two-year academic program at a junior or community college. The two-year program leads to an associate's degree in library technology. Many people working in libraries take courses part time to become certified or to get their degree.

Junior and community college programs generally include one year of liberal arts courses and a year of library-related study on purposes and organization of libraries and on procedures and processes involved in operating a library. Students learn to order, process, catalogue, and circulate library materials. Some receive training in data processing as it applies to libraries. Many learn to use and maintain audiovisual materials and equipment.

For information concerning career opportunities and training programs in this field, write:

Council of Library Technical Assistants
6800 South Wentworth Avenue
Chicago, Illinois 60621

American Society
for Information Science
1140 Connecticut Avenue, N.W.
Washington, D.C. 20036

Special Libraries Association
235 Park Avenue South
New York, New York 10003

SALARY AND EMPLOYMENT OPPORTUNITIES

A library technical assistant receives between $10,000 and $12,000 a year. A person with an associate's degree can further his or her training in a university-sponsored program to become a full-fledged professional librarian. The professional librarian oversees all the activities of a library and can earn up to $20,000 annually. Librarian and library technical assistants are employed in public libraries, school libraries, medical, legal, and scientific libraries, and libraries in government and industry. Many find positions with commercial and industrial firms, such as pharmaceutical companies, banks, advertising agencies, and research laboratories.

The increase in population, expansion of research, and increased information in many established and new fields will add to the demand for people trained in library work.

CLAIMS ADJUSTER
(INSURANCE ADJUSTER)

Practically everything in existence today is subject to loss or destruction due to accidents, fire, catastrophies, or theft. Anything of reasonable value is usually insured by its owner or owners through insurance companies. When any of these items, which can range from a piece of jewelry costing $100 to a gigantic building costing millions, is damaged or lost, the replacement value must be determined in order to settle the insurance claim. This type of work is performed by a specially trained person known as a *claims adjuster* or *insurance adjuster*.

The work of the claims adjuster is complex. He or she must first determine who is at fault. Whether or not the damage is covered in the insured's policy (and, if so, to what extent) is another item to be assessed. The adjuster must be familiar with legal and insurance terminology, have a thorough knowledge of the replacement cost of the damaged articles, and know the labor costs involved in repairing the damage.

Some adjusters work with all types of properties and all types of disasters. Properties coming within an adjuster's domain may include consumer merchandise, automobiles, airplanes, ships, trains, farm crops, buildings, machinery, and just about anything of value whose loss would provide hardships for the owner. Because health is of great value to everyone, a claims adjuster may become involved in assessing the physical damage incurred by victims of accidents and disease and attempt to arrive at a fair monetary fee to be paid to the victim.

Adjusters may also become familiar with various types of accidents and tragedies such as fire damage, marine losses, hurricane or flood damage, and frost damage to crops.

Some adjusters will handle all types of properties and disasters; others will specialize in just certain areas. For example, one adjuster might specialize in marine losses, while another is concerned only with automobile damage. Likewise, an adjuster may specialize in certain types of disasters, such as fire or bodily injury, or certain types of weather damage, such as floods, tornadoes, and hurricanes.

The work of a claims adjuster can become even more complex. Not only are material goods insurable, but situations are also insurable. For instance, promoters of athletic and entertainment events may insure against financial loss due to bad weather or from the entertainers not showing up. If this type of situation should arise, you can readily see the complexity in determining the loss value to the promoter. Some policies may cover embezzlement by employees of a firm. To settle this type of claim would take a great deal of business expertise.

In performing their tasks, adjusters are required to work with many people other than those involved in the actual loss. This includes witnesses to accidents, physicians in regard to determining the extent of damage in bodily injury cases, and people in various industries who can give assistance in determining loss value for products manufactured or associated with their industry.

Adjusters may be employed in several ways. Many will work for insurance companies investigating claims against their employer. Others will work for independent adjusting firms who limit their activity to doing outside claims work for any insurance company desiring their services. This is sometimes done to expedite a speedy and impartial settlement. Many small insurance companies who do not find it practical to have permanently employed adjusters in every locality will often use the services of a private firm. A large insurance company that temporarily faces an overflow of work may hire an outside firm to alleviate the burden on its own employees.

A well-trained claims adjuster can open up an office and make contracts with insurance companies to do their claims work on a fee-for-service basis. This can lead to a lucrative income for the talented individual.

There is another aspect to claims adjusting—the area of the *public adjuster*. Whereas the regular claims adjuster works for or represents the insurance company (the firm whom the claim is made against), the public adjuster represents the insured (the claimant). Such an adjuster investigates, prepares, negotiates, and adjusts claims with the adjuster representing the insurance company. Public adjusters are usually retained by banks, financial organizations, and other institutions who want to make sure that they are getting a proper settlement. Public adjusters normally work for a percentage of the settlement, usually 10 percent.

TRAINING REQUIREMENTS

An insurance adjuster does not have to be a college graduate, although it is always helpful. A person with reasonable intelligence who possesses the ability to work with others can join an insurance company as a trainee and learn this career on the job. Frequently a person with specialized training is sought by insurance companies. For example, a person experienced in automobile repair work may qualify as an auto adjuster. A person with some medical background will find the training helpful in adjusting bodily injury claims.

Many insurance companies conduct their own training programs for their employees. This training should be supplemented by taking a special six-semester study program given by the Insurance Institute of America. This course is given in locations around the country and prepares the student to handle all phases of insurance adjusting. After completing the course, the student takes a series of examinations to receive a professional certificate in insurance adjusting. This certificate can open the way to higher paying supervisory and executive positions in the insurance industry. Anyone planning to enter private practice should also plan to take this course. For information concerning the times and locations of the course, write:

Insurance Institute of America
Providence & Sugartown Roads
Malvern, Pennsylvania 19355

SALARY AND EMPLOYMENT OPPORTUNITIES

The salary of an average adjuster is approximately $13,000 per year. However, adjusters in supervisory and executive positions can earn over $20,000 per year. Also, the self-employed adjuster (as previously discussed) who can develop a good rapport with small and overburdened insurance companies can earn well over $20,000 per year. As also mentioned, the special field of public adjusting can bring in a sizable income.

The future for a good claims adjuster is excellent. Everything purchased and built today is becoming more and more expensive; consequently, it is becoming advisable to insure these properties. And when property is insured, there are sure to be claims against the policies.

BOOKKEEPING
SERVICE OPERATOR

All businesses and professional offices require financial records. Accountants are usually called in to design and install individualized accounting systems enabling the clients to keep accurate financial records. Once a system has been set up, it must be maintained to peak accuracy at all time. This is done by a *bookkeeper*. Large firms usually maintain their own full-time bookkeeper. Some may even have a complete bookkeeping department employing many bookkeepers.

However, many small businesses and professional practices do not require bookkeeping services on a full-time basis. Examples of such facilities are small retail stores; small manufacturing companies; service organizations such as independent plumbers, electricians, and all types of repairmen; professional practices of doctors, dentists, and lawyers; and businesses such as small advertising agencies, etc. The people who practice in these fields all have one thing in common—they need bookkeeping services but only for about five to ten hours a week. Full-time bookkeepers require approximately $175 to $200 a week in salary, a large outlay if their specialized services are not utilized full time.

Consequently, to meet their needs, many small employers hire a part-time bookkeeper, but they often quit after a short period of time. If business people attempt to handle their own bookkeeping chores (and many do), it takes them away from performing the truly creative and productive work they are in business for in the first place. What should the businessperson do? This dilemma has produced vast opportunities for alert individuals to set up professional independent bookkeeping services to handle the burdensome paperwork of small businesspeople and independently employed professionals.

TRAINING REQUIREMENTS

Good bookkeeping procedures can be learned in high school, night school programs, correspondence courses, and junior-college programs. In addition, a course in tax law and tax-return preparation would be very beneficial for a bookkeeping student. A person going into the field should be good in mathematics, like to work with figures, and be a methodical person who looks after the smallest of details.

A full-time bookkeeper employed by a business organization, as noted previously, earns approximately $175 to $200 a week. However, as the owner and operator of an independent bookkeeping service, it is possible to earn a lot more.

The cost of opening a service is small; only $300 to $400 in equipment is needed to start. At the beginning the service can be operated from one's home or apartment. When business expands, the operation can be moved to a commercial office or to a store.

The client is generally charged a flat fee for the work performed. For small firms the rate might be $30 a week. However, the operator of the bookkeeping service may be able to handle all of the required work in about two hours, thus earning a hourly fee of $15. A well-organized bookkeeping service can utilize various mass-production techniques in processing accounts. Paperwork that takes a long time to process can be done quickly by a professional service, thus freeing the independent operator to do only the work he or she can perform. Clients do not care who does the operation as long as it is done properly and does not cost them additional money.

Some of the bookkeeping responsibilities handled by the operator of an independent bookkeeping service are the following:

1. Examine invoices for accuracy, and if there are any discrepancies, contact the vendors.

2. Match invoices to the monthly bills submitted by the vendors and write checks to pay the bills.

3. Enter charges on customers' charge account cards, compute and send out monthly bills, and later record payments.

4. Compute employees' salaries and make up payroll checks.

5. Prepare records for the client's accountant.

As a bookkeeping service grows, the operator can utilize outside computer services to help facilitate paperwork (as previously mentioned), thereby handling large amounts of work in relatively short periods of time. A service can also handle the personal finances of busy individuals by paying their bills and keeping their records. A good bookkeeper with some basic tax preparation knowledge can handle tax-preparation procedures for many people outside the business world. This service alone can bring in thousands of extra dollars during tax time.

Many accountants have informed me that they welcome and encourage their clients to utilize the service of professional bookkeeping organizations. It allows them to communicate the bookkeeping format they desire for their client to someone who can comprehend and carry out their requests. When it comes time for the accountant to review his/her client's records, everything is in order, and the tasks become easier. Upon entering this field, call on accountants to announce your service. Many will be glad to recommend you to their clients.

The role of the bookkeeper employed by a business organization has usually been a dull one. However, when adapted to a business of one's own, bookkeeping can be creative, stimulating, and financially rewarding.

ELECTRONIC COMPUTER OPERATING PERSONNEL

Once a computer has been set up and programmed to handle data, various types of operators are required to prepare and feed the data into the computers (input), operate the computers, and interpret and handle the data given out by the computer (output). These responsibilities can usually be learned in a short period of time through on-the-job training programs or through short-term technical programs.

Input is data to be processed, plus a programmer's step-by-step instructions to the computer. In many systems, keypunch operators or data typists prepare input.

Keypunch operators use machines similar to typewriters that punch holes in cards to represent specific items of information. *Data typists* use special typewriters to prepare input data that the machine converts to holes on cards or magnetic impulses on tapes.

Some computer systems get their input from "direct-access" devices that use magnetic surfaces for recording data. These systems use machines called converters to transfer data from punched cards or paper tapes to magnetic surfaces. *Card-to-tape converter operators* wire plugboards and interpret signals from a panel of lights on the machine. They also must understand the whole system to recognize errors in input or other situations that prevent proper operation.

Once facts and figures have been coded, data is ready to be processed. A *console operator* examines the programmer's instructions and makes sure that the computer is loaded with tape, cards, or other input. The operator then starts the computer. During the processing the operator manipulates switches and observes lights. If the computer stops or lights signal an error, he or she must locate the problem.

Output is translated from machine language to words and numbers. In some systems machines directly connected to the computer do this. In others converters and high-speed printers run by auxiliary equipment operators do this work. The people who operate this type of equipment are known as *tape-to-card converter operators* and *high-speed printer operators*. With the increasing use of telephone lines to transmit data, many auxiliary equipment operators run communications as well as computing equipment.

TRAINING REQUIREMENTS

Keypunch and auxiliary equipment operators can usually attain the necessary skills for the performance of their jobs through on-the-job training programs supplied by their employers and supplemented by four to five weeks of classroom instruction.

Console operators need a longer period of instruction, which can amount to a one-year training program in a junior college or vocational school. Trainees attend classes to learn to mount tapes and operate the console. The classroom training is supplemented by instruction on the job, where operators become sufficiently familiar with the equipment to trace mechanical failures when they occur.

SALARY AND EMPLOYMENT OPPORTUNITIES

Console operators receive approximately $200 per week. Keypunch operators and operators of auxiliary equipment usually receive about $170 a week.

As they gain experience, console operators may work on more complex equipment. Eventually, they may be promoted to supervisors. Through on-the-job experience plus additional study some console operators may qualify as programmers.

Changes in technology will have different effects on the employment growth in computer operating personnel. The demand for console and auxiliary equipment operators will grow rapidly as new computers are installed and existing systems increase their capabilities. The demand for keypunch operators is not expected to keep pace with the growth in computer installations because faster and more efficient methods of data entry will increasingly replace card-punch equipment.

In addition to law enforcement officers, there are several technical specialists indigenous to and necessary for the proper functioning of law enforcement agencies. In this book we have space to discuss only three specialists in the law enforcement field. However, there are many other opportunities in law enforcement that should be explored by those interested in police work.

Latent Fingerprint Expert

Technicians known as *latent fingerprint experts* are trained to treat surfaces with a special process so that unseen fingerprints left on objects by suspected lawbreakers will be made visible and transferable for later identification. This procedure has proved to be highly successful in identifying and convicting criminals. The specialty can be learned through on-the-job training in a police laboratory. There is always a demand in the law enforcement field for this type of work.

Fingerprint Classifier

Closely associated with the latent fingerprint expert is the *fingerprint classifier*. In small police organizations one individual may perform both functions. The fingerprint classifier physically identifies and classifies prints according to individual patterns created by each print. When newly lifted prints arrive at the police department or other law enforcement facility, the classifier matches the new prints with existing prints in the files to identify a possible felon. There is always a need for this specialty.

Radio Telephone Operator

Incoming complaints and outgoing police calls are handled through the *radio telephone operator*. This position requires an individual who is calm, cool, and collected and can handle crises in a swift and organized manner. When a complaint comes in, the caller is often upset and confused. The operator must know how to calm him and extract the pertinent information. The operator must then classify the information into a police call code number, which informs the police officers on duty of exactly what type of situation has taken or is taking place. The operator then contacts the police unit or units in the vicinity of the problem, informing them of the nature of the problem through the code numbers and giving them the location of the occurrence. All of this must be done calmly and swiftly so that the police units can get to the problem as swiftly as possible to apprehend the felons or to avert further trouble.

TRAINING REQUIREMENTS

The specialties of becoming a latent fingerprint expert and a fingerprint classifer can be learned in a one- to two-semester curriculum consisting of six hours per week of combined classroom and laboratory work. This training must then be supplemented by on-the-job training in a law enforcement agency. Conversely, the initial training can be started on an on-the-job basis with a law enforcement agency and then supplemented with the college work. There are many law enforcement agencies with complete training programs in these activities combining classroom instruction with laboratory work.

Radio telephone operators must learn their specialty almost exclusively through an on-the-job program in a law enforcement agency.

For more information concerning career opportunities and training programs in police work, contact your local police department. The following organizations may also be able to provide you with information concerning training programs and career opportunities:

The Federal Bureau of Investigation
10th Street and Pennsylvania Avenue
Washington, D.C. 20005

International Association
of Chiefs of Police
11Firstfield Road
Gaithersburg, Maryland 20760

SALARY AND EMPLOYMENT OPPORTUNITIES

A latent fingerprint expert can usually start at a salary of approximately $1,050 a month and can advance through supervisory levels to about $1,850 a month. A fingerprint classifer can start at an approximate monthly salary of $750, and earnings can rise to $1,345 a month through promotions. A radio telephone operator can start at approximately $750 a month and, with seniority, advance to approximately $1,000 a month.

One thing is sure—with the increasing crime rate plus a renewed awareness of the importance of "law and order," the demand for law enforcement specialties will continue to grow.

9

Food Service
Industry

Although extremely competitive and hard work, the food service industry offers tremendous opportunities for financial success to the individual willing to work and put forth a sincere competitive effort. There are many opportunities to be self-employed in one of the many facets of the food business or to be employed by others in one of the many levels of food preparation, food management, supervision, and executive management.

Everyone eats at least three meals a day. With the increased pace of today's life-style and with more women working to supplement the family income, thus cutting down on the time and energy available for cooking at home, more and more people are eating in restaurants and other types of commercial food establishments. In fact, recent statistics show that the average person eats one out of every four meals away from home.

The food service industry is the third largest in the United States, with annual sales of about $50 billion. Approximately 750 million meals are served a week in this country through more than 367,000 individual establishments. There are approximately 3 million people employed in the industry, and it is predicted that over 4 million will be needed in the next two years. About 75,000 people will be employed in new jobs that do not even exist today.

The food service industry comprises a great variety of establishments. They are located in different types of facilities, and they offer different types of foods, services, and prices. Yet, they all have two things in common—(1) each requires a highly trained team of individuals with specialized skills, and (2) each offers financial success and advancement to the individuals involved. Some of the business establishments included in the food service industry are

Restaurants

Hotels and motels

Cafeterias

Drug store lunch counters

Vending operations

Employee cafeterias (plant and office)

Military feeding operations

Hospitals

Schools and colleges

Airlines, steamships, and railroads

Drive-ins

Coffee shops

Soda fountains

Tea rooms and sandwich shops

Taverns and cocktail lounges

Snack bars at athletic events

Catering establishments

Construction camps

Retirement homes

Institutions

Mobile kitchens

FOOD SERVICE PERSONNEL

The food service industry is a good place to work and can provide good income, opportunity for advancement, and a sense of personal gratification not always available in other industries. Furthermore, the industry offers a great deal of security. In good times and bad, people have to eat. Their choice of restaurant types may vary with economic conditions. Yet the fact remains that people have to eat every day, and the people skilled in the profession of providing the best food for the money spent will always have a job.

A young person can decide on the branch of the industry in which he or she wants to work. One can pick geographic area and can even have some choice in working hours. Many an experienced cook, chef, waiter, or other type of skilled restaurant worker has traveled around the world practicing his or her specialty in a good establishment located in the area visited. There is always a need for good restaurant personnel. In addition, working in different types of restaurants in different areas of the world adds to experience and proficiency and increases chances for employment wherever one goes. Moreover, it also increases chances for success when in business for oneself.

The reputation of a restaurant, or any food service establishment, depends on *people*. The men and women who manage, who prepare the food, and who come into contact with the customer each make a significant contribution to a restaurant's reputation and success.

There are many special positions available in the restaurant industry. They will vary in different restaurants. Some positions are available only in large chain-type operations. Others are combined and may come under the responsibility of one individual, such as the restaurant manager, food service supervisor, or chef. Some positions pay a relatively small amount of money and require little training, whereas others require a great deal of experience and pay a great deal of money. A brief description of some of these positions will be presented, as even the lesser positions can aid someone in determining if the restaurant profession is for him or her. Such a position can even provide a starting point for a successful career in the upper echelons of the food service industry.

Restaurant Manager

Every commodity today is expensive; the cost of doing business in a restaurant is high. Therefore, it is important, more than ever before, to have proper supervision in the restaurant business to make sure that no money is wasted and that the maximum financial return is received for every dollar spent. This is probably the reason for, and the most important function of, the *restaurant manager*. It is the manager's responsibility to coordinate the entire operation of a restaurant or other type of food service facility for efficient, courteous, and profitable food service.

The manager hires and trains working personnel, plans and coordinates work schedules to make sure there is maximum help during peak hours and minimum help during lulls, and plans and coordinates the duties of the help to obtain maximum performance per payroll dollar to keep the restaurant operating at peak efficiency. A manager should be intuitive in observing working personnel in order to find talented help for promotion to higher and more responsible positions. Promoting the right people not only makes a manager's job easier, but also instills a greater feeling of camaraderie and concern among the staff, thus providing for a smooth and efficient operation. The manager may also determine the prices of food to allow a legitimate profit for the restaurant and at the same time remain competitive with the same type of restaurants in the area. The manager handles complaints of customers and seeks ways to improve service.

In a large organization there may be supervisory staff members working directly subordinate to the manager in charge of lower echelon staff. In a smaller restaurant the manager may deal directly with the kitchen and dining room personnel.

TRAINING REQUIREMENTS

Restaurant managers may attain their position through on-the-job experience in a restaurant working their way up from busboy, waiter, or cook's helper. If they go this route, they should take some restaurant management classes at a nearby college or trade school to supplement this training and gain a broad knowledge of restaurant operations. Many restaurant chains offer management training programs to qualified individuals.

Probably the best and quickest way to achieve managerial status in a good restaurant is to undergo a one- to two-year training program in restaurant management at a good junior college or vocational school. A good academic program combines actual work situations with a relatively heavy load of related classroom work, giving the student a working knowledge of the basic principles of successful restaurant operation and the latest practices in the field. In addition, the school should provide a background in liberal arts to provide the student with the polish and sophistication needed to work with customers, help, and upper management. This can eventually lead to excecutive management positions in large restaurant chains.

A restaurant manager can earn from $10,000 to $25,000 a year (and sometimes even more), depending on the size and complexity of the restaurant served.

There is an extreme shortage of adequately trained personnel. A talented manager should have no trouble finding a job. Even managers of many small, limited-menu, fast-food restaurants earn approximately $18,000 a year. There is even a chance of going into business for oneself or, if sufficient capital is lacking, of operating a good service concession in one of the many facilities previously listed. Concession opportunities will be discussed in a subsequent chapter under the heading Food Service Concession.

Food Production Manager

The position of *food production manager* is usually found in a large chain-type operation or cafeteria. This executive is in charge of all food preparation and thus must have a knowledge of food preparation, understand and practice good food standards, and be proficient in cost control. He or she may also supervise the kitchen staff and so should know how to work with and direct people.

TRAINING REQUIREMENTS

On-the-job training may be sufficient to attain the job of food production manager. However, some academic training in restaurant management or institutional cooking is a preferable adjunct to on-the-job training.

SALARY AND EMPLOYMENT OPPORTUNITIES

The average salary of a manager, depending on the size of the establishment served, is approximately $9,000 to $13,000 a year. As the number of fast-food and cafeteria type of establishments grows, there will be an increased need for good food production managers. Such people also have the background to go into business for themselves in a concessionaire capacity in one of the many types of food service establishments to be discussed later under Food Service Concession.

Restaurant Chain Executive

The food service business is very intricate and requires many levels of sophisticated management for success. Restaurant chains are becoming more and more prominent. Many coffee shops and fast-food take-out restaurants are components of large chains, even national ones. In fact, many elaborate and high-class restaurants, although they may have different names and serve different cuisines, are also members of large chains or business conglomerates. Just as an individual restaurant needs a manager, so does a group of restaurants need division and executive managers to oversee the entire operation.

The *restaurant chain executive* does primarily administrative work and does not come in direct contact with food preparation and service. However, a thorough knowledge of food service, in addition to executive management ability, is necessary for this executive successfully to carry out responsibilities.

TRAINING REQUIREMENTS

There is no definite training program designed for attaining executive levels in a restaurant chain. Organizations have their own criteria for advancement. Many chains promote their executives from within. It is a common practice to promote successful and personable individual restaurant managers to executive positions in a chain. For a restaurant manager to be in line for consideration for advancement to an executive level, it is advisable to take outside courses leading to a bachelor's or master's degree in business administration. Not only is a knowledge of food preparation necessary for a chain executive, but one must also know the principles of cost control, accounting, merchandising, real estate, and financing. There are several schools in the country offering four-year programs leading to a bachelor's degree in restaurant administration. This, too, can prepare and add credentials to someone desiring an eventual position as a chain executive.

SALARY AND EMPLOYMENT OPPORTUNITIES

A restaurant executive can receive a salary of from $25,000 to even $100,000 a year, depending on the size of the chain and the executive level held. The median salary range is approximately $40,000 to $50,000 a year for such a position.

Executive positions are not a "dime-a-dozen." However, as restaurant chains expand and new ones are formed, there will always be openings for thoroughly trained and experienced restaurant chain executives.

Food Service Supervisor

One of the supervisors under the immediate direction of the restaurant manager is the *food service supervisor*. This position may also have the title of *dining room supervisor, head waitress or waiter,* or *counter supervisor*. Such supervisors coordinate all dining room activities. They may also function in hospitals, nursing homes, schools, colleges, or similar establishments. These individuals instruct workers in methods of performing duties and assign and coordinate the work of employees to promote efficient operations. They supervise meal serving in the dining room, oversee kitchen and dining area cleaning, and are responsible for kitchen utensils and equipment meeting hygienic standards. Supervisors keep records, such as amount and cost of meals served and employees' working hours. They requisition or purchase supplies and equipment. They may direct food and beverage preparation, assist in planning menus, and may interview and select new employees. They must possess leadership qualities and be able to be fair and objective.

TRAINING REQUIREMENTS

The training and experience for this type of position can come from on-the-job training. A waiter or waitress with leadership abilities can often achieve this post.

SALARY AND EMPLOYMENT OPPORTUNITIES

The average salary range is approximately from $7,000 to $12,000 a year, depending on the size of the operation supervised. Large restaurants and cafeterias are the primary sources for employment in this category. Furthermore, this type of position is one of the steps on the ladder to becoming a full-scale restaurant manager.

Dietetic Technician

It is the function of a professionally trained *dietetic technician* to plan diets and supervise the service of meals to meet the individual and general nutritional needs of patients in hospitals, nursing homes, and clinics. In this capacity the technician works with nutritionists and physicians in devising meals that not only provide individuals with the nutrition they need, but also meals that are appetizing and appealing. Such services are also utilized in large commercial food service establishments such as cafeterias and in the food programs in schools and colleges.

To be qualified as a dietetic technician, an individual must undergo a two-year academic program and receive an associate's degree in dietetic technology.

SALARY AND EMPLOYMENT OPPORTUNITIES

The salary of a dietetic technician can average $12,000 a year. There are vast opportunities open in hospital work, school and college food service facilities, chain restaurants (in the capacity of menu planner), and in research work in university and government nutritional programs. Also, the dietetic technician, with some business background, can possibly obtain the food service concession in a small hospital.

Director of
Recipe Development

Some large restaurants, especially chains, employ college-trained men and women to work in testing kitchens creating new recipes to feature on menus. These people are sometimes given the title of *director of recipe development.* Creative ability and a thorough knowledge of food preparation are prerequisites for this position, and chef training is definitely needed.

SALARY AND EMPLOYMENT OPPORTUNITIES

The salary will vary widely with the size of the organization served, anywhere from $10,000 to $25,000 a year. Very often the one thing that puts one restaurant or restaurant chain far ahead of its competition is the unique and creative dishes it can concoct. Often a very appetizing dish can be devised at a relatively small cost by a creative and imaginative cook or chef. As competition grows among chain restaurant operations, this position will grow increasingly in importance.

Executive Chef

The "bottom line" in any type of restaurant operation is the professional *chef*. The chef is the nucleus and focal point of any successful restaurant operation. He or she is what makes the place GO. Many a restaurant is successful due to the creative talents and skills of its chef. This is not to understate any of the other positions already discussed. As mentioned, they are most important to any successful and profitable restaurant operation. However, it is the talented chef that can bring in the business, thus allowing the rest of the personnel to utilize fully their capabilities. Many cooks and chefs are able to prepare food that is palatable and presentable. However, there are a few that seem to have a natural talent with food. The meals they devise and prepare possess savory qualities far superior to meals served in many other restaurants. Just as certain actors and actresses have a talent of adding deeper meaning to a character they are portraying, so do some chefs seem to be able to add more taste to the food they prepare.

It does not really take any magical abilities to become a fine chef. What it probably takes more of is a fondness for food. This fondness plus hard work (and imagination) can allow an individual willing to learn the technical characteristics of food to prepare the food as a true "artist."

A true *executive chef* is just what the name implies: the head executive of the entire kitchen staff. It is the chef's job to develop new recipes, plan the menus, and supervise the purchasing of quality foods and ingredients necessary in the preparation of the meals created. The chef also develops and supervises the preparation and cooking of the food. Several cooks may work under his or her supervision in a large establishment, or the executive chef may do most of the actual cooking if the restaurant is small. In larger restaurants the chef will generally have cooks prepare some of the basic dishes on the menu, while the head chef personally prepares some of the more exclusive and unique dishes. The executive chef must also possess leadership abilities in order to coordinate and supervise the activities of the entire kitchen staff.

TRAINING REQUIREMENTS

First, an aspiring chef must have a real feel for, and a strong desire to work with, food and be creative at it. One way to test this desire out is to get a job as a kitchen helper or cook's assistant in a large restaurant. If the work and kitchen atmosphere agree with you, it is very possible that you have the attributes necessary to pursue a career program in becoming a full-fledged executive chef. Many junior colleges and vocational schools offer excellent two-year training programs covering all the responsibilities of the executive chef. This training should then be backed up with work experience in a restaurant operation known for its excellent food.

SALARY AND EMPLOYMENT OPPORTUNITIES

The salary for an executive chef ranges from $15,000 to $30,000 a year and in some of the larger restaurants or hotels up to as much as $50,000 a year.

The well-trained and experienced chef has almost no problem in finding suitable employment. As mentioned, the reputation and profit of a restaurant is highly dependent on the talents of its chef. Therefore, whenever a new restaurant is opened or an existing one is not doing the business it would like to, an intense search is often conducted to find a chef who can provide meals of the highest culinary standards to give the restaurant an excellent reputation and potential for profit.

A chef who desires to go into business privately can do so by opening a restaurant. If one lacks the capital to do so, it is possible to operate a restaurant on a concession basis or to go into the catering business, which requires a relatively low initial investment and provides the opportunity for huge profits. Both options will be discussed under "Independent Careers" in the Food Service Industry.

Cook

A *cook* works under the direction of the chef and directly prepares the food according to the instructions of the recipes used by the restaurant. In large restaurants one may find individual roast or dinner cooks, cold-meat cooks, vegetable cooks, sauce cooks, short-order cooks, or soup cooks. In small establishments that do not employ chefs and serve basically simple menus, the cook will be in charge of all food preparation.

The line separating a cook from a chef is a fine one. Basically, however, a chef and cook differ in the amount of supervisory responsibilities they assume and in the complexity and creative elegance of the meals they prepare, with the chef performing more in each category. This is not to understate the role of the cook. It takes a good cook to follow the directions of a top chef. Furthermore, many people like to dine on the simple basic foods. It takes a good cook to properly prepare simple meat, poultry, and fish dishes. Many restaurants are prospering serving simple, limited, and well-prepared menus.

TRAINING REQUIREMENTS

An individual with a knack for preparing food can learn to be a good cook by working under a top chef or learn the craft through a one- to two-year chef training program in a good junior college or vocational school. After graduation from a good program, a cook may reach chef status by working under the auspices of an executive chef, by keeping up with the latest techniques in food preparation, and by experimenting with his or her own new dishes.

SALARY AND EMPLOYMENT OPPORTUNITIES

A good cook can earn approximately $15,000 a year. By developing talents to assume the role and responsibilities of a chef, the cook naturally can expect a much higher pay scale. A good cook can get a job in almost any restaurant in the world or can even go into business operating a coffee shop, fast-food restaurant, catering service, sandwich shop, or food service concession in a large establishment.

Waiter or Waitress

Many people think of a *waiter* or *waitress* as just a person who serves food. Obviously, he or she is a food server, but a good waiter or waitress is a lot more. A good waiter is a connoisseur of food and can give advice to customers on what foods on the menu might be most apt to satisfy their culinary desires at the moment. He or she must be a psychologist, be an actor, and possess poise and self-control in order to get along with people. A waiter on the dining room floor is like an actor on the stage. He must act in a manner to inspire confidence and add to the aesthetic atmosphere of the restaurant. A good waiter must be able to take orders accurately, work quickly, and coordinate orders so that each course of the meal does not arrive too early or too late. The attitude of a waiter can add greatly to the pleasure of the guests and make their meal more enjoyable.

TRAINING REQUIREMENTS

There is no formal or academic training program required to become a good waiter. Waiters usually start out as busboys or busgirls clearing tables and resetting them with fresh linen and tableware. They assist the waiter in filling water glasses and in serving appetizers, desserts, and beverages. An individual starting out as a busboy or busgirl can learn to become a full-fledged waiter or waitress by observing the methods and techniques of the better waiters and waitresses and then disciplining themselves to perform in their capacity. Generally, many experienced waiters will always be glad to give guidance and instruction to an individual aspiring to become a good waiter.

SALARY AND EMPLOYMENT OPPORTUNITIES

The financial rewards of a good waitress or waiter are excellent. Generally, the basic minimum wage is about $100 a week, plus tips. Tips will generally average from 15 to 20 percent of the total bill. In a fine, high-class restaurant this can add up to quite a sum of money.

Today in most medium- to high-class restaurants dinner for two, plus a couple of drinks, will easily come to $20 or over. Therefore, if there are two couples at a table, the total bill will amount to approximately $40. With the basic 15 percent tip, the waiter or waitress will receive $6. If a total of fifteen different foursomes are served during the course of an evening, it is easy to make $90 to $100 on a shift. Multiply this by just five nights' work, plus the basic salary, and the take-home pay at the end of the week is quite substantial.

Waiting on tables not only can provide a good living for people who want to engage in this work on a full-time basis, but also can provide earnings for students wanting to work part time to earn money for college or living expenses. It is an excellent source of income for young people who want to travel and be able to earn good money wherever they go.

TRAINING REQUIREMENTS FOR THE INDUSTRY

That the food service industry offers a diversity of opportunities to the ambitious individual is quite obvious. Becoming proficient in the many facets of this industry is a continuous learning process. However, a good two-year junior college program is highly advisable to the individual who wants to make food service a career and reach the upper echelons of the industry more rapidly.

Hundreds of jobs are open to the person who completes this type of training. However, an individual may also decide to transfer credits to a four-year college for more advanced work.

Primarily, the two-year program includes study in such areas as food preparation, menu planning, food purchasing and storage, equipment purchasing and layout, personnel management and job analysis, food standards and sanitation, diet therapy, catering, beverage control, food cost accounting, and record keeping. Also included are such general courses as psychology, communication skills, physical education, sociology, economics, chemistry, and nutrition. Classes, laboratory work, and practical experience with part-time work in a food service operation comprise most programs.

For the individual desiring to become a cook or chef, the basic two-year program is tailored to place emphasis on all types of food preparation.

Junior college classes are constantly being revised and expanded to keep pace with the new concepts and developments in the industry. Courses may be taken on a full- or part-time basis. Tuition and fees are usually low in most junior colleges. Food service administration graduates are qualified for such positions as assistant manager, manager, food production supervisor, purchasing agent, food cost accountant, food service director, director of recipe development, personnel director, sales manager, and banquet manager.

For information concerning training programs in the food service industry, write:

Director of Education
National Restaurant Association
1530 North Lake Shore Drive
Chicago, Illinois 60610

Council of Hotel, Restaurant,
and Institutional Education
1522 K Street N.W.
Washington, D.C. 20005

For scholarship information, write:

*National Institute for
the Food Service Industry*
120 South Riverside Plaza
Chicago, Illinois 60606

INDEPENDENT CAREERS

Besides the many fine employment opportunities in the food service industry, there are also many opportunities for an individual to be an independent entrepreneur in the industry. The most obvious area to become self-employed is that of a *restaurant owner.* The only problem is that this usually requires an initial investment of from $50,000 to $100,000 and in some cases even more. If you have access to that kind of money, fine. But if you do not, there are many other areas of self-employment that can be very profitable and that require a relatively small initial investment. The following are some examples.

**Food Service
Concessionaire**

There are many business establishments that find it necessary to maintain food service facilities as part of their total operation. We have already noted that the operation of a food service facility is very complex and requires a great deal of management. Many organizations whose primary function is other than food service find it more feasible to purchase and set up the necessary equipment for food service and then lease it out on a *concession* basis to an individual capable of operating it profitably and making it an attractive adjunct to the primary organization. Examples of this are hotels and motels, employee cafeterias in large business institutions, manufacturing plants, and government agencies, schools and colleges, construction camps, vacation resorts, hospitals, and retirement homes.

For example, a medium-size hotel or motel may want to concentrate its efforts on just running the lodging facilities without having to worry about the intricacies of operating a food service. On the other hand, however, it is necessary for most hotels and motels to operate a fine food service facility to add to the comfort and enjoyment of its guests, thus contributing to the total "merchandise package" of the establishment. When such a situation occurs, the hotel establishment may set up a kitchen and dining room and then lease it out to a highly experienced restaurant manager or chef. The lease agreement is usually for a percentage of the volume done by the *food service concessionaire.* This volume usually varies anywhere from 10 to 20 percent. Sometimes the lease calls for a percent sharing of the profits. In any case, in a proper location there is usually enough profit left over to satisfy both parties. In many instances once the restaurant concession develops a reputation for fine food and service, many people from the surrounding areas who are not guests of the hotel establishment will travel to dine at that particular restaurant. The results are excellent profits with relatively little capital investment.

Very often small- to medium-size hospitals do not want to become involved in food service. They, too, will lease the food service requirements to an individual qualified to prepare food meeting the dietary needs of the patients. This concessionaire will usually be a dietary technician. In an arrangement such as this, the hospital will pay for each meal served. This can add up to quite an attractive financial package. The same can also apply to nursing and retirement homes.

Schools, colleges, and industrial plants may also prefer not to be bothered with the actual food service. They would rather concentrate their efforts on their primary functions, but they realize the importance of maintaining proper food facilities for their students or employees. They, too, will very often follow the concession principle in providing food service. They will lease out the cafeteria facilities to a qualified individual for a percentage of the volume or profit or pay a flat fee per meal served and collect the money from the patrons themselves. In any event, a large cafeteria facility, operated under a suitable contract, can prove quite profitable for the qualified operator.

The concession principle can apply to any type of organization requiring a food service facility.

TRAINING REQUIREMENTS

The ideal background for operating a food service concession in most facilities would be to have training as either a cook or chef, supplemented with some courses in cost accounting and management. If a concession is to be an elaborate one in a fine hotel, chef training is definitely recommended.

Many junior colleges offer two-year programs in institutional cooking, which combine the techniques of large-scale food preparation with the management skills required in these operations.

If you are adept at management and have some direct experience in the food preparation industry, this will usually suffice. Just make sure you are adept at handling cooks and chefs. They can be very temperamental, and the success of any operation depends heavily on their expertise and dependability.

For operating a concession in a hospital, an associate's degree as a diet technician is almost essential. In general, however, any junior college with a complete food preparation curriculum will be able to provide you with any type of training you might need.

Caterer

An excellent business for the creative chef or cook to go into on his or her own is *catering*. There is a relatively small initial investment plus low overhead. It can be exciting and challenging for the enterprising individual. Catering can entail preparing a small birthday party on one day and then arranging a gourmet feast for over 300 people the next day.

Catering is the preparing and serving of food to custom order for the special occasion, and the successful *caterer* is one who can make his or her talent reflect credit on the customer.

A caterer's job is to save trouble, add style, and handle a situation beyond the scope of the customer. The caterer is expected to provide superior food and to answer every question in the book from how many servings in a cake to where to rent a marquee or tent. Catering has to do with parties, celebrations, occasions, and traditions. There is always a new twist to add to a party or dinner, and for that reason catering is never dull. However, to make it profitable, catering must be based on sound business practices, and proper training, therefore, is of the utmost importance.

TRAINING REQUIREMENTS

Men and women who go into catering should have a natural talent for, and interest in, food preparation and have a flair for its presentation, whether it be individually served at dining tables or buffet style. A basic chef or catering course taught in a junior college or accredited vocational school is an excellent beginning. This should then be augmented by working for a first-rank caterer until a well-rounded knowledge of both the preparation and business aspects of catering are acquired. If you have a natural talent for this type of work, it should not be long until you are ready to go into business for yourself.

The salary and employment opportunities of a chef or cook involved in the catering business as an employee in someone else's business is approximately the same as it would be for the other areas of the food service business. However, catering presents many opportunities for the creative chef or cook to earn large sums of money as a self-employed individual.

When a luncheon, party, or dinner is catered, the food is either prepared at the site of the affair or in a remote food preparation facility and then transported to the affair via a catering truck. This eliminates the need for operating in a "high-rent" area, the necessity for expensive illuminated outdoor signs, and the need for expensive dining facilities, as is required in a conventional restaurant operation. In fact, all that is needed is a food preparation facility that meets the standards of the catering codes of the community's public health department.

The public health department sets standards that must be met for cooking, storing, and refrigerating foods. The stoves, storage, and refrigeration equipment needed to start a small catering service meeting the codes can be purchased for approximately $5,000. More food preparation equipment can be purchased as business grows. Some caterers even build and furnish special facilities for people to have parties. This will obviously cost a lot of money, but it can be financed from the profits created by your initial operation.

When the food is prepared in a catering facility, it is transported to the location of the affair via catering trucks. Such trucks contain heating and refrigeration equipment allowing the fully prepared food to be transported distances of up to 400 miles without spoiling or losing its flavor. The operator of a catering service can rent these trucks until he or she is in a financial position to own one.

If an individual wants to see what the chances for success

317

are before investing $5,000 in a food preparation facility, he or she may possibly solicit the catering business of people who are giving dinner parties in their homes and are willing to let the caterer use the cooking facilities in their own kitchen. Likewise, many organizations such as churches, synagogues, lodges, and civic groups, such as YMCAs, have kitchens located in their facilities that a caterer can use. If one operates on this basis for a while, and builds up a reputation of preparing fine dinners, the caterer can then open his or her own food preparation facility. Once an individual has his or her own catering kitchen and attracts a lot of business, it is possible to prepare meals for several affairs being given at the same time, sending them out to the various locations where service staffs will see that they are properly served.

Many caterers employ a permanent full-time staff of waiters, waitresses, and other personnel to see that the food is properly served once it reaches its destination. Small caterers or caterers who on occasion may not have enough staff members on hand to take care of all the affairs catered on one particular day can hire the services of part-time outside service people to handle all of their obligations. Very often college students and other people looking for part-time income avail their services to caterers. It is an excellent arrangement for both parties.

Catering does not necessarily mean preparing meals for parties and dinners. Many workers in office buildings, factories, and retail establishments like to enjoy a well-prepared sandwich or salad for lunch and do not like to fight the noon-hour crowds waiting for a seat in a crowded restaurant or coffee shop. Many caterers specialize in preparing sandwiches and salads of a higher quality than is usually found at most typical lunch counters. They solicit people to distribute their sandwiches and salads to workers in the various establishments just described. In most cases the people who distribute the food pay for it after they have completed their routes and keep part of the profit derived from their sales for themselves. In a way, they, too, are in business for themselves. Most caterers require their salespeople to rent portable food warmers for storing hot sandwiches during transportation. These food warmers can be taken in and out of automobiles very easily. A successful lunchtime caterer will usually hire an individual to go to new areas to solicit new business. This is done by distributing free samples to potential customers. Also, it is a good idea to require a salesperson to maintain a certain sales quota in order to keep a route. This will induce the salesperson always to arrive for work on time and to do a good selling job. Some caterers will do both party and dinner catering, plus lunchtime sandwich catering. This can insure maximum utilization of time and equipment.

Most caterers will usually double or triple their food costs when charging for the meals that they prepare and serve. Naturally, they cannot pocket all of this profit as they also have overhead to maintain. However, it is not uncommon for a successful caterer to make $50,000 to $100,000 a year. This is an exceptionally attractive arrangement especially when you consider the relatively low initial cost of going into business and that the food (inventory) is not purchased until after the catering order has been obtained. This allows for an immediate return on money invested with little excess surplus left over.

When one starts in the catering business, things can be slow at first, as is true for most new ventures. However, once a reputation for preparing and serving fine foods is built up, people will then seek out the caterer to handle their affairs.

There are many steps one can take to stimulate business. First, advertise in the yellow pages of the telephone book and in local newspapers. One should go to every church, synagogue, lodge, and headquarters of every civic organization to advise their officers and staff of the talents and services being offered. A caterer should advertise in all newsletters and journals of all religious, civic, and business organizations in the community. Most important of course, is to do the best job possible once the business starts rolling in. All this can lead to one thing—*success!*

Fast-food Restaurant Operator

Establishments that cook and dispense foods to be taken out or consumed on the premises at very simple and inexpensive tables and chairs, or to be eaten in the car are classified as *fast-food restaurants*. The menus usually consist of hamburgers, hot dogs, fried chicken, tacos, fried fish, ribs, sandwiches, and beverages. Many meals eaten away from home are eaten in these types of establishments. Even when people are in a hurry and are looking for a quick snack at a moderate price, they appreciate quality and good taste.

Did you ever see a large crowd in front of a very small and modest food stand, while a large, ultra-modern food facility nearby is almost empty? This is quite a common occurrence. There is also a reason for it. Even a simple hamburger or hot dog can be improved by spending a few extra cents on the ingredients and then using a little ingenuity and creativity in seasoning and preparing it. When the owner of even the simplest and smallest food stand does this, eventually the word gets around, and many workers and residents in the area will patronize such an establishment to treat their appetites to something extra. Even a hamburger can be a delicacy if prepared properly with quality ingredients.

A simple cooking course along with some practical experience can prepare an individual to operate a first-rate, fast-food establishment. Approximately $20,000 of new and used equipment is required to set up this type of facility. Although $20,000 is not a small amount of money, it may be a worthwhile investment as the simple and moderately priced fast service meal is quickly becoming a very popular form of dining in our rapid-pace society.

Sandwich-shop Operator

If the cost of opening up a fast-food restaurant serving both hot and cold foods is too much, the *sandwich shop* may be the answer to the budding entrepreneur trying to establish a foothold in the restaurant business.

There are even creative ways to prepare sandwiches to make them look and taste better. There are special breads to serve them on, better ingredients to be used, new combinations to be discovered, and flavorful condiments to serve them with. Who would not go out of their way for a really *good* sandwich? Furthermore, the serving of high-quality and good-tasting soups, cakes, pies, and beverages along with these sandwiches can provide a meal "fit for a king." There are a lot of people working in office buildings, small factories, and stores, in addition to shoppers who like being treated like royalty, who will patronize a shop that will give them something better than "average."

The cost of opening this type of establishment is a lot less than that of a typical fast-food restaurant as it is not necessary to have a grill, stove, and stove hood, since no hot meals are being prepared. It may be profitable, however, to purchase a microwave oven to be able to heat some sandwiches adding to the delight of many patrons.

The cost of equipping a sandwich shop is as follows:

Slicer	$ 600
Microwave oven	600
Refrigerator	1,200
Freezer	1,500
Seating	2,000
TOTAL	$5,900

It is highly advisable to open a sandwich shop in a commercial area consisting of many offices and stores as this type of operation caters favorably to the needs of the employees and shoppers of such an area. If you have fundamental background in cook training and some basic management courses, you have what it takes to operate a good sandwich shop.

The fundamental opportunities in the restaurant field have been presented as concisely and accurately as possible. Food service is more than a business, it is an industry. As in most industries, there is always room for new developments, which, in turn, lead to new positions and new sources of profit. Food service can provide an exciting and profitable career to the individual with the aptitude for this type of work.

10

Special Service Businesses

JANITORIAL MAINTENANCE

The maintaining of clean interiors in a home, factory, office building, hospital, school, or retail store can act as a hallmark of quality and excellence for that particular facility and its inhabitants and personnel. Well-kept floors, carpets, windows, and upholstery convey the message to clients, customers, and employees that the firm they are dealing with is conscientious in everything it does. It shows that the organization "cares" and takes pride in itself and in everything it does. The responsibility of maintaining clean and elegant interiors is primarily the responsibility and function of the people in the *janitorial maintenance business.* The proper carrying out of this responsibility can also be very profitable to qualified participants.

Very often janitorial service personnel are thought of as broom pushers and mop pushers. At one time this was probably true, but not anymore. Modern technology has entered the janitorial field. Today, scientifically compounded waxes and detergents, along with modern cleaning machines, have eased the physical burden of cleaning interiors and have increased tremendously the amount of work one janitor can do in a certain amount of time. This has also made the janitorial business more profitable.

There are many facets to janitorial servicing. A janitorial service person may handle all types of jobs, handle just one, or become involved in a combination of several that allow the most potential profit for the effort. The following are examples of the different types of work that comprise the janitorial maintenance business:

- Floor cleaning and waxing
- Rug and upholstery cleaning
- Steam carpet cleaning
- Drapery cleaning
- Window and wall washing
- Furniture cleaning and polishing
- Spot removal service
- Insect exterminating
- Selling and changing light bulbs
- Selling janitorial supplies

TRAINING REQUIREMENTS

To be proficient in janitorial maintenance, one must know the cleaning characteristics of various types of wool and synthetic rugs, the composition of modern floor coverings, and the different types of wall and upholstery coverings. Janitors must know how to operate many types of cleaning machines and be able to plan their work requirements to get the greatest amount of work done in the shortest amount of time. Janitorial work is definitely a science.

An intelligent person can learn, in a relatively short period of time, the skills needed to run a successful janitorial service. Excellent sources of information are the manufacturers and distributors of janitorial equipment and supplies. These people will be only too happy to train you in the proper use of today's modern cleaning machines and detergents and waxes. Janitorial equipment suppliers can be found in the yellow pages of the local telephone book. Call on several suppliers until you find one that you are most comfortable with and can receive the most service from.

There are several correspondence schools offering short-term courses in janitorial maintenance. The names and addresses of these schools can be obtained by writing:

National Home Study Council
1601 18th Street, N.E.
Washington, D.C. 20009

In addition, working in a full-service maintenance company for awhile can also provide a valuable background in janitorial work.

SALARY AND EMPLOYMENT OPPORTUNITIES

A staff janitor working in the employ of a commercial janitorial service, school system, or large factory or office building makes only a very modest salary ($3.00 to $3.50 an hour). However, there are other areas for an experienced janitor to prosper. Commercial janitorial services, school systems, and large office and factory systems employing 100 janitors or more need janitors to work in supervisory capacities. Janitors with administrative and leadership abilities who can effectively plan large work assignments and supervise personnel can earn from $15,000 to $18,000 a year. In addition, there are tremendous opportunities for a good janitor to start and operate a janitorial service business, one that offers a complete janitorial service or one that specializes in a particular area, such as carpet cleaning.

There are several good reasons for an individual to start his or her own janitorial service. First, the initial cost is modest. For an initial investment of from $2,000 to $5,000 an individual can purchase the most modern machinery and equipment for cleaning floors, rugs, and upholstery. Second, the owner and operator of a moderate-sized janitorial service business can realistically make $20,000 a year and more, plus the satisfaction of being independent. Third, it is easy for the small independent operator to compete successfully with the large janitorial services. In fact, in many instances the smaller operator can compete more effectively than the "big operator," as the overhead is lower and large sums of money are not needed to pay for large janitorial staffs, clerical staffs, and office headquarters. Usually the small operator can work out of his or her home. With several good machines plus one or two assistants, the small operator can cover a lot of ground.

HOW TO GET STARTED

A good personality plus a neat appearance can do a lot to inspire the confidence of potential customers when soliciting their business. If you can convince businesspeople that you can improve the appearance of their facilities at a reasonable cost, thereby improving their business potentials, you are well on your way to obtaining their business.

Many commercial institutions require daily janitorial care plus weekly or monthly care in "stripping" the old wax from floors and applying new wax, plus complete carpet cleaning. The newcomer to the janitorial business should call on and "sell" himself and his services to restaurants, supermarkets, beauty shops, office buildings, banks, all types of retail stores, and management companies for apartment houses and office buildings. These organizations alone can provide the newcomer with a sound basis for success. Also, do not forget the homeowner or apartment renter. General residential cleaning has experienced a steady increase in demand as household incomes rise and as more and more housewives leave the home for outside employment.

FACTS AND FIGURES

A rotary-action floor cleaning machine with cleaning and polishing attachments can be purchased for approximately $500. To this basic unit a carpet shampoo attachment can be added for about $300. If desired, a separate carpet cleaning unit employing a rotary brush plus shampoo dispensing unit can be purchased complete for approximately $700. A vacuum for wet and dry work costs about $600. If desired, a machine that steam cleans carpets can be purchased for $1,000. This type of machine offers one of the most effective advances in professional carpet cleaning. On the forward stroke of the applicator wand, a mist of steam with cleaning and conditioning agents suspended into it is propelled deep into the pile of the rug; the steam and the cleaning agent emulsifies the dirt in the rug; and on the back stroke of the applicator wand, the steam, cleaning agents, and suspended dirt are vacuumed up into a receptacle tank in the machine. There are many other types of machines that perform this operation. For about $2,000 there are electrically propelled floor cleaning machines that you just guide along the floor. As one of these moves along, it dispenses its own cleaning solution, scrubs the floor, and then vacuums it dry, all in one easy operation. This type of machine is worth its weight in gold when handling service contracts for facilities with large floor areas, such as factories and supermarkets.

If the occasion arises, an upholstery cleaning machine can be purchased for about $375 and a wall cleaning machine for about $275. You do not have to start out with every type of machine there is, just the ones immediately necessary to handle your initial work orders. One nice thing about the janitorial service business is that once you establish yourself as a reputable account, many equipment distributors will lease or rent you various pieces of additional equipment until you find it feasible to purchase them outright. This alone can reduce your initial investment immensely.

HOW TO CHARGE CUSTOMERS

There is no one accepted formula for charging customers. One method for the beginner to establish rates is to check the fees charged by competing services. Janitorial maintenance operators do not generally charge by the hour; they usually charge a flat rate per job. However, because with modern janitorial equipment many large jobs can be completed quickly, it is very easy for an independent operator to average $10 to $11 an hour for work performed.

Some types of work pay more than others. For instance, carpet cleaning can net an operator $15 and more an hour. The fee for carpet cleaning charged to commercial firms such as banks and restaurants is from 5¢ to 10¢ a square foot. The average fee for doing the carpets in a one-bedroom apartment is approximately $50—it only takes an hour and a half to complete. For a three-bedroom home it is about $70; the total job requires only about two and a half hours to complete. This is why many people specialize in carpets only. The typical fee for cleaning a sofa and chair is about $50. As indicated, the operator can rent the necessary equipment from a supplier until ready to purchase such equipment outright.

Sometimes it is very hard for businesspeople to find competent and honest maintenance personnel. Therefore, when the owner or manager of a business finds a service operator who is good, dependable, and honest, there usually is no quibbling over service fees as long as they are in the normal range.

There are several things the owner of a maintenance service business can do to increase income. One can offer extra services, such as exterminating insects, changing bulbs, selling sanitation supplies, and offering a spot-removal service.

Many areas of the country are prone to insect infestation. Because of this, many buildings require regular exterminating servicing. As long as a janitor has to cover the entire area of a building in the janitorial duties, he or she might as well offer an insecticide service. The chemicals and sprayers needed are very inexpensive.

When light bulbs burn out, it frequently is an inconvenience for the owner or manager of the business or building to locate and install a new unit. This presents the opportunity for the service operator to arrange with an electric light wholesaler to purchase bulbs at wholesale and then install them in the facility serviced, for a fee.

There are many sanitation accessories that a janitorial service operator can obtain at wholesale cost from equipment suppliers and sell at retail to the customers serviced. Such equipment includes:

- Paper towels and dispensers
- Hand soap and dispensers
- Drinking cups and dispensers
- Toilet bowl and urinal deodorizers
- Toilet bowl covers
- Toilet paper
- Sanitary napkins and dispensers
- Waste paper baskets

A stain-removal service is a natural adjunct for a janitorial business. Very often something is spilled on a carpet, couch, or chair that leaves a stubborn and unsightly stain. Many times the rest of the carpet or upholstery fabric is clean, and it would be silly to clean the entire fabric just to remove one ugly stain. Most janitorial supply firms sell special stain-removing kits along with directions for their use. With such a kit, a service can advertise a special stain-removal service. For this one could very well charge $20 for a job that takes only 15 minutes to complete. Although it may seem high, many people would rather pay $20 to have a stain removed than pay for a complete cleaning job that could run well over $100.

Mobile Car-washing Service

Although automobile cleaning does not directly come under the category of janitorial maintenance, it is a form of cleaning maintenance and so will be discussed here.

Many people wash their cars once a week. This is especially true in snow areas where it is important to wash off the corrosive road salt that accumulates on automobiles.

It costs a car owner approximately $2.50 to have his or her car washed in a stationary commercial car wash. In addition it is a time-consuming process to find a car wash and then wait in line for servicing. This presents many potential income-producing possibilities for individuals owning mobile car-washing equipment. The equipment is taken to parking lots and garages to clean people's cars while they are at work. This system works as discussed in the following paragraphs.

The approximate cost of a mobile car-washing unit is about $3,000. The price is broken down as follows: $1,500 for the basic unit which includes a pumping system, hot water heater, electrical connections, and a detergent tank; $1,000 for a generator; and $500 for a 200-gallon water tank if there are no water facilities on the premises. Also needed is a van or pickup truck to transport the unit to various cleaning locations.

The owner and operator of the equipment goes to large

office buildings, factories, and any large institution where all employees use the same parking facility and arranges with as many people as possible to wash their cars while they are parked in their usual parking spaces. This is usually done on a weekly basis. It takes approximately ten minutes to wash a car with the equipment described. A typical fee for a car is $1.00 to $1.50. This can add up to a tidy sum of money at the end of the day.

Office building employees are not the only source of revenue in this type of business. New and used car lots usually wash every car on the lot on a weekly basis in order to make them look attractive to potential buyers. This is quite a chore for most automobile dealers. Either they have to transport each car to a commercial car wash or hire a maintenance crew to handle the cleaning requirements on the lot. An individual with a mobile car-washing unit can contract with many automobile dealers to handle their cars on a weekly basis. More cars can be handled per hour on this basis than in a commercial parking facility as all the operator has to do is to go right down every row of cars washing one after the other. In this type of mass-cleaning operation it takes only about five minutes to wash each car.

Other potential customers of such a service are cab companies, police departments, trucking companies, and owners of mobile homes. Naturally, more money has to be charged for trucks and mobile homes.

In large cities the yellow pages of the telephone book can direct you to this type of equipment. Look under the heading of "Car-Washing Equipment." If there are no such distributors, go to the public library and look in the *Thomas Register* or a similar directory under Car-Washing Equipment Manufacturers. There you will find practically every manufacturer of this equipment in the country listed along with their addresses. If you have any trouble finding this information, ask the librarian for assistance. Write to numerous manufacturers for information on equipment and prices. Do not purchase any equipment until you have contacted several manufacturers to shop for the best deal. Before purchasing a unit, it is a good idea to ask for the names and addresses of other people who have purchased the same unit and then contact them by mail or phone to ask for their comments on the equipment that you plan to purchase.

As you can see, even the running of a janitorial service can allow someone to be creative; it can provide the chance for independence and the opportunity to make a sizable income by using ingenuity and hard work.

FILM SHOWING

Almost every week in every community in the country, various types of social, business, religious, and civic organizations hold meetings. In addition to discussing activities intrinsic to the functioning of the organization or club, most organizations like to provide a form of entertainment for its members. This entertainment should be informative and interesting. Very often guest speakers are used to provide such entertainment. However, sometimes guest speakers are hard to get, or when obtained they may be very expensive and very often boring to the audience. There is an ideal solution to this—a solution that you can profit from. In lieu of guest speakers informative and entertaining movies can be shown. They can be obtained free of charge and shown with your own movie projector.

There are movies available on almost every subject matter imaginable. What is more, as mentioned, they can usually be obtained free of charge. Many types of athletic organizations, industrial associations, and manufacturing organizations produce public relations films informing the public of the functions of these organizations and associations. These films are made to promote the image and activities of such groups. The organizations making these films are only too happy to allow various groups to view them at no expense. Most public libraries, in addition to books, also contain films covering a wide variety of subjects. These films, too, can be obtained free of charge. There is one stipulation, however; most organizations providing free films for viewing do not want the viewers to be charged an admission fee for seeing them. Therefore, the operator of a *film-showing business* must be careful not to charge for the film per se; rather the operator merely points out to all parties that the charge is for the use of the projector and the labors involved in traveling to the viewing site and operating the projector.

Having your own projector and knowing how to operate it are the only requirements in entering this field. The personnel of the store where you buy your projector can usually instruct you in this task in approximately a half hour's time. This can be supplemented by the owner's manual which comes with every projector sold. If you buy a used projector, write to the manufacturer for the owner's manual, giving the model number.

FEES AND EQUIPMENT COSTS

The cost of a good 16-mm sound projector is approximately $750 new and $500 used. It is feasible to charge from $30 to $50 a session for the use and operation of the projector. Although it may not be feasible to depend on this type of service for a full-time income, it can provide the operator an excellent part-time income. It is very possible to add an extra $100 a week to the family income in the providing of such a service. A film-showing service is also ideal for a husband and wife team. When the volume of business warrants it, it may be practical to purchase an additional projector so that both spouses can provide viewing services to two different organizations on the same night. In this manner, a rather large income can be accumulated.

FILM SOURCES

When starting a service, it is advisable first to research what types of films are available to you and then to contact every organization in the community to advise the staff and officers of your services. Just the reading of every local newspaper can provide a projectionist with the names and locations of many organizations. Sometimes the editorial office of a newspaper can provide a list of many local organizations. Again the telephone book's yellow pages is a good source of information under the heading of Organizations.

To find sources of films, libraries plus major manufacturing companies should be contacted. An excellent source of manufacturing companies is the *Thomas Register* found in most public libraries. In addition, the *Encyclopedia of Associations* listing the names and addresses of official associations representing all types of industries should be consulted. Just write to as many companies and associations as possible as to whether or not they have films available for loan.

Many major athletic associations provide free films covering highlights of many famous athletic contests in the sports represented by them.

The following are the names and addresses of the major athletic associations representing the major sports played in this country. Contact these associations for availability of films:

American Baseball League
280 Park Avenue
New York, New York 10017

National Baseball League
20 Montgomery Street
San Francisco, California 94104

National Hockey League
920 Sun Life Building
Montreal, Quebec, Canada H3B 2W2

National Basketball Association
2 Pennsylvania Plaza
Suite 2010
New York, New York 10001

National Football League
410 Park Avenue
New York, New York 10022

SPECIAL-PURCHASE BROKERAGE

When reading the newspaper you often notice that retail stores are advertising fantastically low prices on special sale merchandise. You see captions such as "Special Sale Due to Manufacturer's Closeout" or "We Have Obtained the Entire Stock of a Manufacturer Going Out of Business and Are Passing the Savings on to YOU." Did you ever wonder how these stores find out about the many sales situations of factories through the United States and even foreign countries? One way is through independent *special-purchase brokers* who make it their business to find out when certain manufacturers need to liquidate overstocked or slightly flawed merchandise known as seconds. This is not that difficult a task for the intelligent and aggressive individual. The fundamental requirement in this field is to be able to sell yourself and your service to both retail-store management and manufacturing companies. This attribute plus acting on the suggestions discussed in this section constitute the background for success in this enterprise.

It is easy to get a list of every product manufacturer in the country. The *Thomas Register,* found in most libraries, contains a list by product category of the names and addresses of almost every major manufacturer in the country. The industrious individual interested in going into the special-brokerage business can have stationery printed announcing his business and send letters to as many manufacturers as one pleases informing them of the service offered—that is, finding a customer for the merchandise that the manufacturer wants to dispose of. Letters are also sent to retail stores announcing that the broker has access to many types of sale items at very low prices. Thus the broker functions as the agent who brings buyer and seller together, for a fee. There are directories listing the names and locations of most major retail stores and chain headquarters throughout the country. Three representative ones are:

Fairchild's Financial Manual of Retail Stores
(published by Fairchild Publications)

Stores of the World Directory
(published by Newman Books Limited)

Sheldon's Retail Directory
of the United States and Canada
(published by Thelan, Sheldon and Marsar, Inc.)

Thelan's Resident Buyers
and Merchandise Brokers
(published by Thelan, Sheldon and Marsar, Inc.)

If these are not available in your library, the library may be able to obtain them on an interlibrary loan. In addition, many retail stores found in the telephone book's yellow pages can be a source of clients.

The astute broker can advertise the services in the various trade journals of different manufacturing industries and retail stores. Your local librarian can help you locate the names and addresses of the various journals. If not, contact the members of the industry or business for the journal names and addresses. The *Encyclopedia of Associations,* found in many libraries, may prove helpful in this task.

INCOME AND EMPLOYMENT OPPORTUNITIES

The broker will most likely be paid a commission based on a percentage of the sale transacted between the manufacturer and the retail store. The broker does not have to become involved in the financing or shipping of the merchandise. After a broker becomes established and personally known by the executives and heads of many manufacturing companies and retail stores, both manufacturers and retail outlets will personally seek him or her when in need of buying or selling services.

The income potential of this type of brokerage service is naturally dependent on the volume of business done. This type of business can be started for just the price of a business license, stationery, and postage fees. The meeting of many people from different industries and businesses can be very exciting and profitable.

DIRECT SELLING

A nonprofessional through *direct selling* has a chance to earn incomes equalling and even surpassing those of many professional people. Income opportunities are limited only to a person's drive and ambition, and there is no shortage of selling opportunities! Hundreds of distributors are searching for new salespersons.

What is direct selling? Direct selling is the selling of a product directly from the manufacturer or distributor to the consumer via an *independent sales agent*. It is the sales agent that this chapter is about.

What types of articles are sold through the direct-sales method? Just about any type of article used by private consumers or business organizations is suitable for direct sale. However, there are certain types of items that are exceptionally successful via the direct-sales technique. These include household articles, such as vacuum cleaners, sewing machines, brushes and brooms, and cleaning supplies; electrical appliances, such as radios, heaters, fans, refrigerator defrosters, and lamps; cosmetic and beauty items, such as facial makeup, beauty creams, lotions, hair brushes, hair dryers, and vibrators; cooking utensils, such as pots and pans, electric skillets, toasters, portable ovens, and food storage containers; jewelry items, such as bracelets, necklaces, rings, earrings, and watches; educational material, such as magazine subscriptions, books, and encyclopedias; and wearing apparel, such as shoes, stockings, shirts, uniforms, slacks, and dresses. These are but a few of the many items suitable for direct selling.

Many of these items are obtained by the salesperson directly from the manufacturer. This eliminates many mid-distribution wholesalers involved in retail store selling, therefore allowing the sales agent to make a sizable profit while still maintaining competitive prices. Furthermore, many products are of superior quality to their counterparts found in retail stores. The profit derived from these sales ranges from 20 to 100 percent of the selling price with the average being about 40 percent.

The sales orientation programs provided by many direct selling organizations plus your own aggressiveness and ingenuity essentially constitute the background required to suceed in this endeavor.

SOURCES OF SUPPLY

There are many sources to choose from when purchasing products for direct sale. First, there are numerous selling organizations that purchase large quantities of goods from manufacturers and then sell these goods to independent sales agents along with merchandising programs designed to assist the salesperson in doing a good selling job. Second, many manufacturers specialize in distributing their products through the sales agent directly. Clothing and shoe manufacturers do this quite often, allowing the sales agent to obtain orders via the manufacturer's catalogue or samples provided by the firm. The percent profit is usually lower than in other types of sales; however, the goods are purchased by the agent after the order is taken from the customer. In this manner no money is tied up in merchandise that sometimes may be unsalable.

Sales agents may obtain information on selling organizations and direct sales manufacturers by writing:

Direct Selling Association
1730 M Street, N.W.
Suite 610
Washington, D.C. 20036

Several periodicals specialize in informing independent sales agents of direct selling opportunities:

Opportunities in Selling
The Council on Opportunities in Selling, Inc.
630 Third Avenue
New York, New York 10017

Specialty Salesman Magazine
Specialty Salesman and Business Opportunities
307 North Michigan Avenue
Chicago, Illinois 60601

Salesman's Opportunity Magazine
John Hancock Center
Suite 1460
875 North Michigan Avenue
Chicago, Illinois 60611

In addition to the selling organizations and direct-sales manufacturers just discussed, there are many major manufacturers in the United States who sell through many channels. Their terms may be different from those of the direct-sales firms; however, the profit potential they provide may be greater and should not be overlooked. Most public libraries in this country have the *Thomas Register,* which lists all types of products manufactured in this country, by category, and then gives the names and addresses of the major manufacturers in each product category. Just browsing through this directory can give an imaginative sales agent ideas for items that may prove to be highly successful when sold by the direct-selling method. Some of the companies listed should be contacted to see if profitable selling arrangements can be made.

Before any buying decisions are made, each source of supply should be investigated as to the quality of the merchandise, prices to the sales agent, number of items required to be purchased in order to obtain a low price, length of time required for shipment, and selling aides and sales training programs offered by the supplier. Very often no one individual supplier will offer the best deal in every category mentioned. Therefore, it is up to the sales agent to compare prices, purchasing policies, and services of each supplier and then decide which supplier best meets the particular needs.

SELLING METHODS

There are several methods of direct sales. In all cases the seller must know the products well, be able to demonstrate them, if possible, and have definite lines of approach in mind. One of the most popular and very successful methods is the *door-to-door approach.* As the salesperson walks from house to house ringing doorbells, the first objective is to be accepted into the homes or apartments. One good way of doing this is immediately to give the home or apartment dweller a free sample of the product along with a brief verbal description of the value of the product. Once this is accomplished and the sales agent is inside the home, he or she can then demonstrate the product and inform the potential customer of the service the product can render and how it outperforms competing products.

If the prospect shows any interest, a good sales agent can often have the order form completed during the last stage of the sales talk. Where repeat sales are possible, such as with cosmetic and beauty aid items, a salesperson should keep notes on the visits in a record book or file cabinet. These records can serve as a reference guide to inform the salesperson on the most opportune time for a repeat sales call.

To be sure of a pleasant welcome at a customer's door, it is sometimes advisable to send postcards or make telephone calls to potential customers giving them a brief description of how the salesperson's product can serve them. In this manner sales appointments can be made, and the customer will be prepared to see and listen to the salesperson, thus improving the chances for a sale.

After a sale is completed, some direct salespersons obtain referrals. Referrals also assure a salesperson of entry into the potential customer's home. To induce a customer to refer the salesperson to other potential customers, the salesperson can offer the customer some extra samples or some free merchandise after a certain amount of sales are completed as a result of the original customer's referrals. In this manner a successful sales territory can keep mushrooming.

In recent years the *party-plan approach* to direct selling has been increasingly popular. Salespersons develop a list of prospective customers willing to invite a group of their friends and acquaintances to their homes for a selling party. Potential party givers can be found by using telephone directories or by placing advertisements in local newspapers.

Through offers of either free merchandise or sales commissions, salespersons can encourage women to invite friends to a "party" at which the salesperson demonstrates merchandise. The agent demonstrates the wares by using the items in the home. Some people who sell cooking utensils prepare meals using the line of cooking utensils they sell. Party demonstrators usually take orders at the parties or later by phone. This method makes it possible to have one time-consuming demonstration serve a number of prospects. Furthermore, hostesses usually invite those they believe will give orders so that their commissions or bonus gifts will be larger.

In recent years a number of salespersons representing fashion companies have sold women's apparel at fashion parties. The guests often model the agent's garments and then place orders for them.

The party-plan method of selling may also be applied to civic groups trying to raise money for worthwhile causes. Examples of these groups are local PTAs, veterans groups, lodges, church groups, etc. Because these organizations receive commissions on all orders taken, this sales approach appeals to the civic mindedness of prospective customers.

Direct selling is suitable for people of all ages who are willing to extend themselves in meeting new people and new challenges. It gives them a chance to make large amounts of money and to be in business for themselves. To be successful in direct selling, one does not have to be a "born" salesperson with a good gift of gab. The most important thing is to know your products well and be able to approach people in a direct and courteous manner.

In addition to products for sale to private individuals in their homes, there are many items suitable for sale to commercial business organizations. Most of these sales usually constitute a large volume of merchandise—net result, a large profit from one sale. An example of items suitable for sale to commercial institutions are advertising products. These include matchbooks, calendars, and other products imprinted with the client's name, address, and advertising message. Such products are used for distribution to the public to stimulate goodwill and promote business. They are ideal for restaurants, banks, and retail stores wanting to get their message across to the people.

Some sales agents specialize in purchasing industrial cleaners from manufacturers or janitorial supply houses and then selling them to gas stations, garages, factories, office buildings, schools, and colleges. This type of merchandise offers excellent opportunities for repeat business.

Uniforms are an item that should not be overlooked. People in many job and career fields wear them, including doctors, dentists, pharmacists, nurses, medical assistants and receptionists, drug store personnel, barbers, beauticians, and auto mechanics, just to name a few. These people are always looking for new uniform designs to enhance their appearance. They spend almost as much time in their uniform as they do in their street clothes. Therefore, they want to look just as well at work as they do during their leisure time.

The sales agent selling uniforms should go to every type of

office and business where people wear uniforms. Very often it is possible to get orders by showing representative samples of uniforms or pictures in illustrated catalogues. In order to insure proper fit, the salesperson will take a customer's measurements at the time the order is placed. To stimulate sales, the innovative salesperson might offer an extra service such as embroidering the customer's name and occupational title on the uniform. This can be accomplished easily with a simple sewing machine and a few embroidery lessons. Uniform sales are exceptionally suitable for party plans. Very often nurses and other medical personnel employed in a medical facility know each other, and there is always one person willing to throw a uniform party in a home or apartment.

As can be seen, the items suitable for direct sale are almost limitless. Once an individual develops a successful sales program, it is also possible to purchase merchandise in very large quantities at extra discounts, and then solicit other people to do the selling. In this manner a person can profit by developing a large sales organization directing and promoting the sales activities of others.

PROCESS SERVING

Practically every procedure performed in the legal system is carried out through legal documents. When a person is directed to appear in court he or she is notified through a *subpoena* or *summons* of the appearance required of him. The subpoena or summons is a written legal order directing a person to appear in court either to answer charges placed against him or her by another party or to act as a witness to an involved party in a legal proceeding.

Most people do not like being served papers ordering them

to appear in court to answer charges placed against them by another individual and often will avoid conventional methods of receiving messages or orders. Therefore, subpoenas are usually delivered and served by a special individual known as a *process server*. The process server works on behalf of attorneys and their clients to deliver and present subpoenas to the designated people. Very often when approaching the recipient, the server will pretend to be someone else other than a process server and, when face to face with the defendant, will then present the subpoena. After presenting the subpoena, the process server returns to the client's office to sign an "affidavit of service."

In many legal proceedings the outcome of a trial often depends upon the testimony given by witnesses representing the interests of either the plaintiff or the defendant. Therefore, it is important that witnesses to a dispute appear in court to give accurate testimony. To make sure that witnesses are properly notified of their obligations to appear in court, subpoenas are also issued to them via process servers. As can readily be seen, the services of the process server makes it very difficult for a defendant or witness to say that he or she was not notified.

Process servers also provide message services for attorneys, delivering important documents for filing in the courthouse or, when two offices are collaborating on a case, delivering important papers from one law office to another. These papers cannot be delivered through the mail because the possibility that they might be delayed or lost in the mails cannot be risked.

TRAINING REQUIREMENTS

There is no formal training required to become a process server. Being alert and conscientious are the most important assets. It might be advantageous, however, for an individual to work for a large process-serving firm for a while to gain experience before opening his or her own practice.

The purpose of becoming a process server is to go into private practice eventually as an independent server. Therefore, the general fees that an independent process server charges will be discussed.

For serving papers to defendants or witnesses, the general fee is a $3 service charge plus a rate of approximately 70¢ a mile for the distance traveled to deliver the papers. Because the defendant usually does not welcome a summons, the process server is sometimes required to stake out a defendant's residence waiting for the party to arrive or leave home. Sometimes the server may have to stake out a location for three full days waiting for the party to be served to appear. When staking out a location, the server may receive anywhere from $7 to $10 an hour for his or her efforts.

Once the defendant is properly served, he may not respond to the charges placed against him. This is known as defaulting. When finally brought to court, the defendant may claim that he was never served. In this case the process server has to appear before the judge, taking an oath and testifying that he or she did actually serve papers on the defendant. The judge then decides who is telling the truth. For time in court the process server will receive up to $25 an hour.

For message service work the server usually charges a low fee, as all that is entailed is the actual delivering of papers to the proper recipients without them trying to avoid the server. All in all, however, a process server in business privately can make a very attractive living. An advantage to this business is that there is very little expense in starting a service. About all one has to pay for is an answering service to handle the messages.

There are several steps you can take to start a successful subpoena business. You can advertise in the telephone book's yellow pages and in various legal publications in your local area. Sending direct mail to attorneys is another good method of keeping them abreast of your services. You might take attorneys out to lunch so that they can meet you personally and discuss the services that you can render. Some people with their own independent subpoena business promote a large clientele by joining social organizations that have many attorneys as members, such as tennis and golf clubs and various civic organizations.

Once a service grows, the originator can hire people to work for him or her and share the fees with them. Even though many people are employed and the fees may have to be shared, the accumulation of a lot of fees can provide the owner of the service with a very lucrative income.

CONSIGNMENT SELLING

How would you like to open a retail business without having to put up any money for inventory? This can be done. Moreover, there are many people who would be only too willing to supply you with inventory. Equally important, there are many people who would eagerly seek out your store as a place to shop for unique items. The store we are describing is a *consignment shop*.

All over the country amateur craftsmen and artists are creating original and high-quality handicraft items. Paintings, needlepoint, jewelry, ceramics, clay, marble, and metal sculpture, furniture, leather goods, wooden articles are only a few of the varied items handcrafted by people in their homes and workshops. Practically every night school program is filled with people from all walks of life learning every type of handicraft imaginable. These people are your suppliers.

Many people who create handicrafts, for reasons of personal satisfaction, would like to see their products for sale in the marketplace. It gives them a feeling of creative worth when they see a public demand for their efforts. Also, many people on limited incomes, if for no other reason, would like to have their products sold in order to add to their income.

These handicraft items usually cannot be sold to the typical retail store, for its merchandise is generally geared for the mass market. A smart entrepreneur can lease a vacant store in an area with heavy foot traffic and accept handcrafted items on a consignment basis. This means that the creator of the crafted article places the item with the owner of the shop to be sold in the store. When the item is sold, the shop owner shares in the purchase price of the item with its creator. Generally, the owner of the item and the shop owner agree on a general price range. The item is then sold by the shop owner at the highest possible price in the agreed-upon range. The percentage of the sale that is retained by the shop owner can vary widely depending upon the item sold and the gross profit derived from it. Generally, the shop owner will retain 30 to 40 percent of the sale price.

There is another side to the coin—the purchaser of these art objects. People are constantly searching for new and different gift items and decorating objects for their homes, apartments, and offices. Many articles mass-produced in manufacturing plants for large-scale retail distribution have that "mass-produced" look about them. An item handcrafted by a private individual generally possesses a unique air about it, which cannot be duplicated by the mass-produced item. This quality is what attracts the discerning customer. Thus, the consignment concept can draw a large clientele. Also, because of their originality, the items found in a consignment shop can usually carry a price tag that allows a great deal of profit for both the creator and shop owner.

HOW TO OPEN A SHOP

When opening a shop of this type, it should be relatively easy to find craftspeople to supply your store. First, you can contact every arts and crafts program in every high school and college in your area. From this source alone there should be numerous people only too willing to place their creations in your store. Advertising in handicraft magazines can also aid in soliciting the work of fine independent craftspeople. And, of course, the advertising of your services in local newspapers can produce an excellent response.

People are always looking for new and different places to shop. Some well-arranged and creative ads can induce a lot of people to go into a consignment shop in search for original and artistic items.

When starting a consignment shop, there are several fundamental principles that should be observed. First of all, do not accept any items that are poorly made or that are in poor artistic taste. Poorly-made items will give a bad image to a store and will hinder the sale of quality-made items. Also, keep in mind that even though you do not have to spend any money on the merchandise up for sale, care should be taken to see that they are properly displayed. The walls of the store should be properly painted, the shelving and other fixtures used to display the merchandise should be acceptable in appearance, and the store should be properly lighted. It is necessary to follow these principles in order to display the merchandise properly and to insure its quick sale at the highest possible price. A suitable display and sales atmosphere can be economically created with some imagination and creative improvisation.

INCOME OPPORTUNITIES

Making money is limited only to one's imagination. If you can provide an important service to society, you can profit from it without having to spend a lot of money in doing so. In the case of the consignment shop, you are providing a valuable service to both the creator and the consumer. There is no surer formula for success.

Professional fabric care is one of the nation's leading service industries. Sales of the textile maintenance industry totals over $6 billion dollars annually. The fabric-care industry allows an individual to set up his or her own sales shop without having to become involved with the actual dry-cleaning procedures. If desired, the actual cleaning of clothes offers some high-paying technical positions in dry-cleaning plants. These opportunities will be discussed later.

Many dry-cleaning plants do dry cleaning for many independently owned and operated dry-cleaning service stores located in neighborhood and commercial areas throughout a city or town. It requires very little room, financial investment, and training to open a dry-cleaning store.

An area of approximately 450 square feet is required to establish a reasonably sized service store. A small store in a busy shopping center makes an ideal location. Also, a dry-cleaning service concession operated in a large variety or discount store can prove very profitable. Approximately $5,000 is required for fixtures, comprised mainly of conveyers that automatically bring the cleaned clothes to the sales personnel when the customers come in for them. Because this is a service business, no money is needed for inventory. A store such as this is capable of grossing $1,100 a week. The typical profit made on dry-cleaned garments is approximately 50 to 55 percent, representing a potential gross profit of $550 a week. This figure can be increased as store expansion becomes warranted.

SOLICITING BUSINESS

It is possible for an operator to supplement the store business by purchasing or leasing a van and offering clients a pickup and delivery service. Naturally, more money has to be charged for such a service. This type of service is especially popular in higher income areas where the residents appreciate and are willing to pay for such extra services. Another possibility for an individual to start in the business is to go solely into the home pickup-and-delivery aspect of dry-cleaning servicing. All one needs is a van, an arrangement with a dry-cleaning plant and some salesmanship. Later on, if desired, the home service operator can also open a permanent retail location.

There are many other ways to promote a dry-cleaning business and make it grow. First, there is the pleasant personality of the sales personnel. This is a definite must. In a world that is turning colder and less personal, a friendly attitude by anyone is greatly appreciated and invites business. There are also extra services that an operator can offer, such as sewing on missing buttons and finding and returning items left in pockets. Every once in a while it is a good business practice to offer a special price sale on the cleaning of certain types of garments, such as ties or wool sweaters. It is also to your advantage for the plant that does your dry cleaning to be able to handle delicate cleaning jobs such as the cleaning of fur coats, fine silks, leather goods, and rugs and draperies. The store that can offer a full range of dry-cleaning services puts itself in a better position to prosper. Restaurants, hotels, medical facilities, and other organizations requiring the cleaning of employees' uniforms and other types of fabrics present excellent sources to solicit business from. The management of the dry-cleaning plant you choose to do business with will be able to give you advice and pointers on operating a successful shop. After all, their success depends on yours.

The growth potential in dry-cleaning servicing, as in so many other endeavors, is limited to only the amount of conscientious work one wants to put into it.

Dry-cleaning Plant Specialties

Clothes, rugs, and draperies are made from a huge array of natural and synthetic fibers. Many types of materials require special handling. Likewise, the many types of products that can stain a fabric require special techniques to remove them from the fabric. This has created a special job class in dry cleaning known as *spotting*. A good spotter can earn from $5 to $10 an hour, depending on the size of the operation worked in.

The dry cleaning of fabrics is a very involved procedure requiring the skills of many people. All dry cleaning plants require the services of a skilled *plant manager*. It is the duty of the manager to be familiar with all procedures in dry cleaning and possess the administrative ability to coordinate and supervise the work of all plant personnel into one smooth working operation. A good plant manager can earn from $15,000 to over $25,000 a year, depending on the size of the plant managed.

Many vocational and technical schools offer programs in dry-cleaning technology. The International Fabricare Institute conducts courses throughout the year in the general and specialized fields of fabric care. Beginners can enroll in the four-week general dry-cleaning course and the one-week spot-removal course. In addition, the institute offers many special programs and conferences.

For information regarding these programs, write:

International Fabricare Institute
Box 940
Joliet, Illinois 60434

JOB AND
CAREER PLACEMENT

This book has discussed many job and career opportunities. Not only is there a demand for many types of workers in every industry and career endeavor, but there is also a demand for skilled professionals to furnish the *job and career placement* requirements of both job seekers and employers.

The success of every business depends on the caliber of the

people employed in it. They must be able to fulfill the technical and professional skills required of a job as well as possess the desirable personality traits necessary to a smooth running organization. When a business organization has an opening for a particular type of worker, instead of taking up valuable time interviewing every applicant applying for the position, they often find it preferable to select applicants who have been screened by a good *employment agency.*

The employment agency serves in the role of broker between job seeker and employer. For the job seeker, the agency can help realize his or her dream of a career. For the employer, it can eliminate the nightmare of screening hundreds of ill-qualified job seekers and give assurance of well-placed employees long into the future. For the prospective agency owner, it can mean a growing business.

In providing its services the private employment agency brings together the job seeker who wishes to sell skills and the employer who is seeking these skills. When such a "marriage" occurs, the agency earns a fee, which is paid either by the employer or by the job applicant, or in certain situations is shared by both.

The methods and procedures discussed in this section, approximately one to two years of experience working for a successful agency, and your own desire and aggressiveness constitute the general background preferable to embarking on this endeavor.

Employment agencies have become very specialized. They are a marketplace for technical, professional, and executive jobs as well as clerical and semiskilled jobs.

In a small community an employment agency may serve all categories of employees and employers. In large cities an agency tends to serve a specialized segment of the work force and the employers of that work force. An exception, perhaps, is the very large employment agency that may have as many as twenty or thirty "desks" to serve every need.

Some agencies work only with a single skill, such as data

processing, advertising, or engineering. Most common is the "white-collar" agency, which places clerical, professional, technical, executive, and administrative personnel. Other divisions serve "blue-collar" workers (factory help, production workers), domestics, unskilled workers, babysitters, farmworkers, nurses, models, theatrical personnel, and teachers. Each is highly specialized and has its own methods of doing business. A person employed in a particular business, profession, or industry who possesses a good personality plus sales ability may find himself or herself particularly suited to starting an employment agency catering to the needs of the occupational field he or she is trained and experienced in.

OBTAINING JOB ORDERS FROM EMPLOYERS

Making a placement involves matching a job applicant and a job opening. There are a number of ways for a new agency to obtain job orders from employers. Once an agency has established good relations with several employers, the employers will generally contact the favored agency when they are in need of personnel. Some of the many sources of securing job orders are described briefly in the following paragraphs.

Newspaper Business Stories.   An article in a local newspaper may show that a company is planning an expansion, that it has just obtained a large contract, that it is introducing a new product or service, or that it is moving to larger quarters. This company may need new personnel. Phone the company and ask the personnel manager if you can be of service.

Business and Industry Conventions.   Many specialized types of businesses and industries hold annual or semiannual conventions. If possible, attend these conventions to contact important organizations to find out their employment needs and to make them aware of your services.

"Help Wanted" Advertisements in Newspapers. Very often a company will place its own ad in the local newspaper for a particular type of individual. If you have an applicant who fits this job, a call to the company that is advertising the job may lead to a placement. Such companies often are flooded with unqualified applicants after placing an open ad in the classified pages. Even if you do not place an applicant, you may have made a contact with a new potential employer-client. It is also a good idea to cut these ads out for future reference, as they identify a company's needs and may be able to provide employment for future applicants to your agency.

Directories. Directories are sources of company names from which you can solicit business. Some are national, some are local, and others cover special industries. Most public libraries contain directories of local, county, or state businesses. Most of these books give general information, such as company name, address, phone number, type of business, number of employees, sales volume, principal products, and names of key personnel. If you cross-index this information by industry, you can locate companies to which applicants with related experience can be referred. State directories are usually broken down into county and city sections, so you can determine just where in your state a company is located and concentrate in a specific section if desired.

Open Solicitation. Frequently an employer who is not necessarily looking for anyone to fill a job vacancy may create a new position if approached with an individual who may be able to improve or promote the business. If you have a job seeker who is very qualified for a particular company, do not hesitate to contact the firm and try to arrange for an interview.

Socializing. Job hiring can become a very personal business. It is always a good idea to join civic, social, and recreational clubs that may include many company executives among its membership. If a good social rapport can be developed with these individuals, they may be inclined to give your clients "first crack" when their companies have job openings. Once this relationship has been established, it is mandatory, of course, that the applicants referred to them are highly qualified for the position offered.

GETTING APPLICANTS TO FILL JOB ORDERS

Finding job applicants is as important to a new agency owner as obtaining job orders. There are a number of ways to achieve this, some of which follow.

Local Newspapers. The classified ads of local newspapers are by far the best source for advertising job openings for blue-collar personnel, skilled craftspeople, clerical and secretarial employees, and most lower salaried administrative workers.

Professional and Trade Publications. For specialized employment you may turn to publications published for specific types of businesses, industries, and professions. Almost every industry, technical specialty, or profession has a professional or trade journal read regularly by specialists in the field.

Institutional Ads. When operating an employment agency, it is important to keep the name and services of the agency in the public image. This will serve to induce future job seekers and employers to contact the agency when in need of employment services. Institutional ads should tell of the general quality and services of the agency without necessarily advertising any specific jobs. They can be placed in newspapers, the yellow pages of the telephone book, and professional and trade publications, as radio and TV spots, and on billboards.

GETTING THE APPLICANT AND EMPLOYER TOGETHER

All job applicants should be personally interviewed by you or one of your employment counselors. Do not refer anyone to an employer unless you are confident of his or her abilities. This practice will establish and preserve excellent relationships with your employer clients. Once you feel that an applicant possesses the requirements for a position, call the employer and arrange an interview for the applicant. It is not necessary for a representative of the employment agency to be present at the interview. However, a representative may act as an intermediary in getting the applicant and employer to come to terms on final salary and other compensations.

When the applicant and employer come to terms and the applicant is hired, the agency owner is entitled to his or her fee. The general fee schedules are discussed in the next section. It has become an increasingly common practice for the employer to pay the complete employment fee. If the employee leaves the job or is justifiably dismissed within ninety days of hiring, a portion of the fee is usually refunded to the employer.

INCOME OPPORTUNITIES

An employment agency may handle low-income employees, such as file clerks and typists, or it may place top executives earning $20,000 a year and more. The fees charged for services vary according to the annual salary derived from the job. The fees range from 7 to 20 percent of the annual salary of the job. In general, a job that pays from $5,000 to $7,000 a year earns the owner of the agency approximately 7 percent of the first year's earnings; a job that pays from $7,000 to $10,000 a year earns the owner of the agency approximately 10 percent of the first year's earnings; a job that pays from $10,000 to $15,000 a year will earn the agency approximately 11 to 15 percent of the first year's earnings; a job that pays from $15,000 to $20,000 a

356

year will earn the agency 15 to 20 percent of the first year's earnings; and jobs that pay over $20,000 annually generally earn the employment agency a flat 20 percent of the first year's earnings.

If the owner of the agency has employment counselors on the staff, they usually receive about 33 percent of the fee collected. It should be obvious that the owning of an employment agency, even working in one, can become very lucrative. In addition, it is interesting and challenging work. It is a field basically for the individual who is friendly, outgoing, inquisitive, and aggressive.

An employment agency is a service-type business where capital requirements to start may be very small. A modest office plus some clerical equipment can start the skilled individual in business.

For more information concerning this field, write:

National Employment Association
2000 K Street, N.W.
Washington, D.C. 20006

11

Professional Sales

The sale of real estate properties, investment securities, and insurance policies is being discussed under one general heading as each involves the selling of a professional service. Each field is extremely competitive. However, each allows the aggressive and intelligent individual the chance to earn large sums of money.

Although it is recommended, a college degree is not necessarily a criterion for becoming successful in these fields. In fact, fortunes have sometimes been made in these endeavors by high school dropouts. It is necessary, however, to become fully informed of all the facets of each field. This knowledge can be gained through company- and institution-sponsored training programs plus self-education on the part of the salesperson through night school programs and the reading of professional literature. The successful salesperson will use his or her academic knowledge of the field and adapt it to a winning sales program. People who can succeed in these areas, which make up the basic foundations of our economy, will always have a secure financial future.

The purchase of real estate, investment securities, and insurance policies is very complex. The salesperson who can properly guide a client through the maze of details involved in making transactions in these fields will generally accomplish more than a sale. In all probability he or she will gain a lifetime client in addition to referrals from satisfied clients.

No matter what we manufacture, we cannot manufacture more land. The activities we perform and the structures we build must be done on the existing land, and when a piece of property changes hands, a real estate agent is usually involved. As communities expand, vacant adjoining land becomes valuable. Conversely, land in vacated neighborhoods sometimes depreciates in value. However, this depreciation does not last long and property values go up if the land is utilized properly. In many instances, creative and futuristic planners and developers obtain areas of depressed land value to build new living and business quarters where functional architecture and attractive landscaping blend to provide an environment conducive to good living. The real estate agent who can keep his/her hand on the pulse of real estate activity can make a fortune.

As in real estate transactions, when a product or service is sold, it also has to be bought. This involves the securities or stock broker. The manufacture and sale of products and services yields billions of dollars annually in profit. Billions of dollars are required for the factories, equipment, and personnel to produce this profit. Entrepreneurs need the support of investors, both large and small, to put up the vast sums of money necessary for business ventures to prosper; conversely, individuals from all walks of life want to share in the profit created by these enterprises. This is accomplished through the sale of *shares of stock,* also known as *securities.* The sale of these securities, whether by the issuing company to an individual or by one individual to another, is conducted by a securities or stock broker. The broker who can keep his/her hand on the pulse of the investment world and give proper advice to clients can also make a fortune.

In today's society, with everything so expensive, the unexpected loss of almost anything could cause the owner extreme hardship. Insurance is a method by which people are protected fully or partially from losses by mutually sharing each other's potential risks. With such protection so necessary and complex, it takes a skilled and knowledgeable insurance agent to professionally guide a client with proper protection. People wishing to insure (protect) themselves against a particular loss purchase an insurance policy against that loss. The premiums they pay go to sustain any other policy owner or themselves when losses occur. The law of averages says that not everyone will incur a loss in any one insurance category. This allows a substantial share of the premiums to be utilized by the insurance companies as profit and eventual investment in other profit-making ventures, such as real estate development. These insurance companies are willing to pay sizeable commissions to the agent who can sell these protective policies. When the insurance agent can wisely guide his or her client in proper protection, the client becomes secure and the agent prospers.

The next three sections will discuss these three fields in more detail.

REAL ESTATE
AGENT AND BROKER

The selling of a piece of property may range from a modest $20,000 home to a luxurious $200,000 mansion. It may involve the sale of a $500,000 apartment house or a $5 million office building.

Property is stationary. It cannot be moved to a common marketplace for sale to the public. Furthermore, only certain categories of people are interested in or are able to purchase certain classes of properties. It takes a special individual to find out what properties are for sale, obtain a contract (listing) to sell the property, and then find a qualified buyer to purchase the property. This can become a very involved task. However, the individual who can perform such tasks can make a great deal of money doing so (approximately 5 percent of the sales price of each sale). These individuals are known as real estate agents or brokers. A *real estate broker* is the person licensed to oversee the complete transaction of a piece of property. A *real estate agent* works independently under a broker and shares the sales commission with the broker. The agent usually receives 60 percent of the sales commission with the broker receiving the remaining 40 percent. If the agent has a broker's license and is in business privately, he or she can retain the full sales commission.

TRAINING REQUIREMENTS

A real estate agent must be licensed by the state. State requirements vary, but usually an agent's license requires three months of training to become knowledgeable enough to pass most state real estate agent's exams. After approximately two years of experience in sales, plus further academic training of approximately one year's duration (varies from state to state), an agent is eligible to take the exam for licensing as a real estate broker. If the broker owns his or her own agency, the broker can handle the complete real estate transactions, thereby retaining the full sales commission, or solicit real estate agents to work under his or her broker's license, thereby obtaining 40 percent of each of their sales commissions. The broker who builds up a successful sales staff can earn an income of up to $100,000 a year and even more.

Agents can work for only one brokerage firm at a time. Many good brokerage firms offer agents excellent sales training programs to develop their sales abilities to their maximum potential. A well-run organization can bring huge profits to both the sales agents and the broker.

Intelligence, sociability, patience, and good humor are assets for the person considering real estate.

SALARY AND EMPLOYMENT OPPORTUNITIES

Inasmuch as most real estate selling jobs are paid via sales commissions, it is difficult to assess definite salaries for agents and brokers. Some agents choose to work only part time. Since a broker's office has to pay a sales agent a commission on sales only and not a fixed base salary, almost any broker's office is willing to solicit the services of an agent.

As previously mentioned, selling properties is extremely competitive. However, there are ways for the ambitious and industrious individual to beat the competition and prosper. First, know every facet of real estate law and each transaction. Just assuring a potential client that you can properly guide him or her through the vast paper work and regulations involved in a real estate transaction can often secure a sales agreement with the client. Advertising in newspapers that you have listings and potential customers of different types of properties can lead to both sellers and purchasers contacting you to avail themselves of your services. The joining of community and civic groups can contribute a lot to making people aware of you and your talents in real estate. The beginning can be tough. However, once an individual successfully handles a number of transactions, he or she soon develops a reputation for getting things sold and eventually both buyers and sellers seek that agent out when in need of real estate services.

Brokers and agents not only sell real estate, but sometimes also rent and manage properties, make appraisals, and develop new building projects. They may provide sources of financial assistance to qualified buyers and aid in such details as arranging for title insurance. Some agents and brokers may become involved in finding site locations for retail store chains and business franchises. Others may become involved in real estate syndication. Once an individual becomes licensed as an agent or broker he or she can function in many phases of real estate operation or just specialize in one or several aspects of the profession. The following are some brief descriptions of some of the many specialties in the real estate field.

Leasing Agent

Property owners who desire to rent or lease their property, both residential and commercial property, may use a *leasing agent* or *broker* to handle the details. After finding a suitable tenant, the agent or broker receives approximately 6 percent of the total lease agreement. For instance, if an agent obtains a tenant to assume a three-year lease for a retail store location at a monthly rental of $500, this adds up to $18,000 for the total lease period of three years. The agent's commission for the lease amounts to $1,080. This, of course, is shared with the agent's broker on a 60/40 percent basis, still leaving over $600 for the agent. Again, if the lease is handled by an independently employed broker, he or she keeps the full commission.

Property Manager

Many people purchase apartment houses and office buildings for investment purposes. They want to profit from the rental fees and possibly from the eventual resale of the property. However, they do not want to participate in the actual management of the property. This involves selecting the tenants, arranging leases, collecting the rents, taking care of tenant needs, and seeing that the property is properly cleaned and that necessary repairs are performed promptly. Such owners hire a *property manager* or a *property management company* to care for the property. Naturally, the owner pays for all of the business and maintenance expense, but the manager or management company spares the owner from having to become personally involved in such details. For this service the property manager or management company usually charges from 3 to 6 percent of the total rental volume for services, with a minimum fee of $200 per month.

Appraiser

The seller of property naturally wants to receive maximum compensation without being priced out of the sales market. To obtain a realistic sales figure for the property, the owner or his or her agent or broker will obtain the services of a professional *real estate appraiser* to compute the best possible sales price. A good appraiser must be aware of the quality variations of different types of building materials and keep abreast of the market prices of similar types of structures in similar areas. One should also be knowledgeable of the potential increase in value of the property being handled. Buyers also may obtain the services of an appraiser to make sure they do not overpay. This is especially true for investors who buy property only to resell it after it has increased in value.

The role of the competent appraiser is vital to the real estate industry. Therefore, he or she is well compensated for services. A good appraiser can earn anywhere from $20,000 to $100,000 a year for his or her services. Real estate appraisal can be learned in many part-time college programs. Academic courses must be supplemented by practical experience. To be an appraiser, one does not necessarily have to have an agent's or broker's license.

Site Locator

Very often a real estate agent will become familiar with the location needs of a particular business or industry and will specialize in finding sites for branch operations of such a business or industry. If the *site locator* obtains the listing in addition to arranging the sale, he or she receives the full sales commission. If the listing is held by another agent or brokerage firm, the sales commission is usually shared between the listing agent and the purchasing agent.

Loan Counselor

The sale of a piece of property can involve thousands, even millions of dollars. Few people or organizations have such sums of money at their disposal. Therefore, most property purchases must be accompanied by real estate loans. Sometimes it is not feasible to obtain these loans through banks. There are people and groups of people who have capital to invest and desire to loan it to worthwhile real estate enterprises for a sum of money known as interest. *Loan counselors* specialize in finding lenders for qualified borrowers and receive a fee from the borrower for this service. Usually it is a percentage of the loan.

Real Estate Syndicator

Often an individual astute in the financial potentials of real estate operations will gather a number of investors together to purchase one or more properties through a partnership, corporation, or trust. The group is known as a *real estate syndicate*. After the properties generate a profit through rentals or subsequent resale, the *syndicator* (the organizer of the syndicate) will share in the profits for his or her foresight and skills in putting the "package" together. This allows a knowledgeable person to profit in real estate growth without having to put up any of his or her own capital.

Title Officer

Whenever a piece of property is sold, the purchaser must be sure that the property is completely owned by the sellers and that there are no liens or encumbrances attached to the property. In other words, the purchaser must be guaranteed that the title is clear. This function is performed by a *title officer* who works for a title insurance company. The title officer traces the ownership of the property back through its previous owners to make sure that it is eligible to be sold by the present seller. After this title search is completed, the title officer writes an insurance policy protecting the new owner from loss if the title is imperfect.

This type of work does not require an agent's or broker's license and can be learned through on-the-job training in the employ of a title insurance company. There is always a demand for title officers. The pay scale is from $1,500 to $1,600 a month.

Escrow Officer

The sale of a piece of real estate can be very complex. The purchaser must submit a deposit, the seller must show proof of ownership, all liens against the property must be submitted, the purchaser must submit financing arrangements, lien holders (people who are owed money from the property) must receive the money due them, and real estate ordinances, such as building inspections, must be satisfied. The handling of all papers and funds connected with a real estate transaction requires an individual skilled in these matters to perform the transaction promptly and accurately. This individual is known as an *escrow officer*. The escrow officer is a disinterested third party authorized to act as the agent of both parties in a transaction. When all the necessary documents are deposited with the escrow officer, the transaction is complete, and the property officially changes hands.

An escrow officer does not need an agent's or broker's license. The skills necessary can be learned through on-the-job training in the escrow department of a bank or escrow company. There is always a demand for an individual possessing these important skills. The average pay scale for an experienced escrow officer is from $1,100 to $1,600 a month.

For information on training programs in the various fields of real estate, write:

National Association of Realtors
Department of Education
155 East Superior Street
Chicago, Illinois 60611

SECURITIES BROKER
(STOCK BROKER)

Today there are few large business organizations that are wholly owned by one individual. In most cases the ownership is distributed among many people who own *shares* of the business. These shares are in the form of stock certificates, also known as *securities*. Individuals can readily purchase or sell these securities through a registered *stock* or *securities broker* employed by brokerage firms. These firms are members of one or several of the major stock exchanges in this country. Two of the largest of such exchanges are the New York Stock Exchange and the American Stock Exchange in New York City.

The seller or purchaser of a stock instructs the broker at what price he or she is willing to sell or purchase a share or shares of stock. As in the sale of any other commodity, when a price is agreed upon by both seller and buyer, a "market price" results. The factors determining market price of a company's stock are the assets of the company, its earnings, and its projected profit picture. The broker transacts selling and buying procedures through agents representing the brokerage firm on the floor of the stock exchange with which the particular stock is listed.

The stock broker earns a commission on each stock transaction. The commission is represented by a percentage of the selling price of the stock. This percentage varies with the type and amount of each sale. The broker may handle individual investors or the investment needs of large corporations, pension and investment funds, and banks.

In order to attract a good clientele, the stock broker must be able to give accurate advice on what stocks to buy and which ones to sell. To do this properly, the broker must keep abreast of market conditions, the local and national economy, trends in many industries, and the financial condition of many companies. Many brokers specialize in stocks of just one industry.

Once a broker has an established clientele, he or she may concentrate on serving this clientele and limit new accounts just to individuals with large sums of money to invest.

TRAINING REQUIREMENTS

Because a stock broker must be well informed about economic conditions and trends, a college education is increasingly important but not always required. Almost all states require persons who sell securities to be licensed. State licensing requirements may include passing an examination and furnishing a personal bond. In addition, stock brokers usually must register as representatives of their firms, according to regulations of the securities exchanges where they do business or the National Association of Securities Dealers (NASD). Before beginners can qualify as registered representatives, they must pass the Securities and Exchange Commission's (SEC) General Securities Examination or examinations prepared by the NASD. These tests measure the prospective representative's knowledge of the securities business.

Most employers provide training to help workers meet the requirements for registration. In member firms of all major exchanges the training period is at least six months.

SALARY AND EMPLOYMENT OPPORTUNITIES

As in the sales of many service-oriented fields, a stock broker is paid on commission. Therefore, incomes will vary. However, it is reported that good brokers can earn anywhere from $20,000 to $100,000 annually depending on the volume of business they transact.

Employment of securities salespeople will expand as economic growth and rising personal incomes increase the funds available for investment. The activities of investment clubs, which enable small investors to make minimum monthly payments toward the purchase of securities, also will contribute to the demand for securities brokers. Growth in the number of institutional investors, such as insurance companies, banks, pension funds, and college and university endowment funds, will also increase the need for knowledgeable securities dealers.

INSURANCE AGENT AND BROKER

The high cost of replacing material possessions, obtaining medical care, and paying financial awards decreed in lawsuits requires everyone to obtain insurance protection on their personal and business property, medical needs, and liability protection for damage they might do to other parties. *Insurance agents* and *brokers* sell policies that protect individuals and businesses against future losses and financial pressures. They help plan financial protection to meet the special needs of a customer's family, advise about insurance protection for an automobile, home, business, or other property, or help a policyholder obtain settlement of an insurance claim.

Agents and brokers usually sell one or more of the three basic types of insurance—life, property/liability, and health. Life insurance policies pay survivors when a policyholder dies; they also may provide retirement income, funds for the education of children, and other benefits. Property/liability insurance protects policyholders from financial losses as a result of automobile accidents, fire and theft, or other hazards. Health insurance policies offer protection against the costs of hospital and medical care or loss of income due to illness or injury. Many agents also offer securities such as mutual fund shares.

An insurance agent may work exclusively as a salesperson for one company or act as an independent agent authorized to represent one or more insurance companies. Brokers, on the other hand, are not under contract with any one company; they place policies directly with the company that best meets a client's needs. Otherwise, agents and brokers do much of the same kind of work.

Agents and brokers spend most of their time discussing insurance policies with prospective and existing customers. Much time is spent planning insurance programs that are tailored to a prospect's individual needs. Some agents specialize in just one type of insurance. Others may specialize in group sales to various businesses and organizations comprising many employees in need of various types of insurance protection.

TRAINING REQUIREMENTS

Although helpful, a college education is not a prerequisite for many insurance selling jobs. Basic intelligence plus a desire to succeed is definitely a requirement, however. All agents and brokers must be licensed in the states where they plan to sell insurance. In most states licenses are issued only to applicants who pass written examinations covering insurance fundamentals and the state insurance laws. New agents usually receive training at insurance company home offices or at the agencies where they will work. Beginners sometimes attend company-sponsored classes to prepare them for the examination. Others study on their own and accompany experienced agents when they call on prospective clients.

Agents and brokers can broaden their knowledge of the insurance business by taking courses at colleges and universities and attending institutes, conferences, and seminars sponsored by insurance organizations.

Information concerning career potentials and training programs as life insurance agents can be obtained by writing:

Institute of Life Insurance
227 Park Avenue
New York, New York 10017

Life Insurance Agency
Management Association
170 Sigourney Street
Hartford, Connecticut 06105

National Association
of Life Underwriters
1922 F Street, N.W.
Washington, D.C. 20006

Information about sales training in life and health insurance is available from:

The Life Underwriter Training Council
1922 F Street, N.W.
Washington, D.C. 20006

Information about property/liability agents and brokers can be obtained from:

Insurance Information Institute
110 William Street
New York, New York 10038

National Association
of Insurance Agents
85 John Street
New York, New York 10038

SALARY AND EMPLOYMENT OPPORTUNITIES

Most agents are paid a commission based on the premiums of the policies they sell. The size of the commission depends on the type and amount of insurance sold and whether the transaction is a new policy or a renewal. After a few years an agent's commissions on new policies and renewals may range from $10,000 to $30,000 annually. A number of established and highly successful agents and brokers earn more than $50,000 a year, with some earning as much as $100,000 annually.

Many new agents start their careers by direct-mail advertisements and phone calls to potential customers. These customers may be recent high school and college graduates, newcomers to a community, newlyweds, professional and business people establishing new practices and businesses, and other established people in the community who probably need additional insurance due to changing times and personal changes in their lifestyles.

As personal incomes rise and life expectancy increases, more families will depend on life insurance for educational funds for their children and for retirement income. Expansion in industrial plants and equipment plus a growing number of major consumer purchases, such as homes and automobiles, will stimulate sales of property/liability insurance. Rising medical costs will increase sales of health insurance. The intelligent and aggressive individual can take advantage of the insurance needs of today's society.

12

Fields Requiring a Four-year College Degree

For all its dynamic growth, the computer field is still in its infancy. Opportunities for advancement are limited primarily by an individual's skill, educational background, ability to communicate, and personal drive.

Today, over 100,000 businesses use computers or computer services. These organizations employ hundreds of thousands of systems analysts, programmers, console operators, keypunch personnel, and technicians who are indispensable in the processing of information.

The two essential ingredients in electronic data processing (EDP) are (1) the computer and computer-related equipment, known as "hardware" and (2) the assembled instructions, or "software," which enable the computer system to perform its task. In other words, the hardware is the machine or computer itself, and the software are the programs that are inserted into the computer. The programs are interchangeable. Many computers are capable of accepting many programs. By this means one computer can service many businesses or a number of different data-processing requirements of one company. The computer makes these different programs (software) operational just as a tape recorder makes different recording tapes operational.

Digital computers perform the most complicated mathematical calculations in a phenomenally short time; for example, some add two large numbers in less than one millionth of a second. An electronic computer can solve a mathematical program requiring millions of calculations in seconds.

Computers perform other functions, such as making comparisons, bringing data together, and choosing between alternatives. Information stored in them is retrieved as needed. Large computers execute a hundred different mathematical, logical, or data-processing operations.

Many business organizations use computers for inventory control. For example, whenever merchandise is brought into an organization, the items brought are coded and inserted into the computer. Whenever these items are shipped out of the firm, the items leaving are recorded into the computer. Thus, whenever an executive of the firm wants to know exactly what is on hand for sale or manufacturing purposes, the computer can give the answer in seconds.

Computers, however, are not magical devices. They cannot think. They must be given careful, detailed, simple instructions. Computers can only give answers that have already been programmed (put into them) by human beings. The main function the computer performs is to give these answers rapidly and accurately.

Basically, a computer accepts data, performs calculations according to instructions (programs), and then provides the results of the calculations.

Computers need people to enable them to function. *Systems analysts* are needed to develop methods of using the machines. They work with all types of businesses and organizations in finding out what their needs are and then decide what questions should be asked of the computer and what answers are needed. *Programmers* prepare the instructions that tell the computer how to handle information and solve problems. It might be said that the programmers insert the answers or formulas for getting answers into the computer. In many situations the work of the analyst and programmer overlap, and very often one person will perform both tasks.

Machine operators feed data into the computers and control their operations. *Keypunch operators* prepare cards that give the computer certain items of information.

Computer service technicians install, maintain, and repair computers and auxiliary equipment. *Sales personnel* are needed to sell computers, auxiliary equipment, and software systems. All of these functions and career opportunities will be discussed. Some have already been considered in the section on electronic computer operating personnel in Chapter 4.

Additional information on career opportunities and training programs may be obtained by writing:

American Federation of
Information Processing Societies
210 Summit Avenue
Montvale, New Jersey 07645

Data Processing
Management Association
505 Busse Highway
Park Ridge, Illinois 60068

Association for Computing Machinery
1133 Avenue of the Americas
New York, New York 10036

Systems Analyst

Many essential business functions and scientific procedures rely on the work of *systems analysts*. Their job is to plan the activities needed for processing data to solve business, scientific, or engineering problems. They use computers to perform these functions.

Systems analysts begin an assignment by first determining the exact nature of the data-processing problem. The analyst structures the problem logically, identifies all of the data needed, and specifies how they are to be processed. Analysts may use various techniques in their work such as cost accounting, sampling, and mathematical model building. After analyzing the problem and devising a data-processing system, they prepare charts and diagrams that describe how the system operates.

Analysts usually recommend which data-processing equipment is to be used and prepare instructions for programmers. They also translate final results into terms that customers can understand.

Data-processing problems are so varied and complex that many systems analysts specialize in one area. For example, analysts who work for scientific or engineering organizations may develop systems to determine the flight path of a space vehicle. Others develop business systems for functions such as accounting, forecasting sales, or marketing research.

Some analysts improve systems already in use. They may develop better procedures or adapt existing systems to handle additional or different types of data. Others do research to devise new methods of systems analysis. These analysts usually have mathematical or engineering backgrounds.

TRAINING REQUIREMENTS

There is no universally acceptable way of preparing for work in systems analysis. Some employers prefer applicants who have a bachelor's degree and experience in mathematics, science, engineering, accounting, or business. Because computers are now being used in every branch of business, industry, science, and medicine, anyone trained in these fields can adapt their training to becoming a computer analyst specializing in these fields.

A beginner can learn to use electronic data-processing equipment on the job or can take special courses offered by employers, computer manufacturers, or colleges. An increasing number of junior colleges offer full two-year college curricula in business data processing.

A number of private electronic data-processing schools appear to offer valid programs and undoubtedly are providing worthwhile preliminary training in business applications, programming, computer operations, and related areas. When choosing a private school, use the rules suggested in the introduction of this book.

SALARY AND EMPLOYMENT OPPORTUNITIES

The average salary for a computer analyst ranges from $15,000 to $25,000 a year and rises as one's experience and proficiency increase.

Employment of systems analysts is expected to grow very rapidly through the mid-1980s as data-processing applications in business, industry, and science expand. Among the factors expected to contribute to a growing demand for systems analysts is the extension of computer technology to small businesses and the growth of computer centers to serve individual clients for a fee.

Systems analysts are employed by industries possessing their own computer departments, by electronic data-processing centers that perform data services for organizations and businesses that do not own their own computer facilities, and by government and university systems.

As each industry grows, so will computer applications and the people who help devise these applications.

Computer Programmer

An electronic computer can process masses of information with great speed and accuracy, but the machine cannot think for itself. Data-processing *programmers* supply the element of intelligence to electronic computers. Their instructions (the program) provide the directions that enable computers to perform a given task. The programmer's job is to prepare step-by-step instructions for the computer to follow.

Before a computer can process a problem, exact and logical steps for its solution must be worked out. A systems analyst (previously discussed) usually does this work. An analyst may work alone or together with the programmer in conducting this preliminary analysis. Frequently, experienced programmers also conduct the preliminary analysis; they are known as *programmer-analysts.*

When this preliminary job is finished, it is the programmer who prepares detailed instructions that tell the machine how to process the data. The way that a program is written depends on the nature of the problem and the type of equipment to be used. The mathematical calculations involved in billing a firm's customers, for example, are different from those required in scientific work. A business programmer works on instructions that tell the computer how to bill customers or make up a payroll.

First the programmer decides what company records contain the information needed to prepare the documents. Next he or she makes a flow chart or diagram showing the computer what order to follow in doing each step. From the flow chart the programmer writes detailed instructions telling the machine exactly what to do with each piece of information. He or she also prepares an instruction sheet for a computer operator to follow when the program is run.

The final step in programming is a check to be sure that the programmer's instructions are correct and will produce the desired information. This check is called "debugging." The programmer uses a sample of the data to be processed to review what will happen as the computer follows instructions. Instructions are changed if any errors appear and then a trial run is made.

Because of the differences in the work, many programmers specialize in either business or scientific applications. Some, known as systems or software programmers, write instructions that tell the computer how to schedule jobs and when to switch from one to another. Although a simple program can be written in a few days, one designed to produce many different kinds of information may require a year or more to complete. Often, several programmers at different levels of responsibility work together under an experienced programmer supervisor.

TRAINING REQUIREMENTS

Just as in the case of systems analysts, there are several avenues open in becoming a computer programmer. A degree from a four-year college is one possibility. Then there are many junior colleges offering excellent two-year training programs in computer programming. Special courses in computer work are available to supplement experience in a field such as accounting or inventory control.

Organizations that use computers for science and engineering prefer college graduates with degrees in the physical sciences, math, engineering, or computer science.

Sometimes computer manufacturers or data-processing organizations will train people in programming, providing that the individuals show an aptitude for logical thinking and exacting analysis. Ingenuity and imagination are particularly important when programmers have to solve problems in new ways.

There are some good private schools offering courses in computer programming. However, these schools should be checked with the Better Business Bureau in the areas where they exist, the accrediting societies, and other school checking procedures mentioned at the beginning of this book.

Large organizations who have their own computing center will very often promote ambitious and industrious clerical personnel to programmers through company-sponsored training programs.

SALARY AND EMPLOYMENT OPPORTUNITIES

Programmers' salaries generally average between $14,000 and $22,000 a year. As their proficiency increases, many programmers can advance to become systems analysts.

As in the case of systems analysts, the demand for well-trained programmers will increase with the expanded applications of computers to science, business, and industry.

Computer Sales Representative

The building of computers and the auxiliary equipment is one of the most progressive industries in our society. New applications of electronic data processing to science, business, industry, and medicine are brought about by the development and building of new computers and computer components. The production of this equipment represents tremendous sales and income potentials to the sales-minded individual possessing a background in computers.

The *computer sales representative* must be well trained in both marketing and computer applications. Sales personnel who specialize in business systems must be familiar with all phases of company organization and the details of modern management. This is a large area to cover. In fact, many sales representatives specialize in a particular industry or scientific applications.

TRAINING REQUIREMENTS

Careers in computer sales are open primarily to college graduates and those who already have experience in allied technical or management fields. Degrees may be in business administration, in engineering or in another science discipline, or in liberal arts. Most computer manufacturers give intensive sales training courses to their beginning salespeople—forty to fifty weeks of paid training, and sometimes more.

SALARY AND EMPLOYMENT OPPORTUNITIES

Computer sales representatives generally earn a base salary plus a commission on the computers or auxiliary equipment they sell. This method of payment can provide a successful representative with an income of from $20,000 to $50,000 per year and more. It should be mentioned however, that if salespeople cannot earn at least $20,000 a year for themselves, they are of little value to themselves or their company, and their employment would probably be terminated.

More and more, many businesses and small industries are turning to computer systems to improve their business operations. This can provide tremendous sales opportunities for the aggressive salesperson who keeps abreast of scientific advances in this field.

HOSPITAL ADMINISTRATOR

As you read through this book, you will notice the many occupations available in the medical profession. Most of these occupations involve procedures carried out in hospitals and large medical centers. Everything that goes on in a hospital, from the performance of the most delicate operations to the cleaning of the floors, must be under the supervision of one chief executive. This person is the *hospital administrator.* It is the responsibility of the administrator to coordinate all of the activities in a hospital into one smooth working organization. Naturally, the administrator cannot supervise each activity personally; but it is possible to oversee each activity through department heads and other supervisory personnel who are subordinate.

The administrator is responsible for developing an effective team of physicians, nurses, dietitians, pharmacists, housekeepers, engineers, and the many others who work in the hospital. At the same time the administrator is responsible for having adequate supporting facilities, services, and equipment available for the hospital staff and patients. In reality, a hospital administrator holds a community trust; it is an obligation to see that the hospital provides an acceptable health services program.

The administrator must be well informed about all hospital functions and services and equipped to select and supervise the staff members who are in charge of all its departments, being able to cope with the special situations and emergencies that arise daily in every hospital.

Administrators of hospitals must be excellent business people. They are given a budget by the hospital board of directors and must be able to work within it to utilize every dollar to supply a maximum amount of equipment and services.

Today hospital personnel receive high wages. In order to pay these high wages and stay within the budget, a hospital administrator must see that there is no overlapping in services. The same principle goes for equipment purchased. While the administrator must be certain that the hospital is provided with the most modern equipment to furnish patient diagnostic and treatment services, he or she must also see to it that the hospital does not purchase equipment whose functions overlap each other. Also important, a fee system must be devised that is fair to the patient and also allows the hospital a reasonable profit.

In a large hospital every department is usually under the "ownership" of the hospital. In a smaller hospital an administrator may find it more feasible to contract out certain hospital functions to private operators. For instance, the administrator of a small hospital may have a private firm handle its laboratory work on a fee-for-service basis. In this type of arrangement the private organization charges the hospital only for work actually done, the hospital in turn charges the patient this fee plus an additional amount to allow the hospital a reasonable profit to carry out its functions. By this method, a small hospital can keep its overhead to a reasonable level. As you can see, the work of a hospital administrator is varied; likewise so is the training.

TRAINING REQUIREMENTS

To be competitive for the top jobs in this demanding profession usually requires a master's degree in hospital administration. There are thirty-four universities that offer this program. Obviously a bachelor's degree is required as a prerequisite to the master's program. Although no specific bachelor's program is needed, it is advisable to take a substantial number of business and science courses. The master's program is generally of two years' duration, which includes not only academic work, but also on-the-job administrative experience in hospitals. The curriculum may include such courses as hospital organization and management, medical care, accounting and budget control, personnel administration, public health administration, and the economics of health care.

A liberal arts graduate who has not been able to settle on a career might consider taking a master's program in hospital administration. It is a well-paying rewarding profession. If it is not feasible for you to enroll in a master's program but you do desire a career in hospital administration, you may find it possible to obtain employment in many of the secondary administrative positions available in personnel administration: records, budget and finance; purchasing; accounts receivable and payable; or data processing. After establishing employment in one of these areas in a hospital, it is always possible to supplement your education and increase your chances for advancement by taking outside college courses in accounting, budgeting and finance, psychology, business analysis and organization, and subjects dealing with health sciences. This method of maintaining a position in a hospital plus supplementing it with outside related courses may prove a strong stepping stone to higher executive levels.

For information on college and university programs in hospital administration, write:

American College
of Hospital Administrators
840 North Lake Shore Drive
Chicago, Illinois 60611

Association of University Programs
in Health Administration
One Dupont Circle, N.W.
Washington, D.C. 20036

SALARY AND EMPLOYMENT OPPORTUNITIES

The number of positions in hospital administration is expected to grow very rapidly through the mid-1980s as health facilities are expanded to provide additional health services to an increasing population. Also, a trend toward more complex organization in hospitals is expected to create new openings for administrative assistants who can later move up to become executive administrators.

There are many areas in which a hospital administrator can employ his talents. First, there is the community hospital with which we are all familiar. Second, there is the private hospital. Medical care is big business today. Many private investors are finding it very profitable to own hospitals. After the money has been raised to build or purchase a private hospital, it is necessary to find a good administrator and administrative staff to insure the proper handling of this huge financial investment and provide reasonable profit. It may seem rather mercenary to think of a hospital as a business investment; however, all money is made in our society by providing necessary goods and services regardless of the type. In fact, in many cases a private hospital will provide even better health care at reasonable rates due to the competitive factor. In many areas a large business organization will own several large hospitals and employ not only an administrator for each one but also a district administrator to oversee all of the hospitals under the ownership of the organization.

There are many administrative positions open to graduates in other health care institutions such as nursing homes and public health departments. Every government agency that provides medical care utilizes the services of hospital administrators. Health care is provided by Veterans Administration, the U.S. Public Health Service, and all branches of the armed services. Administrators in the U.S. Public Health Service and armed forces hold ranks of military officers and get paid according to their rank. Naturally, they advance in rank as their experience and seniority increases.

Administrators in the federal veterans hospitals can earn up to $36,000 per year. Positions in community and private hospitals will pay anywhere from $15,000 a year to about $50,000 per year, depending on the size of the hospital. In the private sector administrators who supervise the operation of several private hospitals can possibly earn as much as $100,000 per year.

Inasmuch as many hospitals are federally funded, it will be necessary for the government to employ administrators to oversee the operation of these institutions to insure their proper functioning and to submit reports and make recommendations on how services can be improved.

To sum up, the opportunities in hospital administration are varied and numerous to the ambitious person willing to keep up with new hospital methods and apply himself or herself to the application of these methods.

BIOMEDICAL ENGINEER

Practically all diagnostic and treatment procedures performed in medicine are accomplished through the use of complex scientific equipment such as X-ray, electrocardiogram, diathermy, heart and lung, and kidney machines. The development and building of these machines involve both engineering and medical principles. In the past engineers would work with medical researchers in the development of new scientific devices. Quite often the engineer knew nothing of medicine and, conversely, the medical researchers knew very little about engineering. This led to the development of a new and specialized field, biomedical engineering.

The *biomedical engineer* possesses training in engineering and medicine and is thus able to bridge the gap between these fields. He or she is able to look for medical applications to engineering knowledge and, consequently, draw upon engineering expertise to develop devices to solve present medical problems.

Biomedical engineering is a relatively new field. To the person entering this field, the potential for pioneering new medical horizons is virtually unlimited. As stressed previously, the health of the human body can always be improved upon; thus, the biomedical engineer will always have a media to develop and expand all talents and, in addition, will always have the emotional satisfaction that the work has a direct bearing on improving the health of humanity.

There are three aspects to biomedical engineering. The first concerns research of biological systems and functions. The second involves the design and development of medical instruments and prosthetic devices. This includes the heart pacemaker that helps regulate the heartbeat and the artificial hip joint implanted in a patient who has an arthritic hip joint removed. The third involves the application of the computer to medical science and its diagnostic methods.

In research the engineering aspects of the biological systems of humans and animals are studies to determine how they interact to enable the human body to function properly. The study of the circulatory, nervous, and respiratory systems has been helpful in developing machines to diagnose and treat diseases of these systems. Biomedical engineering research also examines the effects that our environment has on us. The work has helped our understanding of the effects of environmental pollution and the adaptability of man to outer space.

In the second aspect biomedical engineers design and develop instruments and techniques that help medical personnel observe and relieve physical ailments. One such recent technique involves the use of ultrasound impulses to locate and identify normal and abnormal masses within the body.

Prosthetic devices for which biomedical engineers are responsible include artificial limbs, arterial pumps, artificial kidneys, and other devices that either replace or assist the body's natural organs.

Biomedical engineers have been leaders in adapting the computer's uses to medical science's needs. Computers are being used to monitor the conditions of patients, control experiments of therapy, and process electrocardiogram data reflecting the heart conditions. Computers are currently being developed to aid in medical diagnosis and to record the patient's medical history. In the future doctors may have the aid of a computer in prescribing medications as well.

Many sophisticated laboratory apparatuses giving new insight into normal and pathological body functions are constantly being developed by biomedical engineers.

TRAINING REQUIREMENTS

There are several ways to become qualified as a biomedical engineer. There are about twenty universities and colleges that offer training in the field on the bachelor's level. If you already have a degree in engineering (preferably electrical or mechanical), you may take additional university-level courses in the life sciences to qualify for a bachelor's, master's, or doctoral degree in biomedical engineering. Likewise, if you have an undergraduate degree in the life sciences, you may take additional courses in engineering to qualify for these degrees. Obviously, the higher the degree, the more education required. A master's program usually takes two years of full-time study to complete. A doctor's degree requires approximately four years beyond the bachelor's degree for completion. Fellowships for Ph.D. candidates in biomedical engineering are provided by the federal government. Those interested in applying for fellowships should write:

Career Development Review Board
Division of Research Grants
National Institutes of Health
Bethesda, Maryland 20014

For information concerning training programs and career opportunities in biomedical engineering, write:

Alliance of Engineering
in Medicine and Biology
3900 Wisconsin Avenue, N.W.
Suite 300
Washington, D.C. 20016

Biomedical Engineering Society
P.O. Box 1600
Evanston, Illinois 60204

Foundation for Medical Technology
Mt. Sinai Medical Center
100th Street and Fifth Avenue
New York, New York 10029

National Institutes of Health
9000 Wisconsin Avenue
Bethesda, Maryland 20014

Engineers Joint Council
345 East 47th Street
New York, New York 10017

American Association
of Physicists in Medicine
Administrative Secretary
335 East 45th Street
New York, New York 10017

SALARY AND EMPLOYMENT OPPORTUNITIES

The employment opportunities for biomedical engineers are numerous. Universities and government agencies offer many fine positions in teaching and research. Individuals with bachelor's or master's degrees in biomedical engineering are reported to start at salaries from $15,000 to $20,000 per year. People with a Ph.D. start at about $21,000 a year. As one's proficiency increases, so does one's salary.

Biomedical engineers who enter private industry working for medical equipment manufacturers have almost unlimited income potentials. There is great competition among medical equipment manufacturers to develop new and improved equipment. The biomedical engineer who can aid in this goal will be rewarded commensurately. Also, because it takes a knowledgeable person to sell this complicated equipment to hospitals and other medical facilities, the biomedical engineer who desires to go into sales can earn a salary of up to $50,000 per year and more, depending upon his or her sales ability.

There is a perpetual goal to increase the human life span and to cure the diseases that go with it. There will always be a future for the biomedical engineer.

STATISTICIAN

In today's complex society, with everything competitive and expensive, very little can be left to chance. Nothing is done in business, medicine, industry, or government without a great deal of research first taking place. Statistics is an important ingredient in research; and it is the professional *statistician* that plans, gathers, and analyzes these statistics to enable executives in all fields to make the best possible decisions.

The beauty of becoming a statistician is that every industry requires statistics in order to survive. So, no matter what your major is in college, with some graduate training in statistics you can apply your major to a corresponding industry. For instance, if you majored in biology, you could apply this training to a statistical position in the medical, agricultural, or chemical field. How many political science graduates are walking around looking for a job? Well, why not apply the political science training doing political research? Many politicians make their campaign and legislative decisions by trying to figure out what their constituents want. This is not easy to do. An alert political science major with a good statistical background could be invaluable here and also in other areas of the political arena.

The possibilities for a good statistician are infinite, especially if he or she has some imagination. Statisticians do more than just collect data. They decide what data should be collected and how this should be done. They then collect, analyze, and interpret the data for further decision making. When this is properly done, it can mean the savings of millions of dollars to various industries, businesses, and government agencies. It can even mean the savings of thousands of lives where the health field is concerned. The statistician is a prime figure in the shaping of our society.

Good statisticians will always have a job as every field requires them. When the country is in an economic slump, as we have recently experienced, it is the statistician who can help show the way to an improved economic plateau.

The following are just a few examples of the many varied applications of a career in statistics:

Actuarial Science: determining premium rates for different insurance risks; designing pension plans for private and public groups; measuring effectiveness of loss prevention and loss control programs.

Agriculture and Fisheries: developing superior varieties of grain; increasing egg and milk production; assessing the effectiveness and potential dangers of pesticides; management and allocation of natural fishery resources.

Biology: exploring the interactions of species with their environment; creating theoretical models of the nervous system; studying genetic evolution.

Business: estimating the volume of retail sales; deciding what products will have the greatest consumer acceptance; designing inventory control systems; producing auditing and accounting systems; improving working conditions in industrial plants.

Economics: measuring indicators such as volume of trade, size of labor force, and standard of living; analyzing consumer behavior.

Engineering: working out safer systems of flight control for airports; improving product design and testing product performance; determining reliability and maintainability of products.

Health and Medicine: developing and testing new drugs; finding the best possible drugs for consumption that will give the maximum therapeutic advantages with minimal side effects, preventing and diagnosing disease.

Psychology: measuring learning ability, intelligence, and personality characteristics; creating psychological scales and other measurement tools; studying normal and abnormal behavior; determining under what conditions people learn and work best.

Quality Control: developing methods to insure product quality; devising sampling and testing techniques of various industrial and consumer products; experimenting with various designs in product development.

Real Estate: observing growth patterns in industrial, commercial, agricultural, and residential properties to aid development companies in selecting the best possible properties for maximum investment return.

Sociology: testing theories about social systems; designing and conducting sample surveys to study social attitudes; exploring cross-cultural differences; studying the growth of human populations.

Stock Market: plotting trends in various industries and observing growth patterns in individual and groups of stocks; integrating this data with economic and political factors to give brokerage firms current data on what stocks will most likely rise and fall.

TRAINING REQUIREMENTS

A four-year program for a bachelor's degree is definitely required to be a statistician. However, one does not necessarily have to go to a special school to learn this profession. Many of the necessary courses can be learned at little financial expense in a junior college after which a university can be used to complete the required program.

Fewer than eighty colleges and universities in the United States offered a bachelor's degree in statistics in 1972. However, most schools do offer a degree in mathematics or a sufficient number of courses in statistics to qualify graduates for beginning positions. Required subjects for an aspiring statistician include mathematics through differential and integral calculus, statistical methods, and probability theory. Courses in computer uses and techniques are useful for many jobs. Computers are relied upon heavily in the collecting, sorting out, and analyzing of data. However, there is no doubt about it—computers will never do the work of a statistician. They can only aid in the execution of the work. It might be said that a computer is to a statistician what a test tube is to a scientist. Therefore, it is wise for a statistician to take some computer courses.

If you have already completed college in a major other than statistics and now wish to direct your talents to a career in statistics, the types of courses just mentioned can be taken in evening programs, if you desire, until enough knowledge is gained to transfer your original education to a statistical position in that field.

Beginning statisticians who have only the bachelor's degree often spend much of their time performing routine statistical work. Through experience they may advance to positions of greater technical and supervisory responsibility in top-management capacities. Your advanced degrees can be earned while holding down a job. This will alleviate heavy financial burdens and give the graduate degree candidate greater appreciation for the advanced studies. Also, many firms will contribute financially to the further studies of their employees.

Most school guidance departments can give you information on schools that offer degrees in statistics. You can also obtain this information by writing:

The American Statistical Association
806 15th Street, N.W.
Washington, D.C. 20005

SALARY AND EMPLOYMENT OPPORTUNITIES

Beginning statisticians with a bachelor's degree will start at about $9,000 to $10,000 per year; those with a master's degree, about $12,000 per year. A Ph.D. may very well start at a salary between $18,000 to $20,000 per year. There are statisticians with advanced degrees and experience earning $36,000 per year, plus excellent fringe benefits, in the federal government.

An experienced statistician can also be self-employed. Statisticians today often engage in private consulting practice with clients from industry as well as from all levels of government. It is probably where the most can be earned. Statisticians with a talent for consulting can earn more than $50,000 per year. This can be readily understood when you consider, as previously mentioned, how industry and government rely on their talents in the investing of millions of dollars.

To repeat, every industry requires statistics to survive. Thus, there will always be jobs for statisticians.

ACCOUNTANT

Everything manufactured in this world and every service performed requires money. We are a long way from the days when an item was manufactured or bought for one price, sold for another, and the difference pocketed by the seller. Manufacturing, buying, selling and servicing merchandise has become extremely complex. There are many facets to consider when selling a product: the cost of the raw materials, equipment costs, advertising expense, and payroll, to mention just a few. These items have to be considered when conducting business. As the business world becomes more complex, so do the financial procedures accompanying it. It is very easy for even the sharpest and shrewdest business executive to become lost in the complex world of finances. As a result, executives turn to the *accountant*—the trained expert in finances—to help with the decisions involving money.

The role of the accountant today has increased in importance to a record all-time high, and it will continue to become increasingly important in all phases of civilized society. Almost nothing can happen in our society without money being involved. The accountant is to the business world what the doctor is to the medical world.

Accountants in public practice serve a wide variety of clients, such as commercial enterprises, industrial firms, government agencies, and nonprofit institutions. They perform numerous services ranging from ordinary record keeping to advising clients on complex management matters. Accountants will design and install for their clients individualized accounting systems enabling them to keep accurate financial records. They will audit a company's accounts periodically and will give their professional opinion as to whether these fairly reflect the company's financial position.

The preparation of periodic financial statements showing profits and losses for the client's business is another important function of accountants. This allows the client to keep tabs on the company's financial position and to make necessary changes before it is too late. The accountant will figure the income tax to be paid and prepare the necessary forms and schedules. He or she must be constantly alert to every change in the tax laws and how they affect each client. Accountants can help their clients by analyzing operating costs and providing them with data and advice concerning profits, loans, pension and profit-sharing plans, tax-deductible trust funds, future tax plans, etc.

Within recent years accountants in public practice have expanded their range of services to include advising clients on a variety of management matters that accountants are particularly qualified to do. Their training and experience and the association with the clients give them a special knowledge and understanding of their complete operations. Such operational advice may also be termed management consulting. It offers a whole new promising field of activity for the accountant.

As can be seen, the work of the accountant is both challenging and vitally interesting. The accountant is virtually the eyes and ears of management. Every organization, large or small, has to keep track of its operations in order to see what it is doing and where it is going financially. To sum it up, the essential work of the accountant is to assemble, analyze, and interpret dollars-and-cents information about a client's operations, thereby helping the client to make important decisions.

It is estimated that approximately 20,000 new accountants will be needed annually to take the place of those that retire and to fill new positions created by the increased complexity and expansion of the financial world.

Electronic computers and automatic data processing offer a completely new field and many challenges to the alert accountant. The accountant who is well versed in these modern and highly specialized developments will undoubtedly be called in by more and more clients to consult and advise them on record-keeping systems that use data-processing equipment. Many accountants will be called upon to find new applications for automatic data-processing equipment.

TRAINING REQUIREMENTS

Accountants are approaching the same financial and social status of other professionals such as doctors and lawyers. Likewise, accountants do devote a great deal of time in studying their profession to achieve such a status. There is one big advantage the aspiring accountant has in training for his profession—accomplishing the necessary training in different achievement levels at one's own pace, possibly including periods of practical work experience in outside industries or accounting offices to gain additional experience and earn money while in training.

The cost of becoming an accountant can be considerably less than it is for a doctor or lawyer. The aspiring accountant can begin his or her career acquiring an associate's degree in accounting during a two-year program at a junior or community college. The student can then continue for another two years at a university-level college. This combined schooling can cut down considerably on the education costs of becoming an accountant. After two years of practical work experience the graduate accountant is eligible to take the exam to become a Certified Public Accountant (C.P.A.)—one of the highest levels in accounting, somewhat analogous to an M.D. degree in the medical field or an L.L.B. degree in the legal field.

SALARY AND EMPLOYMENT OPPORTUNITIES

As we have suggested, the employment opportunities in accounting are almost limitless. An accountant may work for a large accounting firm, or go into business privately (handling the financial affairs of the clients), or may work for large organizations and advance to such positions as chief plant accountant, chief cost accountant, budget director, senior internal auditor, or tax preparation officer. Some accountants become controllers, treasurers, financial vice presidents, or corporation presidents. Many prominent government and industry officials have achieved their high positions as a result of training and experience as accountants in public practice. In fact, several members of the Congress of the United States are former accountants.

Because every type of industry, business, or profession has its own particular problems and idiosyncrasies, it is sometimes advantageous for a new accountant to specialize in the accounting needs of a particular group of people, profession, or industry. In this way one will become extremely knowledgeable in a particular field and will be able to develop a reputation as an authority, thereby attracting a large number of clients from that field.

A staff accountant in an accounting firm or business organization can achieve a salary level of approximately $25,000 a year. Accountants that open their own practices, become senior partners in large accounting firms, or reach executive levels in large business organizations can achieve earnings of $50,000 a year and much more. The achievement levels and financial rewards are almost unlimited.

Practically everything purchased today, whether by an individual consumer or by a large organization, is paid for at a later date. This system is called "credit." Webster's dictionary defines credit as meaning "trust." And that is exactly what it is all about. The seller trusts the buyer to pay for the merchandise at a later date.

There are many good reasons to sell merchandise on credit. Credit allows a person who has the potential ability to pay to have what he or she needs at the present and to pay for it at a time which is more convenient and economical for the consumer. In the commercial world an organization can purchase goods on credit, utilize these goods for manufacturing or resale purposes, and then pay for the goods after they have been utilized to make a profit. Because of these business practices, it makes good sense for a firm to sell their products on credit. Selling goods on attractive credit terms can add greatly to the total sales picture of a firm.

Because credit selling and buying are so attractive, a firm must take intelligent steps to extend credit to those people or firms whose ability and chances of payment are good, and must refuse those firms who present too much of a risk. Establishing who is a good or bad credit risk is a complex task and is turned over to a *credit manager*. A credit manager may work for the firm that sells the goods or may work for or own or manage a firm that specializes in making credit decisions for firms without their own credit departments.

In deciding on whether or not to extend credit to a firm, a credit manager goes into a thorough investigation of the candidate's financial affairs and takes into account the state of the economy in the area which the client deals in. The credit official analyzes detailed financial reports submitted by the applicant, interviews company representatives about its management, and reviews credit and agency reports to determine the firm's reputation for repaying debts. He or she also checks at banks where the company has deposits or previously was granted credit.

In extending credit to individuals (consumer credit), detailed financial reports usually are not available. In this case the official must rely on personal interviews, credit bureaus, and banks to provide information on the person applying for credit.

Credit officials working in banks are *loan officers.* They are responsible for the distribution of loans to businesses and individuals. Some officers may specialize in certain industries, such as agriculture, chemical, real estate, retail merchandising, etc. By specializing in a certain industry a loan officer can become very familiar with the inner workings of that industry and thus become more proficient in determining the chances of repayment by organizations in that field.

Credit managers in retail and wholesale trade usually cooperate with the sales department of their firm in developing credit policies liberal enough to allow the company's sales to increase and yet strict enough to deny credit to customers whose ability to pay their debts is questionable.

Everything in business is a risk. The credit manager is not judged by how small the credit losses are, but rather by the ratio of successful loans to unsuccessful loans. Anyone can reduce the number of credit losses by becoming very restrictive on credit to everyone. However, by being overrestrictive, you are also inhibiting possible sales opportunities that will be beneficial to a company. As you can see, the successful credit manager must use business knowledge plus analytical judgment in taking the best calculated risks.

Obviously, there are going to be risks that will not pay off. In these cases the credit manager must take steps to encourage payment and may send letters or talk to the debtor to arrange for payment. If this does not work, he or she then must take legal action to receive the amount due.

Through training and experience a credit manager also functions as a business analyst and may be required to service as a "business doctor" for financially sick customers. Many times a

400 Fields Requiring a Four-year College Degree

credit executive will advise an ailing company how to straighten out its financial problems and proceed on the road to recovery. In this manner a company with financial problems can recover and become a good customer and credit risk for a supplier of goods or money.

Besides making a fine salary, a credit manager can derive a great deal of satisfaction in making positive credit decisions that can enable a small business to grow. Many times it is an intelligent credit executive with a keen sense of the future that gives assistance to a small struggling company and makes it possible for this company to grow into a large and successful industry.

TRAINING REQUIREMENTS

It is possible for a high school graduate to take special courses in various university and junior college programs to obtain a beginning job in credit management. However, to get ahead in this field, it is better to have a college degree behind you. What is nice about this field is that you do not have to have a specific major in your undergraduate years. If you took a liberal arts program in the hopes of "finding yourself," this is fine. Most companies just want to know that you have a degree; they will see to it that you receive the specialized training necessary. This training may be through company-oriented programs or by special courses given by several recognized credit organizations in this country.

The National Association of Credit Management operates the National Institute of Credit—a study program conducted in over 100 colleges and universities in the United States that offers an Associate Award for beginners and the Fellow Award for those with experience. These courses are also available on a correspondence basis for those not able to attend classroom instruction. For information regarding these programs, write:

National Association of Credit Management
475 Park Avenue South
New York, New York 10016

Another study program, offered by the Society of Certified Consumer Credit Executives (SCCCE), is a three-level certification program in consumer credit and is recognized throughout the credit world. The first level is that of the Credit Counsellor (CC) and is open to the beginning student. The next level is the certification as an Associate Credit Executive (ACE), which is an intermediate level of recognition and is open to people with three years' experience in credit work. The third and highest level is that of the Certified Consumer Credit Executive (CCCE), which has as its prerequisite five years of consumer credit experience plus the attainment of the first two levels. These courses may also be taken on a correspondence basis. For information, write:

Society of Certified
Consumer Credit Executives
7405 University Drive
St. Louis, Missouri 63130

For general information regarding training programs available in commercial credit, write:

Credit Research Foundation
3000 Marcus Avenue
Lake Success, New York 11040

SALARY AND EMPLOYMENT OPPORTUNITIES

Salaries for credit managers range from about $12,000 per year up to about $50,000 per year, depending upon the management level reached.

The employment of credit officials is expected to increase rapidly as the number of individual credit transactions continues to grow. At no time in the history of the world has credit played such a major part in international affairs as at the present.

Credit is the energy that vitalizes business, that constructs the foundation of a fine standard of living, and that makes it possible for businesses to grow. It offers great opportunities for qualified people. Credit management is a profession that will be more and more in demand and become more and more important in business life.

TRAFFIC MANAGER

Everything bought and sold in this world must go through one very important step—transportation. In the manufacture of goods the raw materials and components necessary to produce the finished product almost always come from sources outside of the manufacturing area. After the manufacturing steps are completed, the finished product must then be transported to various wholesalers and distributors until it reaches the final consumer.

There are many different methods to transport goods, each varying in time and expense. Also, there are many different carriers involved in each method, and they too will vary in the fees charged.

As you can start to see, the transportation of goods can become very complicated and expensive. If not handled properly, a company can go out of business due to its transportation problems alone.

It takes a highly skilled and intelligent person to handle a company's freight problems and guide the delivery of merchandise through the maze of the various transportation methods and carriers involved. All of this must be coordinated so that the merchandise reaches its final destination in a modest length of time and at a reasonable cost—enter the *traffic manager*.

The industrial traffic manager analyzes various transportation possibilities and chooses the most efficient type for the company's needs. It may be rail, air, road, water, or a combination of these. He or she then selects the route and the particular carriers. To make these decisions, traffic managers must consider delivery schedules and costs to insure the product's delivery in a reasonable length of time and at a modest cost.

Some traffic managers will become involved in researching and deciding on the best type of packaging materials to use and in the designing and operation of shipping, receiving, and warehousing facilities.

A good traffic manager should be experienced in the basic use of computers. Computers are used to trace a shipment from its beginning, through the maze of various carriers, to its final destination.

There are other avenues of employment open to a traffic manager other than the industrial firm. Many traffic managers are employed by the carriers contracted by the industrial firms to move or take part in the moving of the company's goods. In this capacity the traffic manager is responsible for the construction of a price structure low enough to attract business and yet return a profit to the carrier company. Many times the traffic executive is involved in the sales of the carrier's services and in coordinating relationships with connecting carriers.

The reason coordinating ability is so important is that no one transportation company owns and controls all of the transportation facilities to move goods around the world. Some companies are involved in trucking, some are involved in rail transportation, others use airline and steamship lines. What's more, many of the individually owned and operated carriers carry on business in just certain localities. You can see how many times goods have to be "piggy-backed" through many modes of transportation and carriers.

There are freight transportation companies that own almost none of their own equipment except for a few local delivery trucks. They operate by taking complete responsibility for a company's transportation needs and then subcontract the assignments to various carriers. Their profit comes from the difference in the price they charge for the complete transportation service and the charges to them by the carriers they subcontract. These companies depend heavily on the talents of the traffic manager for their efficient operation.

Since traffic managers are fundamentally trained in transportation rates and the coordination of the many transportation methods, they are highly qualified to become involved with the transportation of humans. Quite obviously, humans are not going to be transported in the same manner as freight, but the same principles of transportation are used to transport people, whether for business or vacation.

A good traffic manager can arrange "travel packages" for businesspeople, conventioneers, clubs, and independent vacationers. This is done by purchasing a large number of seats or accommodations on airplanes, trains, or steamships at wholesale prices, arranging special wholesale group rates with hotels and sightseeing tours, and then coordinating everything into one "travel package." The package is then sold to the special group. The deal allows not only a savings to each group member, but also a sizable profit to the traffic manager or the company.

TRAINING REQUIREMENTS

A traffic manager does not have to be a college graduate. It is possible to reach executive positions in traffic by on-the-job training and rising through the ranks. Naturally, a college degree is always helpful. It is desirable, however, to take some courses that offer special preparation in traffic management. If you decide to learn this vocation on the job, it is advisable to take outside courses in data processing, statistics, accounting, and economics. These subjects can be learned at night in many of the junior or community colleges throughout the country.

There are several schools in the United States offering specialized programs and courses in traffic management:

The Academy of Advanced Traffic
One World Trade Center, Suite 5457
New York, New York 10048

or

One East Penn Square Building
Philadelphia, Pennsylvania 19107

The Traffic Manager's Institute
14 New England Executive Park
Burlington, Massachusetts 01803

College of Advanced Traffic
22 West Madison Street
Chicago, Illinois 60602

You can obtain a booklet entitled "Directory of Transportation Education in U.S. Colleges and Universities," by writing:

The American Trucking Association
1616 P Street, N.W.
Washington, D.C. 20036

SALARY AND EMPLOYMENT OPPORTUNITIES

Traffic managers working in companies whose transportation requirements are moderate can earn approximately up to $18,000 per year. Those employed in very large companies can receive anywhere from $25,000 to $50,000 per year.

An experienced traffic manager can also go into business privately with very little capital investment. A transportation company can be started by soliciting shipping assignments from small companies and subcontracting the work to the individual carriers. Also, as mentioned previously, a good traffic manager can go into the business of putting together various "travel packages" for groups of individuals.

In each of the two situations there is practically no limit to the amount of money the independently employed traffic manager can make.

ADVERTISING

Everything produced in today's society, whether it be a manufactured product or a service, depends on advertising for its sale to the consumer. *Advertising* is simply a method of informing the public of a product or service in a truthful and appealing manner designed to stimulate its sale.

Advertising serves consumers by telling them immediately about existing and new products offered for sale. It gives them information so that they can compare the values offered by competing advertisers and thus buy efficiently. Through advertising the manufacturer can reach thousands of prospects at once with a sales message, something no individual salesperson could ever achieve. Thus, advertising lowers the cost of selling.

Over $22 billion dollars are spent annually on advertising products and services. This volume provides for a lot of varied and interesting jobs in advertising agencies, advertising media, and even in advertising departments of large companies who do their own advertising. By stimulating sales of goods, advertising serves to keep thousands of people employed in the production of these goods, and thus is greatly responsible for our high standard of living.

Advertising agencies are firms devoted entirely to the creation, preparation, and placing of advertisements for the advertisers who are their clients. Many people with specialized responsibilities are employed by these agencies to carry out the complex task of soliciting, creating, and producing advertisements.

Advertising media are vehicles of communication through which advertisements are presented to the public. These vehicles (or media) include radio and television stations, newspapers, magazines, direct mail, billboards, and anything else that can be used to carry an ad. Advertising agencies decide on which media is best suited to carry the message of their client. Very often, agencies and media will employ the same type of people. This will be discussed in detail later.

Advertising service and supply houses take the creations of the advertising agencies and media and render the finished product to be carried by the media. These products include newspaper and magazine mats, posters, film, and videotape. Supply houses employ printers, engravers, photographers, layout men, etc. Large advertising agencies will usually have their own production departments, whereas smaller agencies will subscribe to the services of these supply houses for the final production of their creations.

Advertising personnel are engaged in diverse areas such as administration, creation, selling, buying, research, and production. They include the following occupational titles.

Advertising Manager

Advertising managers are generally heads of an advertising department, providing overall direction for the planning and buying of advertising for manufacturers or dealers. They are employed by both advertisers and advertising media. In companies that do not employ advertising agencies they have direct control in preparing the advertisements and may even do part of the work themselves.

Most advertising media (newspapers, magazines, and broadcast stations) have an advertising manager, who functions as a sales manager in selling advertising space or broadcast time to advertisers.

Account Supervisor

Account supervisors are usually seasoned advertising people employed by an agency and are responsible for the administration of one or more major accounts. They are experienced in marketing techniques, planning and campaigns, and in making successful contacts with clients. They must also be good business administrators. This is especially important in large agencies that employ hundreds of people.

Account Executive

Account executives can be employed by agencies or media and are responsible for all advertising created for a particular client. There may be a number of account executives in one agency, each handling one or more clients. An account executive studies the client's sales and advertising problems, develops a plan to meet the client's needs, and seeks approval on the proposed program. These executives must be able to sell ideas and maintain good relations with clients and must be able to judge copy, understand the use of graphics, and plan complete advertising campaigns. Much of this work, of course, is delegated to assistants or other agency departments. However, the account executive must have a firm knowledge of the entire operation in order to serve the clients properly.

Advertising Copywriter

Advertising copywriters create the headlines, slogans and text that attract buyers. They collect information about products and potential customers. Copywriters use a knowledge of psychology and writing to prepare copy that will stimulate the reader to buy the product advertised. A copywriter may specialize in a type of copy that appeals to certain groups—heads of households, businesspeople, scientists, teenagers, engineers, etc. Some copywriters specialize in a particular product or industry—food, automobiles, engineering products, appliances, beauty products, etc. It is possible for a person with training in another occupation, such as engineering, chemistry, or medicine, to couple this training with creative and writing talents to become a copywriter specializing in products associated with the original field. The original training plus the creative ability of such a person would be a great asset in appealing to the buying potential of people engaged in that particular field. In advertising agencies copywriters work closely with account executives to develop an advertising program best suited to their client.

Media Buyer

The *media buyer* works for an advertising agency and decides on what type or types of advertising media the client's money would be best spent. After deciding which media to use (newspaper, radio, TV, magazines, etc.), then the buyer must select the particular vehicles in each media that would reach the greatest number of potential buyers of a particular product. For instance, if the decision is to use newspaper or television advertising, then which television shows will give the client's products the best possible exposure for the money spent? The media buyer must have a general knowledge of advertising rates in order to stay within the client's budget. A good buyer must also know how to negotiate contracts for advertising space or time.

In recent years specialized firms offering independent media buying services have performed this function for given agencies. Thus, if one becomes proficient in media buying, it may be feasible for that person to open an office and solicit advertising agencies to handle their media buying needs.

Research Director

Research directors and their assistants assemble and analyze information for advertising programs. They study possible uses of a product, its advantages and disadvantages compared to competing products, and ways of reaching potential buyers. These workers may survey buying habits and motives of customers or try out sample advertisements to determine the best selling methods.

Art Director, Artist, and Layout Artist

The *art director, artist,* and *layout artist* plan and create visual effects in advertisements. They are employed by advertisers, advertising agencies, and advertising media. In addition, many artists and art-production firms work for agencies and advertisers on a free-lance basis. Often it is the art director who conceives the basic idea for an advertising campaign.

A layout technician provides rough sketches to show the arrangement of an illustration, text material, and other elements of an advertisement. The manner in which an ad is laid out determines the amount of attention it will get from the observer and potential customer. The effectiveness of an entire campaign may depend on how well the layout job has been performed.

Production Manager

The *production manager* and the assistants are responsible for the mechanical production of all materials necessary for the final processing of the advertisement. Their production department deals with printers, engravers, mat services, and outside service and supply houses that contribute to the production of the advertisement in its final form. A production person may work for a large agency or even set up a private firm to handle the production needs of many small agencies.

Public Relations Person

The *public relations (PR) person* handles news about the company, whether employed by an advertiser, agency, or media. When agency PR people are responsible for publicity for clients, they maintain close contacts with the account executives and clients in order to be informed of all newsworthy developments. The PR man or woman must be able to judge news values and prepare stories in a professional journalistic manner.

Promotion Manager

The duties of a *promotion manager* in advertising media extend to all phases of promoting the company, including advertising. The manager compiles statistical information proving the value of the advertising facilities that the company has to offer and then presents it in an attractive and convincing form to potential advertisers. The manager is also responsible for the preparation of advertising literature and the sales material that salespeople use in an effort to obtain contracts for advertising space and radio-television time.

Space or Broadcast-time Salesperson

The *space* or *broadcast-time salespeople* work in media and call on advertisers and advertising agencies to sell newspaper space and radio-television broadcast time. They must be familiar with the respective sales advantages of their medium and its relationship to other media and competition. They should possess the same qualities of sales expertise required in other sales fields. As salespeople of advertising space and time, they should be well versed in research and statistics about the reading and viewing habits of the audience expected to be reached. One of the largest segments of the advertising industry is made up of salespeople. And sales is where many successful advertising executives start their careers.

Direct Mail Specialist

The *direct mail specialist* is employed by companies that sell their products directly by mail. The specialist is usually an expert in writing sales letters and designing printed advertising literature that is to be sent by mail.

We have given only a brief description of the many specialties found in the advertising profession. A large advertising firm may employ one or many of each specialty. Smaller firms may have one person carrying out several related functions. For instance, an account executive may also function in sales, promotion, and even public relations. Likewise, one person may handle most of the production tasks. A copywriter may even handle some of the artwork. At any rate, each job provides the creative person with a great deal of challenge and chance for success.

TRAINING REQUIREMENTS

There is no specific training program for advertising. The most important requirement is to possess imagination, creativity, and ambition. Since each advertising campaign presents its own set of challenges, a flair for problem solving is essential. The ability to get along with people and sales expertise are two other important prerequisites.

Although a college degree is not essential, it is a great asset in getting your first job, as advertising is an extremely competitive field. A liberal arts background is sufficient to enter the advertising profession. It will be helpful to include courses in business administration, marketing, merchandising, journalism, English, advertising principles and research, advertising copy and layout, and any other courses that would be of value in your future work. If you plan to go into specific areas of production such as artwork, printing, photography, or television film, it would be advisable to take specific courses in the specialty desired.

Over 900 accredited colleges and universities in the United States offer courses in advertising, with about 80 offering a major in advertising. Even after the most extensive education, however, the real training program occurs working in an agency or media, performing the various tasks mentioned previously. Some businesses conduct in-house training programs where beginners can acquire the needed skills.

Many people in advertising come from other occupations and backgrounds. These include accountants, salespeople, engineers, teachers, journalists, and even lawyers. Advertising is a very complex field, and people with creativity and imagination can adapt their primary profession to fit the needs of the advertising world.

If you cannot afford a four-year college program, but desire to be in advertising, do not despair. Many of the fundamentals needed to get a beginning job in an agency can be learned in a two-year junior college program. When going for your first job, the manner in which you present yourself can contribute greatly toward getting hired. A well-written employment application letter to various concerns can make a personnel director sit up and take notice of you. After you are hired, the rest is up to you. You can always supplement your education with night school and correspondence courses.

Further information on a career in advertising can be obtained by writing:

American Advertising Federation
Educational Services
1225 Connecticut Avenue, N.W.
Washington, D.C. 20036

Association of Industrial Advertisers
Education Committee
41 East 42nd Street
New York, New York 10017

*American Association
of Advertising Agencies*
200 Park Avenue
New York, New York 10017

SALARY AND EMPLOYMENT OPPORTUNITIES

The salary for most beginners in the various advertising specialties detailed is approximately $10,000 per year. After a couple of years of experience, an employee should earn approximately $16,000 per year. Salaries for people with five years' experience who reach middle management generally range from $20,000 to $22,000 per year. Upper management salaries can reach $50,000 per year and more.

It is possible to open an agency if you have some experience and contacts in the field. A small agency can devote itself to the creative aspects of advertising and send out its production to the specialized production companies mentioned previously. You could even open your own small production company doing work for the agencies involved in the creative end. If your forte is media buying, you can open your own office and specialize in media buying for small agencies and advertisers.

To give you a general idea of the financial potential in owning your own agency, here are some of the fee schedules charged by agencies: the creative and production work is usually charged to the client at approximately $50 per hour plus materials. After the ads for the campaign have been produced, a fee of approximately 15 percent of the amount spent on the various advertising media is charged to the client. In other words, if an advertiser spends $100,000 on newspaper, magazine, or television advertising, an additional $15,000 is paid to the agency.

This is in addition to the $50 per hour charged for creating the ad. Keep in mind, however, that the owner of the agency does not keep the entire fee and must pay the employees and/or other people who were contracted to perform special services, such as media buying or production. In any case, the owner or partner of a successful advertising agency can make a sizable income. Some incomes go up to and over $100,000 a year. You may think that some of the fees charged for advertising are rather exorbitant. Actually, they are not when you consider the results that are accomplished. A good advertising campaign can result in the sales of millions of dollars worth of a client's product. When you consider this, the amount spent on advertising can represent a relatively small amount of money. In fact, it has been calculated that the cost of advertising many products accounts for less than 1 percent of the sales price!

In summing up our discussion we would like to emphasize that the advertising field is extremely competitive. It takes a strong person to succeed in this profession. However, since everything produced in our society is sold through advertising, there will always be room for creative, ambitious people who can promote the sale of a client's products.

TECHNICAL WRITER

Are you now taking a variety of science and technical courses and searching for a "way to go" with them? Are you now in a technical, scientific, engineering, or business field and trying to find a new application for your skills and knowledge? If the answers to these questions are "yes," a career in technical writing may be for you.

Technical writing is writing that conveys scientific and technical information precisely, accurately, and clearly. In the broadest sense, any presentation of factual information constitutes technical writing. The information developed by science and technology has to be recorded. Sometimes it must be written in clear, uncomplicated language for lay readers, and other times it must be presented in great detail for specialists.

The many technical and scientific developments and new consumer products of recent years have created a need for skilled writers to interpret these developments and write instructions for their use. *Technical writers* organize, write, and edit materials about science and technology in order to establish clearer communication between scientists, engineers, and other technical specialists. They write articles for people who use scientific information or need technical instruction. These people include repair personnel, mechanics, technicians, and housewives.

Technical writing must always be clear and easy to follow. When it is to be used by specialists, it must include technical detail and a highly specialized vocabulary.

Technical writers may also write for students and the general public about scientific, medical, and technical subjects. The writer, in these cases, must write in terms lay people can understand.

In preparing an article, writers generally research the subject and background of the technical information needed. They may consult authorities regarding policy and details. They may observe or participate in the operation of a project to gain an understanding of what they are to write about. They may make field trips to libraries, agencies, and other places to find material.

The technical writer's product takes many forms, such as publicity releases on a company's scientific or technical achievements or on a manufacturer's contract proposals to the federal government. It may be manuals that explain how to operate, assemble, disassemble, maintain, or overhaul components of a missile system or a home appliance.

Technical writers may prepare scientific advertising copy

for manufacturers of highly technical products whose ads are to be read by industrial buyers. They may write for educational publications or publishers of "do-it-yourself" books. Technical writers usually arrange for the preparation of tables, charts, illustrations, and other artwork, and they may work with technical illustrators, draftspeople, or photographers.

Experts in various fields of business frequently write articles and publications on finance, accounting, and business. Many stock brokerage firms employ full-time writers to write articles concerning growth and earning potentials of various companies and industries.

TRAINING REQUIREMENTS

The training requirements for technical writing are varied. When writing for some types of publications, the writer has to be highly trained in the industry or subject being written about and possess secondary training in journalism. For other assignments it is necessary to be trained primarily in journalism and have a talent for investigating and researching scientific data. In any case, a technical writer should have training in both technical and scientific subjects plus journalism training.

The most important qualification for technical writers is to enjoy writing. They should be able to work with words and present organized ideas in clear, logical sentences, offering old facts in fresh ways and new facts in familiar ways.

Generally speaking, an applicant for a position as a technical writer should have an associate's or bachelor's degree in a scientific or technical field and then obtain supplementary training in journalism.

Beginners often assist experienced technical writers by doing library research and by editing and preparing drafts of reports. Experienced writers in organizations that have technical writing staffs may advance to positions of technical editors or other supervisory and administrative positions. After gaining experience and contacts, a few may go into business for themselves doing free-lance work.

For more information concerning careers and training programs in technical writing, contact:

Society for Technical Communications, Inc.
1010 Vermont Avenue, N.W.
Suite 421
Washington, D.C. 20005

SALARY AND EMPLOYMENT OPPORTUNITIES

Thousands of business firms and industries employ technical writers. Some firms specializing in the preparation of technical reports for all types of organizations have numerous technical writers on their staff. In recent years there has been a proliferation of technical magazines, and all use the output of technical writers.

The need to put the growing amount of scientific and technical information into language that can be understood by managers for decision making and by technicians for operating and maintaining complex industrial equipment guarantees an expanding employment market for technical writers. Since many products will continue to be assembled from components manufactured by different companies, technical writers will also be needed to describe, in simple terms, how the components fit together. Others will be needed to improve and simplify operating and maintenance instructions for consumer products.

Experienced writers may earn from $12,000 to $24,000 a year. People employed in technical fields may do free-lance writing for various technical publications to supplement their income, or they may work full time as a free-lance writer. Free lancers may be paid by the word, published page, or a flat rate per article. Generally, a free-lance writer receives approximately $12 for a typewritten page consisting of approximately 300 words plus $8 for a black-and-white photo. For special articles a magazine may pay from $50 to $500 depending on the contents. A technical writer may also write his or her own do-it-yourself books for those wanting to undertake certain technical tasks themselves, such as the repair of autos or TVs.

The future is unlimited—all you need are your brains and your typewriter.

MEDICAL ILLUSTRATOR

You are working your way through, or have just completed, a college program involving the biological sciences and do not know where to go from there. If you possess artistic ability, there is a chance to harness your academic training to a career as a *medical illustrator.* Medical illustrating is a very closed profession. In 1977 there were only about 300 medical illustrators in the country, and the facilities for training more are limited. However, if you are now taking or have already completed a program in the biological sciences, can draw well, and are willing to take some drawing and illustrating courses, do try for admission into an accredited training program in medical illustrating. This profession can be financially rewarding and can offer a great deal of satisfaction in its performance.

Medical illustration is a profession that combines the finest artistic talent and training with a keen interest in and knowledge of the biological sciences. Medical graphics are used to communicate medical information to students and other members of the medical community. As mentioned in the chapter on commercial art, "A picture is worth a thousand words." This is especially true in presenting medical information. Very often a drawing illustrating a medical procedure can clarify and add meaning to a long dissertation on the subject.

The trained medical illustrator is a specialist artist who can create graphics that meet the requirements of medical and scientific communication media, including publications, projecturals, film, television, exhibits, tridimensional models, and visual instruction materials for classroom or lecture use. The illustrator is capable of drawing with extreme accuracy and realism the most minute details and, when called upon to do so, can reduce a complex idea to a simple explanatory diagram or schematic concept. Because of the broad scope of medical illustration, the artist must be accomplished in a variety of drawing, painting, and modeling techniques and be able to use the tools and materials of fine and commercial art.

The ability to convey information clearly and effectively through pictures and models is possible only when the illustrator is thoroughly familiar with the subject matter and possesses imagination and versatility in presenting it. The artist must determine which styles, methods, and techniques of presentation are best suited to the project at hand. Illustrations may be in black and white or in color. The finished illustration may be reproduced for textbook use or medical advertisements or to explain an accompanying article in a medical journal. An illustration may be adapted to classroom teaching or the newer self-instruction units that require films, film strips, transparencies, slide tapes, and videotapes. Illustrators are often asked to prepare animation sequences for motion pictures.

In addition to illustrating medical procedures and clinical specimens, medical illustrators present facts, data, statistics, and research findings graphically, by creating charts, diagrams, and graphs that help a reader or viewer "get the picture" clearly and quickly. Occasionally, they make three-dimensional figures or models of plaster, wax, plastic, or other suitable materials for exhibiting and teaching purposes.

Sometimes medical illustrators are asked to design and develop new medical equipment or instruments. They may make rough sketches of new technical equipment that exists only as a concept. These preliminary drawings help the manufacturer plan and make the new device. For this work artists almost never have models to work from. They must draw from their own mental images of what the physicians and other members of the research team describe.

Medical illustrators must have a thorough command of fundamental art skills and an extensive knowledge of anatomy and certain other biological sciences.

TRAINING REQUIREMENTS

Schools of medical illustration are purposely few in number to maintain a balance with the existing demand for trained graduates. As the demand increases, however, so should the number of teaching facilities. All of the present accredited schools of medical illustration are in medical school complexes. The length of most programs are from one to two years. Instruction is given by the staff of the medical illustration department, professors and instructors from the medical school, and guest lecturers.

To become eligible for admission to a medical illustration program, one should have had science and art courses in undergraduate school. The science courses should include biology, zoology, comparative anatomy, embryology, physiology, and histology. Art courses should include drawing, painting, design, color theory, illustration techniques, lettering, layout, and typography.

For information on schools of medical illustration, write:

Association of Medical Illustrators
6650 Northwest Highway
Chicago, Illinois 60631

SALARY AND EMPLOYMENT OPPORTUNITIES

A good medical illustrator makes approximately $22,000 a year. Most medical illustrators work for large medical centers emphasizing teaching and research. These facilities include university medical schools and hospitals or Veterans Administration hospitals. Some illustrators work for biological laboratories, large pharmaceutical companies, and advertising agencies handling pharmaceutical accounts. A few work for publishing companies devoted largely to publication of medical textbooks and teaching materials. Some illustrators who live near large medical institutions, advertising agencies, and pharmaceutical firms often contract for free-lance illustrating jobs and work in their own homes or studios. As a free-lance illustrator, an artist can charge approximately $50 an hour for work. It is even possible for an illustrator to go into business designing and developing teaching aids in the biological sciences for high school and college students.

The demand for medical illustrators should increase. New advances in medicine and new concepts in medical education are encouraging a multimedia approach to learning. The medical illustrator has a unique background and multiple talents that are particularly suited to fill this role.

NURSERY SCHOOL INSTRUCTOR

With so many mothers involved in full-time employment, the role of the well-run nursery school (child-care center) and its instructors is becoming exceedingly important to today's society. Even in situations where a mother is not involved in outside endeavors, exposure to a preschool training environment can add greatly to a child's emotional and physical development.

The task of educating children is an important one. It is estimated that 50 percent of a person's personality is developed by age five. The early years of childhood are important not only for future development, but also for the value of a child at the moment.

A person does not have to have a long list of academic degrees to be an effective *nursery school instructor*. A good instructor should be sensitive to a child's needs and be able to relate to children. One should be able to exert discipline over a child but at the same time make the child realize that the discipline is out of love and concern for him or her. In general, an instructor should be an intelligent, alert, and intuitive person with a genuine interest in each child's development. It is necessary to have an understanding of a child's needs and of the methods useful in meeting them. A good sense of humor and the ability to get along with parents and other staff members characterize all good nursery school instructors.

The work in a nursery school can be very stimulating, and a person can obtain a beginning position with a minimum amount of academic training. The initial training can then be supplemented with advanced degrees leading to higher positions such as director of a nursery school or other child-care facility.

TRAINING REQUIREMENTS

An individual can become qualified for a beginning position in a nursery school or other child-care facility by obtaining an instructor's certificate in early childhood education through a one-year academic program in child development taught in many community and junior colleges throughout the country. This training can then be supplemented by one more year of training to obtain an associate's degree in early childhood education. The associate's degree can be further supplemented with approximately two more years of training for a bachelor's degree in education. Those individuals who want to teach childhood education at the college or university level can continue this education at the graduate level in a master's or even doctor's degree program in the field.

A beginning instructor with an instructor's certificate will usually earn from $650 to $750 a month. After obtaining an associate's degree and some practical experience, this salary can rise to $1,000 a month. The individual with the bachelor's degree can earn as much as $14,000 to $15,000 a year as the director of a large child-care facility or as a teacher in the elementary school system. It should be noted, however, that the obtaining of the associate's degree is often enough qualification for the talented individual to obtain a directorship of a child-care facility.

There are many types of child-care facilities. The fundamentals and principles of running each type, however, are basically the same. A child-care facility may be an independent (private) nursery school, a church school, a community-run facility, such as the Head Start programs, or even a care facility operated by a business for its employees' children.

It is even possible for an experienced individual to start his or her own private child-care center. Very often an existing structure such as a large home or small apartment complex can be rented for such a purpose. The structure should provide approximately 50 square feet of inside space for each child and about 100 square feet of outside recreational area for each child. Cooking facilities are also required. It has been estimated that to equip a school properly for thirty children approximately $5,000 to $7,000 worth of recreational equipment is needed. The teacher-to-student ratio should be approximately 1 to 10. Practically all states require a child-care facility to become licensed and set definite standards for licensing. These standards can be obtained by writing to the department of social welfare in your state. In some cases the cost of setting up a good child-care facility may be partially funded by government agencies. This is especially true in low-income areas. Check with your local office of the Small Business Administration regarding any possible government funding.

The following represents some of the typical *monthly* rates charged by child-care centers in 1977.

All day care for a five-day week	$125 to $150
Half day care for a five-day week	80 to 100
Half day twice a week	50 to 65
Half day three times a week	50 to 70
Before and after grade school	70 to 85

Sometimes these fees are partially subsidized by local, state, and federal government agencies for the children of working parents.

The role of day-care centers will become increasingly important to our society, not only to provide supervision for children at times when direct parent supervision is not possible, but also to provide a basis for future strength and emotional growth in a society that is sometimes confusing to grow up in. The nursery school or child-care instructor is a primary force in such a program.

MARRIAGE, FAMILY, AND CHILD COUNSELOR

A human being is a complex animal. In addition to the pressures originating within ourselves, the complexity of today's life-styles causes external pressures to be exerted upon each one of us. Consequently, the stability of some of our basic institutions has been threatened—namely, marriage and the family relationship. Likewise, the behavior of children has been affected.

Almost one out of three marriages are now ending in divorce. Families are undergoing crises unheard of only ten years ago. These situations alone, plus many other factors in today's environment, have created problems for children. Many of them, too, have reacted adversely to their problems. These crises have led to the development of a special career field known as marriage, family, and child counseling.

Many of the problems that we create we can solve. Furthermore, many people have expressed a distinct desire to resolve their conflicts within themselves and with others. To help them solve their problems, increasing numbers of people have consulted a *marriage, family, and child counselor.*

Many of the conflicts between married couples and family members result from the inability of family members to communicate with each other. Very often inner conflicts will cause one marriage partner or family member to react in a manner not truly representative of his or her true character; yet it will illicit untoward responses from other family members. Likewise, children affected by a hostile environment not only by family members, but also among other children their own age, will often show the results of the negative aspects of their social environment.

Marriage, family, and child counselors through private counseling and sessions in which family members are allowed to interact with each other strive to get at the causes of the various problems. In this manner they can show each person why he or she is acting a certain way and how it is affecting not only his or her life, but also the lives of those around them. This can go a long way toward resolving many conflicts.

There is no one set formula for resolving personal conflicts. This offers the innovative and conscientious counselor an interesting and challenging field in which to work. It gives one the chance to try out new techniques based on professional experience and intuition in aiding people in the resolving of their problems. For the counselor there will always be new horizons to understand and conquer. Furthermore, seeing a marriage or family achieving happiness can be a very satisfying experience for the counselor.

Most states require counselors to be licensed. The requirements for this license vary from state to state, but most often a master's degree is required to become eligible for taking the licensing examination. There are several educational programs that may provide the necessary training. Some universities and graduate schools offer a specialized master's degree program in marriage, family, and child counseling. Generally speaking, a psychologically oriented educational program is a requisite to pass the exam and then engage in a professional practice.

A suitable master's degree program must include clinical experience with patients in a therapy situation. Courses in this field are directed toward an analysis of individual experience, environmental influences, and the physiological processes underlying human activities. Clinical techniques, diagnostic procedures, psychopathology, and correlated internships in clinical settings are provided. After completion of such a program the student is prepared to assume the responsibilities and duties of clinical practice.

A person may be more qualified for this type of work than he or she may realize. Personal experiences, good judgment, analytical ability, and logic are important attributes in becoming an effective counselor. In most cases a liberal arts background including a good selection of psychology courses is sufficient for getting accepted into a master's degree program offering preparation for the state exam. In many states the state board responsible for the marriage, family, and child counseling license may be able to recommend good schools for the preparation for this work. This organization is usually located in your state capital.

For further information regarding training and licensing for marriage, family and child counseling, write:

*American Association of Marriage
and Family Counselors*
225 Yale Avenue
Claremont, California 91711

There are tremendous amounts of work to be accomplished in this field. The person possessing common sense and intuition plus the academic qualifications should be able to succeed in this counseling field. The clinician who practices successfully generally develops a prominent reputation in the community in which he or she practices and thus will receive many referrals.

A beginning practitioner might charge $20 an hour for services. He or she may see each family member individually or as a group. Once a clinician develops a moderate practice and reputation, it is quite common to receive $40 an hour and even more for services rendered. When a student completes the academic qualifications, he or she may practice under another counselor's license until the state exam is taken and passed.

In starting and developing a practice, it is possible for the beginning practitioner to obtain referrals from professors he or she has studied under. Very often patients who see a counselor during clinical training will continue to patronize the therapist when he or she opens an office. Since pediatricians and family doctors are often the first to notice abnormal behavior among children or other family members, it is a good idea for the beginning clinician to call on members of the medical community to acquaint them with his or her services.

School teachers and other school personnel are also among the first to encounter problem behavior in a child. They too should be contacted. Probation officers may also be a good group to contact. Many civic groups welcome marriage, family, and child counselors as guest speakers. This gives the practitioner the chance to become known to many people who may eventually be in need of service. Patients are another excellent source of referral to others in need of counseling services. Before long, a full schedule and satisfying career is launched.

As our society changes and advances, new problems will constantly accompany these advances. There will always be a need for qualified people to aid people and societies in analyzing and solving their problems.

Index

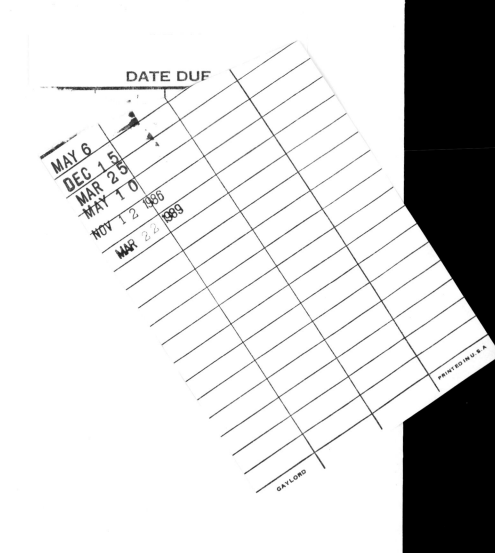

DATE DUE

MAY 6
DEC 15
MAR 25
MAY 10
NOV 12 1986
MAR 22 1989

PRINTED IN U.S.A

GAYLORD